THE
GEEK'S
GUIDE

To Internet Business Success

THE GEEK'S GUIDE

To Internet Business Success

The Definitive Business Blueprint for Internet Developers, Programmers, Consultants, Marketers and Service Providers

Bob Schmidt

 VAN NOSTRAND REINHOLD
I(T)P® A Division of International Thomson Publishing Inc.

New York • Albany • Bonn • Boston • Detroit • London • Madrid • Melbourne
Mexico City • Paris • San Francisco • Singapore • Tokyo • Toronto

International Thomson Publishing Company.
The ITP logo is a registered trademark used herein under
license.

The ideas presented in this book are generic and strategic. Their specific
application to a particular company must be the responsibility of the management of that company, based on management's understanding of their
company's procedures, culture, resources, and competitive situation.

Printed in the United States of America.

Visit us on the Web   www.vnr.com

For more information contact:

Van Nostrand Reinhold   Chapman & Hall GmbH
115 Fifth Avenue   Pappalallee 3
New York, NY 10003   69469 Weinham
                               Germany

Chapman & Hall   International Thomson Publishing Asia
2-6 Boundary Row   60 Albert Street #15-01
London SEI 8HN   Albert Complex
United Kingdom   Singapore 189969

Thomas Nelson Australia   International Thomson Publishing Japan
102 Dodds Street   Hirakawa-cho Kyowa Building, 3F
South Melbourne 3205   2-2-1 Hirakawa-cho, Chiyoda-ku
Victoria, Australia   Tokyo 102 Japan

Nelson Canada   International Thomson Editores
1120 Birchmount Road   Seneca, 53
Scarborough, Ontario   Colonia Polanco
M1K 5G4, Canada   11560 Mexico D.F. Mexico

1 2 3 4 5 6 7 8 9 10 QEBFF 01 00 99 98 97

Library of Congress Cataloging-in-Publication Data

available upon request.

ISBN 0-442-02557-2

Production: Jo-Ann Campbell • mle design • 213 Cider Mill Road • Glastonbury, CT 06033

*This book is dedicated to my parents
and my wife and children.*

Table of Contents

Acknowledgments

So many people provided inspiration for this book in one way or another, many without realizing it. The work and seminars of the late George Johnson of St. Louis, a consultant's consultant and veteran ad man, provided the inspiration for the concept.

Discussions in 1994 with David Kaleky, Paul Bertram, and Tom Manley made clear the opportunities the Internet would bring for Web developers, programmers, and marketers. Likewise the vision of Frank Viverito, Dennis Bell, and George Nobiletti with whom I participated in the founding and startup of A-Net Web, an effort that, though no longer in operation, offered an opportunity to think through almost every Internet business and marketing opportunity that has since come to pass, and many still to come.

This book also grew from my participation in discussions about Internet marketing and the Web development business on CompuServe's Smallbiz forum in 1993–1994, and later on the Internet Marketing list and the HTML Writers Guild lists. Posts to these lists highlighted the challenges facing Web developers and Internet marketers everywhere and the need for a book that addresses the business realities and recognizes the new professions which have emerged.

And it would never have been written at all were it not for the patience and understanding of my wife Diane and children Jennifer and Robby whose love and support made this book possible.

The cooperation and support of Jane Eto of Signature Sites and Max Croft of CFI-Westgate Resorts is acknowledged.

And finally, I would like to acknowledge my editor, Noah Shachtman, whose confidence, good advice, and support was always available, along with Gene Busnar the entire VNR editorial staff and production team whose extra efforts made the timely publication of this book possible.

Introduction

WHO SHOULD READ THIS BOOK?

In short, creative, marketing, design, and computer professionals working on Internet and new media projects, including:

- Web designers
- HTML writers
- Web consultants
- Internet marketing consultants
- Web-hosting service owners and managers
- Internet service providers
- Internet storefront owners
- CGI programmers
- Java/JavaScript programmers
- copywriters
- art directors and graphic designers
- account executives
- production managers
- advertising and public relations agency owners and managers
- marketing directors
- publishers
- editors

HOW TO SUCCEED IN BUSINESS

You should read this book if you're interested in learning what it takes to succeed with a business based on developing Internet projects. Because practically all forms of Internet businesses use the World Wide Web and require the development of Web sites and the design of Web pages, the goal of *The Geek's Guide to Internet Business Success* is to equip you with a solid understanding of the Internet-consulting, Web-development, Web-design, programming, and Web-site promotion business.

Whether you are a freelance Web designer, a small Web consulting team, or a twenty-person firm, you'll gain essential insights into the business and a firm foundation on which to make important business decisions.

If the Internet is only a sideline for your business or organization, as is the case for ad agencies, public relations firms, publishers, and associations—all of whom can have significant Web development activities—you will find that most of the topics covered apply to you, as does the separate chapter devoted to your interests.

If you're a new media creative professional specializing in graphic design, CD-ROM, virtual reality, or other forms of multimedia development, you'll find this book of interest as well because those businesses are similar in many respects to the Web development business.

SECRETS REVEALED

No matter what your background, you'll gain valuable insights into the Web site creative process and learn how to work with or manage the sales and marketing, creative, and production professionals you'll deal with everyday—not to mention your clients. At the very least, you'll have a better understanding of what they're doing and why they're doing it, what they expect from you, and what you can expect from them!

ILLEGAL INFORMATION

Some of the information in this book could actually be illegal if used in the wrong place (for instance, discussions on setting rates bumps up against antitrust laws when discussed by members of the same industry in online forums and Internet mailing lists). So you see, this book could actually keep you from getting into trouble with the law. How many books can make that claim?

YOU'LL LEARN...

- how to set up your business
- how to sell Web design and Internet marketing services
- how to find and keep customers
- how to set prices
- how to manage the Web site development process
- how to budget for success
- how to bill customers and get paid on time
- how to grow your business

You'll discover all the ins and outs of Internet marketing on and off the Web including Web site promotion techniques such as search engine registration, Internet public relations, and more.

And, oh yes, just to comply with the truth-in-reading laws, here's some of the stuff we won't be covering:

- how to hook up to the Internet
- how to send e-mail to Mars
- how to design really slow-loading Web pages
- how to set PERL before swine
- how to stake a claim in the Internet gold rush
- ninety-nine more things to do with AOL disks

There's nothing wrong with books on those subjects, but there are plenty already written (if you're reading this in a bookstore and you're looking for one of those, that's OK—they make great bookends).

THE CREATIVE SHALL INHERIT THE WEB

Marrying words and images has always been the province of the creative professional. Graphic designers, copywriters, photographers, typesetters, filmmakers, video and multimedia producers, and many others operate in this realm. Creative professionals are responsible for developing finished products that get attention, inform, persuade, and entertain. Your own background may be very similar to this. Then again, perhaps "artistic background" doesn't quite describe you. Many Web developers come from more technical backgrounds in programming, interface design, or networking, applying similar creative problem-solving skills. In any case, those who are creative problem solvers will have the best chance of succeeding with Internet projects.

NOT ELSEWHERE CLASSIFIED

Whatever your background and experience, this book will show you how to sell, build, and manage the creative side of what you may think of as a strictly technical enterprise.

OVERVIEW

When the Web began, there wasn't much in the way of graphics, and commercial applications were certainly not the focus. In fact, if you weren't in the military, the government, a university, a research organization, or working for a defense contractor or a computer company, you probably had never even heard of the Internet.

If you wanted to sell travel packages or the latest music CDs with a shopping cart or promote or sell anything except the most advanced computer technology in the most low-key manner imaginable, you weren't even welcome and if you told them you wanted to advertise something over the Internet, they'd probably take you out back and shoot you. Of course, it was only a matter of time before creative communications and marketing types, along with savvy programmers, took rightful control over the content of this new medium.

But enough history. Today, the Internet is no longer the province of rocket scientists. For you, that's good thing and a bad thing. It's good because lots and lots of people are flocking to the Internet to see pages you're building for your clients. It's not so good because many people think they can design their own Web pages on a do-it-yourself basis—and if they're going to do it themselves, why do they need you? (Don't worry, they're not very good at it and you could have a long career ahead of you just specializing in fixing their screwed-up Web sites. There is actually a coming boom in this type of work!)

WELCOME TO THE REVOLUTION

In the early 1990s, when the simultaneous display of text and graphics was made possible by the development at the University of Illinois of the Mosaic graphical Web browser (now known as Netscape) by Marc Andreesson (now known as one of the founders of Netscape), a revolution began. And today, *you* are the most important part of that revolution.

Getting Started as an Internet Professional

ONE EMERGING INDUSTRY

Since 1994, a new industry has sprung up. HTML writers, Web page designers, CGI and Java programmers, Web site promotion, and Internet marketing consultants were unheard of before then.

Though precise statistics are not available, there are tens of thousands who are engaged full time or part time in the Web site creation and promotion business, and their ranks are growing daily.

For instance, the HTML Writer's Guild, http://hwg.org, or HWG, as it is known to members, was founded in October of 1994 as a loose affiliation of Web designers, programmers, and marketers. It has grown to well over fifty thousand members in more than one hundred countries and far outnumbers any other professional group. Members congregate on fifteen or so mailing list discussion groups covering every conceivable aspect of Internet projects. According to Bill Spurlock, a founder of the Guild who has also served as its president, the membership continues to increase by several hundred new members every month.

Other organizations include:

Internet Developers Association	http://www.association.org
Webmaster's Guild	http://www.webmaster.org
Webgrrls	http://www.webgrrls.com
Web Consultants Association	http://just4u.com/webconsultants

MANY EMERGING PROFESSIONS

Beyond rough estimates, there is not much in the way of information on the size and scope of the industry. One thing is certain, however: The Internet/Web development business is creating a number of recognizable professions.

Programmers, network specialists, value-added resellers, and systems administrators built the underlying hardware and software of the Internet and they remain a vital part of it. But today they are far outnumbered by those with a far different skill set.

Indeed, Web development means much more than simply designing Web pages. What began as a functional task—part typesetting, part text formatting—has become a hybrid of skills including graphic design, programming, marketing consulting, advertising, and public relations.

Those in the Web development profession must provide all the pieces of the puzzle needed to put businesses (and other organizations) on the Internet. The Web developer may be called upon to create sites for any of a wide variety of purposes including advertising, product sales, electronic publishing, investor relations, public relations, customer service, entertainment—all external communications via the Internet intended to reach some or all of the general market—and a variety of internal corporate communications purposes including employee relations, employee training, human resources benefits information, vendor communications, enhancement of group workflow and decision making—all communications applications that are intracompany (on Intranets) or between companies and authorized outsiders (on Extranets).

In order to meet client expectations it is certainly necessary to have the technical skills that enable one to do so. However, it is one thing to have the technical capabilities and a different matter to successfully run a business.

Once a sideline added to existing skills, today Web design has become something larger. Design skills alone are not enough. One must have a larger skill set to properly sell Web design/development/programming/promotion services and to supervise and produce Web sites on behalf of clients.

Rather than *Web design*, the more appropriate term has become *Web development*, sometimes also called *Web consulting*. By any name, it is now clearly identifiable as a profession in its own right, meeting the needs of clients in all aspects of Web site creation. Indeed, even those unfamiliar with the Web development business tend to assume that the term *Web Design* encompasses the full range of Web development skills, even though those within the profession would separate the two into separate areas. Clients are demanding that Web designers become Web consultants. They are making the same demands on all of the specialized professions within Web development.

Certainly, some Web development is taking place within other organizations such as ad agencies, graphic design firms, publishers, and associations, but we can clearly see the emergence of a new and separate profession dedicated to the successful use of the Web for a variety of business communications and marketing purposes. While one would expect ad agencies to move into this area and take it on as simply another advertising and communications medium, the fact is that they have been, by and large, slow to do so. A few of the larger agencies have set up "interactive" divisions, but most still have not. The typical smaller agency probably doesn't even have an e-mail account. The emerging Web developers have staked a claim and are already years ahead of the ad agencies. The agencies will not be the ones to take their clients to the Internet. And although the ad agencies could learn a few things from the Internet, Web developers and Internet professionals can learn a few things from the agency business as well.

The range of skills involved is broad. All of the following capabilities may come into play in the overall development of a typical Web site:

Content Development

- copywriting
- art direction
- graphic design
- illustration
- photography
- HTML coding
- computer programming including:
  - CGI scripts
  - server side executables written in C
  - database development
  - Java, JavaScript
  - Visual Basic, VB Script, ActiveX
- Multimedia development including:
  - Shockwave
  - VRML

     – streaming audio/video

Site Hosting

- domain name registration/site hosting
- systems administration
- e-mail services
- mailing list administration

Site Promotion

- search engine registration
- traditional public relations
- Internet public relations
- media buying including:
  - banner ads
  - print and television ads

Obviously, Web design, meaning HTML coding or coding and graphics, is only one of the services needed in developing a site. Some of the areas may be handled or supplied by the client. Copywriting often falls in this category; existing electronic art for logos and photos is often supplied by the client as well. Still, just as client-supplied graphics must be scanned, reformatted, converted, have the color palettes adjusted, etc., requiring significant expertise, so too, client-supplied copy will require editing or a complete rewrite by an accomplished copywriter.

There is every reason to believe that Web development will grow to become a permanent force in business and marketing communications, every bit as important as graphic design, advertising agencies, and public relations firms.

While some firms will grow to have large staffs, the typical Web development firm will employ fewer than a dozen people. Many firms will have no more than six or seven on staff and another group will be composed of even smaller businesses that offer a wide variety of services through strategic alliances with other key firms.

BUILDING A BUSINESS AROUND YOUR PERSONAL LIKES AND DISLIKES, STRENGTHS AND WEAKNESSES

We all have areas of strength and areas of weakness. The important thing is to recognize and understand what your strengths and weaknesses are. Often your strengths are a natural outgrowth of what you enjoy doing, meaning that your weak areas often lie in the things you enjoy doing the least.

However, a client is not going to hire you for your weak areas, and while individuals have strengths and weaknesses, a business should have only strengths. So it is important to inventory one's personal strengths and weaknesses and then devise a strategy to provide for the strengths you're in need of.

Here is a list of the areas a Web development firm will need to cover, either within the organization or from outside sources:

	Like?	Dislike?	Strength?	Weakness?
New Business				
Sales	❑	❑	❑	❑
Account Service	❑	❑	❑	❑
Proposal Preparation	❑	❑	❑	❑
Content Development				
Copywriting	❑	❑	❑	❑
Art Direction	❑	❑	❑	❑
Graphic Design	❑	❑	❑	❑
Illustration	❑	❑	❑	❑
Photography	❑	❑	❑	❑
HTML Coding	❑	❑	❑	❑
Proofreading/Testing	❑	❑	❑	❑
Computer Programming				
CGI Scripts/Perl	❑	❑	❑	❑
Java	❑	❑	❑	❑
JavaScript/VB Script	❑	❑	❑	❑
Database Development	❑	❑	❑	❑
Shopping Carts	❑	❑	❑	❑

	Like?	Dislike?	Strength?	Weakness?
Site Hosting				
Domain Name Registration	❏	❏	❏	❏
Server Setup/Administration	❏	❏	❏	❏
E-mail Setup/Maintenance	❏	❏	❏	❏
Mailing List Setup/Maintenance	❏	❏	❏	❏
Site Promotion				
Search Engine Registration	❏	❏	❏	❏
Traditional Public Relations	❏	❏	❏	❏
Internet Public Relations	❏	❏	❏	❏
Media Buying	❏	❏	❏	❏
Administration				
Reception	❏	❏	❏	❏
Bookkeeping/Billing	❏	❏	❏	❏
Online Transaction Support				
Merchant Account Services	❏	❏	❏	❏
Accounting/Transaction Reporting	❏	❏	❏	❏
Management				
Goal Setting	❏	❏	❏	❏
Work Planning	❏	❏	❏	❏
Hiring/Supervising	❏	❏	❏	❏
Financial Management	❏	❏	❏	❏
Decision Making	❏	❏	❏	❏

ARE YOU A SPECIALIST OR A GENERALIST?

Take a look at your likes and dislikes, strengths and weaknesses in
the checklist. If all of your favorite or strong areas are grouped

together, then you're going to be considered a specialist in those areas. If you checked off items across all or most of the areas, then you're going to fall into the generalist category. Both are needed in the Web development business.

Specialists are needed who have the desire and patience to concentrate in one or a few areas, working on them every day, straight through if necessary, to get the job completed.

Generalists are needed to keep the big picture in mind: the overall goal of the site, the creative goals, the coordination of the various stages of production, client communications, and the financial aspects. Without one or more generalists in the firm, the left hand won't know what the right hand is doing. Important things will fall through the cracks, and the client will become skeptical or unhappy.

In making the transition from specialist to Web Developer or business owner, programmers, designers, and other specialists are forced to take on additional areas of responsibility to meet all the expectations of the client and the requirements of the business. Yet not all specialists can become generalists. Those that can't must fill in the missing areas with partners, outside contractors, or alliances with strategically selected outside sources. In any case, the wide range of information presented in this book will aid anyone facing the task of developing a broad range of skills.

A PART-TIMER OR FREELANCER CAN BE A SPECIALIST. A BUSINESS OWNER MUST BE A GENERALIST.

Part-timers and freelancers who desire to specialize in design, HTML coding, programming, or site promotion can do so while also handling the big picture of overall site development, if they so desire. But if you're leading a team, or if you are accountable for more than one or two specialized areas, you have little choice but to be or become a generalist. It will be extremely difficult, if not altogether impossible, to focus on a narrow area and meet all of the client's needs. Indeed, just from the standpoint of communicating with the client, generalist skills will be required in order to speak the client's language. Clients' hot buttons can vary from newbie Internet user questions to marketing statistics, from corporate identity to concerns about competitors, from credit card transactions to shipping products to customers.

BEING THE RIGHT KIND OF GENERALIST

Being a generalist doesn't mean being a jack of all trades, master of none. You don't have to be able to do everything. You don't have to know *how* to do everything, but you do need to know *why* everything needs to be done. You need an appreciation for *when* something needs to be done and you need to be able to communicate these things to clients, employees, and others on your team.

You must keep the big picture in mind. This means understanding what clients hope to achieve with their Web sites or other Internet project and it also means understanding what it takes to operate your business at a profit.

The Big Picture

What should you do if you're not yet the right kind of generalist? One option is to assemble a team that covers the areas you're weak in. This is discussed in chapter 4. Another option is to acquire the critical skills you need to broaden your own capabilities. You'll find tips to help you do that throughout the following chapters.

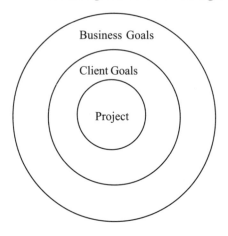

Business Goals

Client Goals

Project

YOU KNOW YOU'RE A GEEK WHEN...

You try to click every underlined word you see in print.

Your Role as a Consultant

The fact is, regardless of what your actual job is, along with just about everyone else in the Web development business, in addition to the actual work of developing Web sites, you're going to end up functioning more or less as a professional consultant as far as the client is concerned—that is, someone who provides expert advice and makes recommendations.

That doesn't mean you have to call yourself a consultant, if you're not wild about the idea. But the way you interact with your clients pretty much dictates that much of the time you'll serve in a consulting capacity. So, whether you're a Web designer, an HTML coder, a programmer, a Webmaster, a graphic designer, a copywriter, an account executive, a production coordinator, or a systems administrator, the minute you start helping other people put their businesses on the Web, you are going to be acting as a consultant.

WHY THIS IS IMPORTANT

In the course of serving clients, you will naturally be called upon on to give advice on a wide variety of Internet connectivity, Web page, and marketing topics. As you make it known that you are knowledgeable in these areas, clients will seek to gain the benefit of what you know. In fact, they'll eagerly listen for hours on end as you expound on all sorts of Internet-related topics—all at your expense, of course.

Now here's where understanding your role as a consultant comes in. Do you just give away the knowledge that you have acquired and consider it a cost of getting or keeping a Web design project or programming? Or can you make money from your expertise by charging clients for your time and advice? Which would you prefer? If you're like me, you'd rather be paid than give things away for free. The fact is, the better you understand your role as consultant, the easier it will be to sell and manage accounts, and make a profit.

When I began my career in advertising and public relations, I was eager to show what I could do and didn't hesitate to give freely of my time and advice if I thought it would lead to an assignment. I was making good money on the jobs I was getting, but not if I counted in all the free consulting I was doing. Even after I had achieved a good volume of business, I was still giving away my time and, what was worse, clients seemed to expect it.

One day I was tied up on the phone generously giving away my free advice to my second-largest client—one that owed me thousands of dollars—when a call came in from my biggest client—a company that always paid well, and on time. I told my staff to take a message; as it turned out, I later learned that in doing so, I lost the opportunity to handle a large assignment.

Now maybe I wouldn't have been able to get that assignment even if I had taken the call, but that incident really woke me up and made me realize what was wrong. Of course, I had no one but myself to blame. From then on, I was determined to stop giving away my time and talents and begin charging for them.

To make matters worse, a few days later I found out that my second-largest client was going broke and I wouldn't get a penny of the money owed me. Less than a week later, the president of that company called me to tell me he had started a another venture and wanted me to handle the new business, but there would be no money coming in from the old. I couldn't believe what I was hearing. All those hours of free consulting time were down the tubes! I politely told him, "No, thank you," but I was thinking, "I wouldn't work for you again if you were the last client in the world." As I thought about this further, I arrived at the following saying, which I call the Professional's Motto:

I would rather starve to death than work for free.

I began to keep this idea uppermost in mind when dealing with clients and it inspired me to learn how to bill for my time like a professional. I do far less free consulting today as a result.

THE IMPORTANCE OF BEING PROFESSIONAL

What is a Professional?

Professionals are those who take their job seriously, who have the necessary knowledge and skills to understand and solve clients' problems, and the ethical strength of character to decline work when they can't solve the problem.

Traditionally, professional occupations were considered those requiring advanced education or training and the application of intellectual skills: medicine, law, and theology, originally, but today also accounting, engineering, architecture, teaching, health cares, real estate, insurance and stockbrokering (all requiring licenses), and a wide variety of nonlicensed occupations including advertising, employment and travel agencies, leasing and financing firms, and of course, computer services.

These professions are distinguished from the skilled trades and crafts that also require special training but do not require the same application of intellectual skills: building trades such as plumbing, electrical, and contracting and others, such as auto mechanics and pest control, fall into this category.

Why You Should Be an Internet Professional

From the time the Internet began in the 1960s until 1993, the term *Internet professional* applied only to computer, networking, and telephone industry occupations.

The Internet as we know it today is still a very young industry, but changes have taken place so rapidly since the early 1990s that we can already recognize a difference between those who merely sell Web pages and those who provide a range of Internet marketing, Web site creation and promotion, and associated creative production services in an effort to properly guide their clients toward a successful and productive Internet involvement.

At a minimum, Internet professionals are those who have the necessary education and training (even if largely self-taught) and the capability of applying intellectual skills in planning, developing, and implementing Internet projects. But, as we shall see, sales and business management abilities are also an essential part of the professional skill set.

Professional Characteristics

What are some of the distinguishing characteristics of a professional? What's the difference between the professional and the nonprofessional? Which are you?

A lot of it has to do with how you conduct yourself, both in front of the client and behind the scenes.

Doing Things Right the First Time

It has been said that a professional is someone who can do it right the first time. That doesn't mean that professionals don't make mistakes. They make just as many mistakes as everyone else, but they correct them before anyone notices. That enables them to give the appearance that few, if any, mistakes are being made.

Of course, being able to do it right the first time implies that you have the skills and knowledge required to do the job. If you don't have the skills and knowledge, your number-one priority should be to acquire them.

Continuous Learning—Another Mark of the Professional

All aspects of the Internet continue to change at a relentless pace. Those who don't stay on top of the latest developments fall behind. The only way to stay on top and maintain a professional edge is to operate in the mode of continuous learning.

Say What You Do, Do What You Say

In front of the client, professionals conduct themselves in certain ways. Although they may be knowledgeable about many things, they do not delude themselves into thinking they have all the answers. They know there are limits to their knowledge and capabilities, and when a subject or question comes up which they don't know much about, they do not hesitate to say, "I don't know."

WHAT YOU *REALLY* DO FOR YOUR CLIENTS

It is helpful to understand the psychology of the client—often referred to as the psychology of the buyer.

Two vital elements of professional services were identified in a *Harvard Business Review* article.* They are equally applicable to Internet consulting and Web development:

---

*Warren Wittreich, "How to Buy/Sell Professional Services," *Harvard Business Review,* March/April 1966.

- minimizing uncertainty
- the ability to understand and solve problems

We'll look at them separately, but they are intertwined.

Minimizing Uncertainty

What does a company gain by hiring an outside firm to assist with its Web development efforts? What benefit does a company get by hiring *your firm* to handle its Internet projects?

Any time we're confronted with new information or a changing environment, it can create a sense of doubt that brings to mind many questions.

- What does it all mean?
- How important is it for my business?
- How important is it for me personally?
- What do I need to do differently as a result of this new information or change?
- Should I stop doing anything I'm already doing?
- Who else in my organization will be affected?
- How will my customers be affected?

Many business people are inherently skeptical, especially of anything the news media seem to be excited about. For the company new to the Internet, barraged by media hype and horror stories, it can seem like a risky area in which to invest their limited resources. Here are a few areas of uncertainty facing the typical Web site client.

- Will the Internet work for my business?
- Do we need a Web site?
- How urgent is it that we get involved with the Internet?
- What kind of Web site do we need?
- What is the best way to take my company to the Internet?
- Will customers be able to find my Web site and, if they do, will they like what they find there and do business with us?
- How will we know the difference between a good Web developer and a rip-off artist?
- How do Web developers charge for their services?

- Should we pay by the hour or by the project?
- How much of the existing information about our company in the form of brochures, ads, product catalogs, etc., is suitable for use on the Internet, with or without adaptation?
- How much new material will have to be developed for my Web site?
- Who will create this material?
- Will the Internet work with my existing marketing strategy?
- Will it work with my existing sales and shipping procedures?

These questions (and a hundred more) are likely to be the same from client to client, with many variations on a theme. The answers you provide, however, must be specific to each individual client, designed to meet their particular needs.

If you are skilled in Web site development and knowledgeable about Internet marketing, you are in a position to offer your clients the confidence and peace of mind that comes from knowing their project is being handled by a competent professional, someone they can rely on to guide them through unknown territory toward success. That *reduces their uncertainty* and changes their perception of the risks involved. In short, it gives them hope that the Internet will work for them.

It will also help them address the other risk-filled areas they have questions about.

- All this Internet stuff sounds great, but why do I suspect there is a hidden catch somewhere?
- How do I know I'm hiring the right people to develop my Internet project?
- Which firm will make me look good and help me get a promotion?

The Ability to Understand and Solve Problems

The second crucial skill clients look in a Web consultant is for the ability to understand their particular situation or problem with respect to the Internet.

This is a very important point and one that sneaks up on the new Web developer, programmer, or marketer who isn't tuned in to it. It requires that the Web consultant have some familiarity with the client company and its present situation, or at least the ability to quickly learn and understand the client's situation.

The alternative is the cookie-cutter or one-size-fits-all approach, where no matter what the problem, you have only one answer to offer as the solution. Some clients will not catch on to this but most will. Therefore, you're in a much better position if you can genuinely listen and respond to the unique problems of each customer. From your perspective, and looking across all clients, it may well seem to be the same problem over and over again. The key is to become attuned to the myriad variations on a theme and recognize how each client is indeed different from the next. Even more important is the need to always develop a unique solution for each customer, even those whose situation and challenges are identical to other clients you have handled. Here again, variations on a theme is the key.

THE PROFESSIONAL SALESMAN VERSUS THE PROFESSIONAL WHO CAN SELL

"I hate selling. I'm not a salesperson. In fact, I hate it when salespeople call to sell me something." If this sounds like you, you're reading the right book!

You don't have to be a professional salesperson. In fact, it is very difficult for professional salespeople to sell Web development services. This brings us to another aspect of professional services identified by Warren Wittreich in his *Harvard Business Review* article, "How to Buy/Sell Professional Services,": buying from the professional.

A significant aspect of professional services is that the client *wants* to buy from the person who will provide the service. Without the necessary knowledge and skill, only rarely can the professional salesperson do the selling without landing in a situation where the answer to every client question is, "I really don't know. I'll have to ask one of our specialists in that area and get back to you." It's one thing to say it occasionally—it's another when it is the *only* answer that can be given to questions of any complexity. That makes it very difficult for the client to believe in the credibility of the person doing the selling and the organization he represents.

Rather than a professional salesperson, what is needed, as Wittreich points out, is *a professional who can sell*—that is, someone who has the expertise, skills, and knowledge of Web development, programming, or Internet marketing needed to achieve credibility and gain the client's trust in addition to the selling skills needed to persuade the client to do business.

ACHIEVING CREDIBILITY

For a professional, then, making the sale really means achieving credibility as a knowledgeable and trustworthy source of expertise. Taking a consultative approach, listening to the customer, engaging in a conversation about the customer's problems, and explaining how your expertise or experience can be helpful will go a long way toward establishing your credibility as an Internet professional in the eyes of your customer.

YOU KNOW YOU'RE A GEEK WHEN...

You're amazed to find out that spam is a food.

Planning Your Business

START WITH A PLAN

While traditional business books will tell you that you need to have a formal written business plan with pretentious corporate mission statements, Ph.D.-level marketing plans, and financial statements only an accountant can read, I have a different opinion. If you're like me, the only thing worse than backing up a 2-gig hard drive on floppies is the idea of writing a business plan! I've spent much of the last twenty years as a professional copywriter and even *I* hate the idea of writing one.

The fact is, most Internet businesses are not rocket science. They are not elaborate businesses. I'm not saying you shouldn't have a plan—you should, but if you can't outline the plan for your business in your head or at the most in a few pages, you're not planning an Internet service business offering Web design, consulting, programming, or marketing.

If you're bootstrapping your business—planning to grow project by project with no outside investment, and no loans other than what you can float on your own good name, credit cards, or home equity—if you plan to keep the business small—no employees, just yourself and a couple of outside contractors—and if you already know exactly who to call to get as much business as you need, you probably don't need a written plan at all. Having one certainly won't hurt, but you can probably live without one and do just fine.

If you seek an investor, if you're throwing in your lot with partners, if you'll need to finance equipment with bank loans, and if you plan to hire employees, you *will* need a well-thought-out and well-written plan and it definitely is worth the time and effort (and agony) to put one together. You'll have an easier time down the road living with your partners and employees, and you'll have a much better chance of getting a bank loan if the loan officer can explain to the bank's loan committee in ten words or fewer what you're going to do with the loan and where the money is going to come from to pay it back. As for investors, while a business plan alone won't persuade them to invest—ultimately, they'll make that decision based more on what they think of you than what they think of the business—your business plan is the first impression they will have of you, and it needs to be a good one.

My Personal Business Plan

I recite the following to myself every morning, just as a reminder.

1.   Find customers.

2.   Sell like hell.

3.   Do the work.

4.   Take the money.

WHAT IS A PLAN GOOD FOR?

A business plan

- forces you to think through the critical areas of the business.
- keeps you organized.
- keeps your sales efforts on track.
- gives you a yardstick to measure performance against.
- serves as the manual for your business when all else fails, and, as they say in the newsgroups, RTFM!

WHAT YOUR PLAN SHOULD COVER

Entire books longer than this one have been devoted to the sole subject of how to write a business plan, and rightly so. In addition, just about every major CPA firm has written its own guide that is available for free, and there is excellent software to help automate the process. Consequently, this chapter will touch on just the major highlights.

Did I say Web sites? There are a few of those with good information, too. *See the resource list at the end of this chapter for more information.* Check them out before sitting down to write your business plan. A sample business plan appears at the end of the book.

Your plan should include the following components:

- *Preliminaries*
    - table of contents—just what it says: an outline of the major plan sections
    - executive summary—A one- to two-page summary of the major points and conclusions of each section of the plan
- *Overview of the Company*
    - a general overview of the company's purpose and strategy
    - legal form of organization
    - detailed description of company products or services
    - office location
- *The Marketing Environment*
    - market research, including market size, major segments, industry analysis
    - the competition
- *The Management Team*
    - key members of the management team
    - team background, experience, strengths
    - weak areas of the organization and plan to strengthen them
- *Marketing Strategy*
    - sales plan
    - advertising and promotion plan
- *Milestones*
    - timeline with dates of major planned accomplishments
- *Financial Statements*
    - funds required by the plan—sources, terms, repayment schedule(s)
    - financial projections
    - financial analysis

CHARACTERISTICS OF A GREAT BUSINESS PLAN

From an 1993 electronic seminar presented on CompuServe's PR and Marketing Forum by Linda Elkins, a professional business plan writer. She is asked to review plans fairly frequently, so she has a pretty good idea of what plans look like before they go to the capital source. Reproduced with the permission of the forum sysops.

1. **Clear, realistic financial projections.** The investigations of many capital providers start and end here. The financials must be in a standard format and presented clearly. Assumptions must be listed for all significant line items. Reasoning for the sales figures projected has to be convincing.

2. **Detailed market research.** You must demonstrate that you know your customers and the problem you are solving for them. You must show the size of your market and know its trends.

3. **Detailed competitor research.** Everyone has competitors, and to run a company effectively you have to know them and respect them.

4. **A strong management team.** If you have holes in ability in your management team, start lining up people ready to come on when the financing comes in, and include them in your plan.

5. **Proof of forethought in every category.** You must show that this really is a plan for running your business. Demonstrate that you know how to sell and distribute your product, demonstrate that you have thought through the hiring needs that come with growth, and demonstrate that you have thought about the kind of company you want to grow, and how the investor fits in.

6. **An executive summary.** Start with a simple statement of what the company is seeking and continue with a clear, upper-level description of your market, management, and product or service.

7. **Excellent formatting.** Make your plan inviting to read—leave white space on the pages, use reasonably large type, write in short paragraphs, and use bullet points whenever applicable. You have five minutes or less to interest the average capital provider, and if she can't immediately understand your plan, she will pass it over.

MOST COMMON ERRORS

Here is a list of the most common problems with business plans, problems gleaned by Linda Elkins from various places, and from venture capital sources or bank loan officers. Plans for internal use will benefit just as much from solving these problems.

1. **No clear plans for progress.** You must prove you can reach the goals outlined in your plan. Show prior successes; write detailed sales plans with numbers and schedules. Talk about previous marketing efforts and compare with future marketing efforts. Many plans describe where the business is now and talk about the markets they will sell to and how much money they will make, but present no step-by-step method to get there. If there is something you don't know the answer to or the method to use, don't avoid it. Attack the blank spot and find out how to fill it in.

2. **Failing to describe the product in layman's terms,** and talking about it too much. In general, product description isn't too helpful for running the business, except in that it leads you to question how you designed your product, and if it is right for the market.

3. **Lack of market and competitor research.** You must show where you fit in your market and you must know the details of your competitors' products. We've talked about this so I won't belabor it.

4. **Incomplete financials.** Provide financials that are detailed enough that a reviewer can make some guesses about your accuracy and for you to use them for management. Most important, include a clear and complete list of the assumptions that form your financials. You must show actuals if you have them.

5. **Huge appendixes.** You don't need to tell the reader everything now. The drop test (the idea that a heavier document is more impressive) doesn't work here. Internal plans, especially, need to be readable and economical.

6. **Bad grammar.** Get a good editor.

7. **Too little detail.** I've run across principals who write four-page plans and feel they have nothing more to say. Use the outline as a crutch and keep researching and

writing. Also, many of you who write four-page plans
think businesses don't need plans and that you can do it
all from your head. If you want investors, you must have a
plan.

8. **The overall plan is too long.** Forty pages or fewer is
ideal for attracting investors; sixty-five pages is definitely
too long. Probably also true for internal plans—how
much are you willing to reread and check progress
against?

9. **Overuse of acronyms.** Don't make the reader go back
and reread the definition. If the full name is too tedious
to type out, consider renaming it.

10. **Redundancy.** Organize your plan carefully and put each
fact and plan in only one place, the place where it tells
the story the best way.

LEGAL FORM OF THE BUSINESS

What Legal Form Will Your Business Have?

Basically, you have three choices when selecting the form of your
business:

- sole proprietor
- partnership
- corporation

The tax differences between the three forms are significant,
and it's beyond the scope of this book to go into great detail. We'll
take a brief look at each of these, but for an in-depth understanding of that form of organization that is best for you, consult a CPA
or an attorney experienced in tax matters.

Sole Proprietorship

A sole proprietor is an individual who is self-employed and owns
his or her own business. It is the simplest form of business organization. The business of a sole proprietor has no existence apart
from the owner. Its liabilities are your liabilities, and your ownership interest ends when you die. Your personal assets are at risk,

whether they are used in the business or used strictly for personal purposes, meaning that if your business does not succeed, all the debts of the business will be your personal debts—or, if someone sues your business, they will really be suing you personally.

Profit and loss is reported to the IRS on Schedule C of your tax return and carried over to your personal Form 1040. Debts of the business are also your personal debts.

A sole proprietor business is the easiest to set up and start. It can work well for someone who is just starting out or running the business as a sideline, has little debt, and does not have any business partners. Typically, as the business grows, there will be tax and liability advantages to converting the business to a corporation.

Partnership

A partnership is a business owned by two or more persons. Each partner typically contributes money, property or equipment, or labor and skill, and each is entitled to receive a share of the profits and losses of the business.

According to the IRS, the term *partnership* includes joint ventures, groups, pools, syndicates, and any other unincorporated organization carrying on a business not otherwise classified as a trust, estate, or corporation.

A partnership agreement should be written and should clearly outline each partner's percentage of ownership and share of income, gain, loss, and deductions. At tax time, the partnership itself will file an "information" return on Form 1065, reporting the income, deductions, and other required information, including each partner's share of taxable income, but the partnership itself pays no taxes. Taxable income is claimed by each partner, according to his share, on his personal tax return.

Liability issues are basically the same for partners as they are for sole proprietors. The partnership does not afford any special protection in the area of personal liability and therefore you should carefully think about whether you will benefit from a partnership or whether you would be better off forming a corporation.

Corporation

A corporation is a business that owned by stockholders and run by officers elected by the stockholders. When you incorporate, you transfer either money or property (equipment, real estate) to the corporation in exchange for shares of stock in the corporation, thereby becoming a stockholder or shareholder. Each corporation is governed by articles of incorporation and bylaws. Typically, the shareholders elect a board of directors and officers. The officers run the business on a day-to-day basis, and all major decisions must be approved by the board of directors.

A corporation exists as a separate legal "person" and may sue and be sued. At tax time, the corporation files a tax return, typically on Form 1020 or Form 1020-A, and corporate profits are normally taxed to the corporation. In figuring its income taxes, generally speaking, a corporation takes the same deductions as a sole proprietorship. In addition, there are special deductions that a corporation is entitled to take. A corporation may decide to pay a portion of its after-tax profits to its shareholders in the form of dividends. If it does, the dividend is taxable income to the shareholders.

There are two major reasons why most businesses incorporate: (1) to obtain more favorable tax treatment, and (2) to limit personal liability exposure.

Some things to keep in mind about corporations:

- You must incorporate in a particular state—usually the state where you will operate the business, though not always.
- Because a corporation is a separate legal entity, you must be careful to conduct the affairs of the corporation separately from your own personal affairs. That means not paying the groceries and the babysitter out of the corporate account.
- To protect and preserve the business as a corporation, you must be careful to comply with the corporation's bylaws and with state law when it comes to holding required meetings of shareholders and the board of directors. This is important because, should the corporation be sued and it is determined that the corporate affairs of the company are not in order, it may be possible for the court hold you personally responsible.

The two basic forms of corporations are the S corporation and the C corporation. Many small businesses elect to be designated as an S corp. This designation enables the income of the corporation to avoid taxation at the corporate level and flow through to the shareholder as in a partnership. In a C corporation profits are taxable to the corporation. Then, if you pay dividends to the shareholders, that income is taxable to them. This is known as the double taxation of corporate profits, because they are taxable first to the corporation and then again to the shareholders. However, your accountant can assist you in minimizing this extra tax hit. An S corp avoids the double taxation and does so without affecting the liability protection you get from incorporating. However, one catch: to be eligible to elect to be treated as an S corporation you must file the necessary forms either the year before you wish to begin the election, or within the first two months and fifteen days of the current tax year.

Limited Liability Corporations

Recently another corporate form has emerged: the limited liability corporation or LLC. An LLC combines characteristics of both the corporation and the partnership and is recognized in forty-seven states. LLCs offer some tax benefits that S corps don't. For instance, you can have more shareholders in an LLC (unlimited) than you can in an S corp (seventy-five). But there are some disadvantages. Among them, the fact that it's a new form means that your state may not have yet decided once and for all how these new entities are to be taxed—laws may change for this new form more rapidly than they will for the established forms. In addition, landlords and investors may not be familiar with the new LLC and may not know what to make of it or how their interests may be affected by your status as an LLC.

Comparing Business Entities

The following table, prepared by David Cartano, a Los Angeles attorney and expert on limited liability corporations, summarizes the main differences between LLCs, C corporations, S corporations, and partnerships. Take this with you when meeting with your attorney and accountant to discuss which form is right for you.

Item	Entity	Comparison
Tax rate	LLC	There is no tax to the LLC on LLC income. All items of income, gain, and loss pass through to and are taxed to the members.

Item	Entity	Comparison
Tax rate *(cont.)*	C corporation	Graduated tax rates up to 35 percent on taxable income over $10 million. Personal service corporations are taxed at the 35-percent rate on all income.
	S corporation	There is no tax to the S corporation except in two limited circumstances (recognized built-in gains and excess passive net income).
	partnership	There is no tax to the partnership on partnership income. All items of income, gain, and loss pass through to and are taxed to the partners.
Eligible owners	LLC	No restrictions on eligible owners.
	C corporation	No restrictions on eligible owners.
	S corporation	An S corporation may not have more than seventy-five shareholders. It may not have nonindividual shareholders, subject to certain exceptions.
	partnership	No restrictions on eligible owners.
Types of ownership interests	LLC	Membership interests. There may be different classes of membership interests.
	C corporation	Stock. There may be different classes of stock.
	S corporation	Stock. There may be only one class of stock. However, there may be voting and nonvoting common stock.
	partnership	General and limited partnership units. There may be different classes of ownership interests.
Special allocations	LLC	Special allocations are permitted if the allocations have substantial economic effect.
	C corporation	Special allocations are not permitted. Dividends must be paid based on stock ownership.
	S corporation	Special allocations are not permitted. Income, gain, and loss pass through to the shareholders based on stock ownership.
	partnership	Special allocations are permitted if the allocations have substantial economic effect.
Liability of owners	LLC	Limited liability for owners and managers.
	C corporation	Limited liability for shareholders, officers, and directors.

Item	Entity	Comparison
Liability af owners *(cont.)*	S corporation	Limited liability for shareholders, officers, and directors.
	partnership	All partners in a general partnership are personally liable. The general partner in a limited partnership is personally liable. There is limited liability for the limited partners in a limited partnership.
Transferability of ownership interests	LLC	There may be restrictions on transfer under state law.
	C corporation	Shares may be freely transferred.
	S corporation	Shares may be freely transferred only to eligible S corporation shareholders.
	partnership	Partnership interests may be transferred in accordance with the terms of the partnership agreement. Ordinarily, a general partnership interest may not be transferred without the consent of the other partners.
Duration	LLC	An LLC dissolves at a time specified in the operating agreement, or on the loss of a member unless the other members agree to continue the LLC.
	C corporation	Continues indefinitely.
	S corporation	Continues indefinitely.
	partnership	A partnership dissolves at time specified in the partnership agreement or when there is a more than 50 percent change in partnership interests during any twelve-month period.
Management	LLC	Managed by all members or designated managers. Members who participate in management are not personally liable.
	C corporation	Managed by directors and officers.
	S corporation	Managed by directors and officers.
	partnership	Managed by general partners. Limited partners who participate in management are personally liable.
Liabilities and basis	LLC	Liabilities incurred by the LLC increase members' basis in membership interests.
	C corporation	Liabilities incurred by the corporation do not increase shareholders' basis in stock.

Item	Entity	Comparison
Liabilities and basis *(cont.)*	S corporation	Liabilities incurred by the corporation do not increase shareholders' basis in stock.
	partnership	Liabilities incurred by the partnership increase partners' basis in partnership interests.
Pass-through of losses	LLC	Losses of LLC may be passed through to and deducted by members subject to certain restrictions (basis, at-risk, and passive loss limitations).
	C corporation	Losses of corporation may not be passed through to and deducted by shareholders.
	S corporation	Losses of corporation may be passed through to and deducted by shareholders subject to certain restrictions (basis, at-risk, and passive loss limitations).
	partnership	Losses of partnership may be passed through to and deducted by partners subject to certain restrictions (basis, at-risk, and passive loss limitations).
Fringe benefits	LLC	Members ineligible for certain fringe benefits.
	C corporation	Shareholder employees are eligible for most fringe benefits.
	S corporation	Two-percent shareholders are ineligible for certain fringe benefits.
	partnership	Partners are ineligible for certain fringe benefits.
Fiscal year	LLC	Must use the tax year of members having a majority interest in the LLC, or the tax year of all principal members if there is no majority interest.
	C corporation	May use any fiscal year. Personal service corporations must use a calendar year, subject to certain exceptions.
	S corporation	Must use calendar year, subject to certain exceptions.
	partnership	Must use the tax year of partners having a majority interest in the LLC, or the tax year of all principal partners if there is no majority.
Tax on sale or distribution of appreciated assets	LLC	There is a single tax at member level on sale of appreciated assets. Generally, there is no tax on distribution of appreciated assets.

Item	Entity	Comparison
Tax on sale or distribution of appreciated assets *(cont.)*	C corporation	There is potential double taxation. There is a corporate-level tax on sale or distribution of appreciated assets. There is a potential dividend or capital gains tax on distribution of sales proceeds to shareholders.
	S corporation	There is a single tax at the shareholder level on sale of appreciated tax. There is also a potential built-in gains tax at the corporate level if the corporation had appreciated property at the time of conversion from a C corporation to an S corporation.
	partnership	There is a single tax at the member level on sale of appreciated assets. Generally, there is no tax on distribution of appreciated assets.
Tax to entity on liquidation	LLC	There is no tax to LLC on sale or distribution of assets.
	C corporation	Corporation is taxed on appreciation in assets on sale or distribution of assets.
	S corporation	There is no tax to the corporation except for potential built-in gains tax if C corporation converted to an S corporation in prior ten years.
	partnership	There is no tax to partnership on sale or distribution of assets. Gain on sale of assets passes through to the partners.
Tax to owners on liquidation	LLC	Gain on liquidating sale of appreciated assets by the LLC passes through to the members. No gain is recognized on distribution except to the extent that the money distributed exceeds member's basis in membership interest.
	C corporation	Gain is recognized to extent that the fair market value of property distributed exceeds shareholder's basis in stock.
	S corporation	Gain is recognized to the extent that the property distributed exceeds the shareholder's basis in stock.
	partnership	Gain on liquidating sale of appreciated assets by the partnership passes through to the partners. No gain is recognized on distribution of appreciated or other assets except to the extent that the money distributed exceeds the partner's basis in partnership interest.

Source: David J. Cartano, Law Firm of Barton, Klugman & Oetting,
333 South Grand Avenue, 37th Floor, Los Angeles, CA 90071-1599,
213-621-4000. E-mail: cartano@msn.com; http://www.loop.com/~cartano/llc.htm.

GET ADVICE FROM AN ATTORNEY AND AN ACCOUNTANT

"It's not what you do, it's how you do it." This is something many clients have heard from their attorney or accountant. It means that the same end can be achieved in different ways, but the way to the end can make all the difference in the world regarding how it is treated for tax purposes.

When considering incorporation, you should make sure you have obtained the advice of an attorney experienced in handling corporations and the advice of a certified public accountant. The attorney will prepare all the necessary articles of incorporation, bylaws, and other documents that must be filed with your state government. Your attorney will also advise you on the best way to handle a variety of issues, including what type of corporate stock should be issued, and will help you understand the special requirements for meetings of corporation shareholders, officers, holding elections, and so forth. She will also help you understand how to keep things straight when you are acting as a shareholder one minute, an officer the next, and an employee after that.

Your CPA can prepare a comparison of your personal and corporate tax situations under different forms of incorporation and advise you on the best overall tax strategy.

The bottom line on the form you choose for your business? Sole proprietor, partnership, one of the types of corporations—any of these forms can potentially work for you. Just be sure to investigate the tax and liability consequences with the help of a knowledgeable attorney and accountant before choosing one.

LOCATION

Make Yourself at Home

Working from home is a great way to start out. It allows you to keep your overhead low, it offers the world's easiest commute, and you're never far from the snack pantry.

Thanks to a booming trend in home offices, you'll find it's easy to obtain the support network you'll need to succeed. Phone companies, UPS, FedEx, office supply companies, and others are growing accustomed to serving small at-home businesses in residential areas if for no other reason than all the deliveries they are making to the growing ranks of big-company telecommuters. You can ride the coattails of this social phenomenon with a surprising amount of efficiency. In fact, the phone company is probably your biggest ally here. Advanced residential and business phone services available in most areas along with special packages of home-business phone plans make it easy to run a business from home that all but a few of your customers will be convinced is really headquartered in an office. If all goes well, you will soon outgrow your humble abode and move out to a full-fledged office suite, but in the meantime there is no reason why you can't make a home location work.

The cost is practically zero and some of your housing costs may be deductible—the square footage devoted to your office or studio area can be prorated. However, the home office deduction is rumored to be an IRS flag for closer scrutiny of your income tax return. Why go through a tax audit if you don't have to? You may be better off skipping the deduction of a few hundred dollars per year and simply enjoying the cost savings of not paying office rent.

And don't feel as if you have to hide where you work. It's very trendy to work from home and your poor, hapless officebound clients will probably envy you what they will perceive as tremendous freedom. Don't be so quick to buy into that idea, though, because as anyone who works from home will tell you, it is not without its pitfalls.

Among the distractions? Temptation is lurking in every room, both on and off the job. When you're working, the refrigerator, television, and backyard are beckoning. If you're the type that can't stand clutter, you'll be tempted to set work aside and clean the house. The mailman will be stopping by any time now, so you probably don't want to make any sales calls—you wouldn't want to miss this daily visit. Well, you get the idea. And, at the end of the day, the tables turn and it is your office which beckons, making it easy to become a workaholic. You may find it too easy to putter away unproductively for hours and fool yourself into thinking you're actually accomplishing something. You may find it actually takes a surprising amount of discipline to separate work from home under these conditions, but for those who can master it, working from home has many advantages.

Virtually Organized

Beyond working from home, the next step is the virtual organization. This essentially amounts to everyone on your team working from home, or some combination of home and office. Again, today, you need not hide this fact. And of course the Web and all its associated tools conspire to make even the most deskbound executive pine for virtual freedom. So play it to the hilt if this is how you choose to locate your business.

Your Executive Suite

Perhaps this home-based and virtual stuff isn't for you. Maybe you don't want a fax machine in your living room or spare bedroom. Maybe the idea of going out on a virtual limb is not your cup of, shall we say, java. Or perhaps you have one or two employees or partners, all of whom work from their own home, but none of the homes is large enough or suitable for everybody.

For you, a good starting point may be an executive suite. These are typically set up by companies that lease a large amount of luxury office space and then sublease to one-person offices. You rent one or two mini-suites, usually large enough to hold only a desk and a filing cabinet. An executive-suites leasing company may provide a variety of convenient and helpful services that you might not be able to afford on your own. Among the services typically offered: expensive or at least expensive-looking furnishings, reception area, conference room, kitchen, secretarial help, a receptionist and dedicated-line phone answering service, voice mail, fax, call forwarding, conference calling, 800-number phone service, and mail pickup. In any case, for usually around $500–$1,000 per month, you'll have an office located in an office building, perhaps even with a prestigious address. You'll have someone to answer the phone and someone to type up proposals and perhaps even type up your invoices, all at a reasonable monthly cost. And, although the actual cost per square foot will far exceed the highest-quality luxury office space, your rent includes services that would cost you far more if you had to hire employees full time—five to ten times as much.

Another benefit of executive suites: you may not have to actually work there in order to benefit from the services. For instance, to help you make the move out of a home office, you may be able to obtain just a few services without actually relocating. You might be able to contract for telephone answering, call forwarding, or use of the conference room while you continue to work from your home—except for the meetings you schedule in "your" conference room!

As a transition from a home-based business to the next level, nothing beats an executive suite. However, this option is probably not the answer for a programmer or Web designer whose expensive equipment may require a higher level of security. Access at odd hours—which may be your best working hours—may also be a problem.

A Corner Office on the Fifty-Fourth Floor

When your business can afford it, look at an address in an executive park or even downtown. Your offices can add to your credibility, especially when dealing with larger companies; despite the trend toward home offices, there will continue to be some who think stability and reliability is measured by location.

As for how much space you'll need, figure 150 to 200 square feet per employee, on average, plus an additional 15 percent to allow for comfortable movement throughout the office and adequate storage space, according to Andrew Johnson, a Southern California commercial real estate broker and author of the book, *Tough Times, Tough Tactics,* published by Johnson Commercial Brokerage (800-270-4848).

According to Johnson, you'll pay anywhere from $15 to $35 per square foot, more in prime downtown areas of larger cities. That's an annual cost, so at $15 per square foot, one thousand square feet of office space will cost you $15,000 per year or $1,250 per month.

You will also typically be assessed a load factor or operating pass-through fee that reduces the landlord's cost of maintaining the building lobby, elevators, hallways, and other overhead—areas she can't lease directly.

Different Kinds of Leases

Triple Net Lease
The triple net lease is commonly found in office buildings. It calls for the tenant to pay for the entire prorated share of all building operating expenses, utilities, taxes, and insurance.

Gross Lease
In the gross lease, a base rental rate covers all of the landlord's expenses in a single cost per square foot.

Modified Gross Lease
The modified gross lease typically works this way: The first year of the lease is considered your base year, during which you pay the base rent only. In the second year, the landlord estimates what the cost increases will be in the common areas and then assesses you your prorated share of the increase in addition to your base rent.

Local customs and laws can have an impact on rent increases. For instance, in California, tenants have what's known as Proposition 13 protection: If the building is sold, the new owner must limit load factor increases to an amount proportionate to the average of the last three years' expenses.

NEGOTIATING YOUR OFFICE LEASE

Office leases can be tricky, especially for the newbie. Negotiation is a critical factor in getting a lease deal you can live with. You can do the homework yourself or get a commercial broker who can guide you through the process. Don't depend on the landlord's broker—she's working for the landlord, not you. Seek out a broker of your own. You want someone willing to do the necessary homework on the market in order to turn up the best deals in the best locations and bring you deals in locations you hadn't thought of. A good broker knows all the tricks landlords play and will help you steer around the fine print in the lease. Use the broker to do your negotiating. A good broker will help you find creative cash and noncash solutions when hammering out a leasing deal.

Leasing Terms to Negotiate Carefully

Free rent. As an inducement to get you to sign a lease, the owner may be willing to offer rent reductions. If the leasing market is off and supply exceeds demand, you may be able to obtain an entire year or more of free or substantially reduced rent. In a tight market or buildings at near 100-percent occupancy, you'll pay full top dollar.

Rent increase. How are increases in base rate handled in the lease? It may be based on increases in the Consumer Price Index, a fixed increase of five or ten cents per month, or it might call for a big jump in the thirty-sixth month.

Length of lease. A landlord naturally wants all space in the building to be occupied by good tenants for as long as possible. It costs the landlord money to lease space. Leasing commissions and vacant space can eat into the bottom line. The longer the leasing term you can afford to agree to, the greater your bargaining power in most cases.

Right to relocate. Typical leases give the landlord the right to relocate you, but it should be specified exactly what space they can move you into. For example, if you're in a corner suite on the top floor, make sure they can't move you to the basement. And in such a situation, the landlord should pay for associated costs such as letterhead, necessary build-out, electrical installations, etc. Andrew Johnson points out, "You should negotiate rights to expand as well as rights to renew. You should ask about the plans of other tenants. Do they have expansion plans, and how will that affect you?"

Build-out provisions. You may be occupying what was formerly an accounting or law firm or maybe it was a boiler-room telemarketing operation. Some adjustments may have to be made in the floor plan to suit your business and that purple shag carpet just might not be your style this year. Don't worry. Your landlord will be willing to make some changes.

Average office build-out can run from $5 per square foot of space leased (paint and carpet) to $30 per foot (moving walls). To negotiate a better overall deal, look for space that's already as close as possible to what you need. "Structural changes are the most expensive," according to Johnson.

Typical lease terms will call for the landlord to "build to suit" or, alternatively, to provide "build-out allowance up to $x per square foot." If the changes you have in mind exceed that rate, then you pay the additional. How do you know what you'll actually get from these deals? "Every building typically has building standards covering carpet quality, number of doors per thousand square feet, etc.," says Johnson. "It's a good idea to always have the ability to have your own contractors, subject to approval by landlord."

Premium locations. You know, that corner office you like so much? Brace yourself—it's going to cost you extra in most buildings. In fact, every subtle little extra detail or advantage the landlord can think of is going to have a price or value associated with it.

Parking. Another crucial area to negotiate, if your building even has parking available. If it does, you'll likely receive a certain number of parking spots based on the amount of space you lease. Additional spaces may or may not be available at additional cost—they may not be available at any cost in some areas.

How Andrew Johnson does it:"Often if you don't utilize all the parking you're entitled to initially, you will lose the right to it. I always negotiate the right for my clients to obtain additional parking."

Amount of space. All of your leasing costs hinge on how much space you're renting. The more space, the higher the total cost. If you can find a way to reduce the amount of space you need, you'll reap the rewards in the form of lower lease costs. There are many ways to be efficient and cut down the amount of space you're leasing. A lot of buildings have storage space either in the basement, adjacent to the building, or in an offsite location. You're better off taking advantage of that than using prime space for file storage. Another way to cut down: Conference rooms typically aren't used that often. It's usually better to enlarge the office of the person who holds the most conferences. Or reception areas can be enlarged to make a conference room.

Building Name. OK, this may be a bit far-fetched, but I can foresee the day when your business will put its name on the top of a major downtown office building. Now, depending on how prestigious your business is, that may cost you big time, or it may be something the landlord will offer as an inducement to get you to take over a major portion of the building.

Other Leasing Considerations

Tenant representation. Don't rely on the landlord's real estate broker. He's not representing you and won't go out his way to negotiate on your behalf. Instead, what you want is someone who represents *you* and looks out for your best interests only. That means using your own broker. Brokers are paid on commission and when buyer and seller each have a broker, the commission is split between them—so it does not cost more to use a broker and have tenant representation.

Finding an agent. As you're driving around looking for good locations, take note of who the more active brokers are. You can tell by who represents the most buildings. Contact their office and ask for their specialist in tenant representation—most large brokers have them. Johnson advises, "Set an appointment and interview them as you would an employee. What is their experience; who has she represented in the past? Sit down with three tenant reps before selecting."

Attorney review. Leases are too technical, too legal, and too binding to sign without a legal review, according to Johnson.

Miscellaneous. It's the little things that can make a difference when you're paying big bucks for office space. Will your office have a separate thermostat or will you be tied into the entire floor or building? Is the area safe at night? Is there security personnel in the building at night? You may pack a pistol and not care, but if you ask your employees to work late, it can be a major factor in their cooperation. After-hours HVAC—do you have to pay extra for weekends? How smart is the building? Adequate phone lines? Wired for fiber? How high tech is it? Can you take advantage of the newest technology?

SCOPE OF SERVICES YOU WILL OFFER

Another vital area that must be thought through from the very beginning is the nature and scope of services you will be offering. For anyone providing Internet consulting or development services, this is a crucial strategic decision because you personally will be selling and performing or supervising the vast majority of services offered by your firm yourself. Therefore, consciously determining the services you offer means understanding how the business will grow from your capabilities and knowledge, and understanding as well the additional skills you will need to learn in order to make the business successful. That in turn means looking at the state of current Internet technology, getting a look at the new technology coming down the pike, estimating when it will become dominant, and keeping tabs on the slower adoption rate of the world at large. Then you must think through where the customer needs will be, and when, and plan your service offerings accordingly.

For example:

> As I write this book, push technology is getting a lot of media attention. A few brave companies have pioneered various forms, mostly as platforms for the delivery of news to Internet users. But there is already talk that push may have even more valuable uses moving information across Intranets to bring up-to-date internal information to the attention of

employees. At the same time, the bandwidth-hogging characteristics of push have been recognized but not yet overcome. The problem may never be solved and that could hold push technology back and reduce its appeal to my clients. In addition, key dominant players have not yet emerged and the future development of the technology is not at all certain.

Personally, I am skeptical that the bandwidth limitations will ever be overcome, but professionally, I recognize that I could well end up being wrong. At present, I am not recommending that my clients do anything other than investigate push technology and think about testing it out starting sometime next year. Meanwhile, I will keep an eye out for any information that comes along on the subject in order to stay at the forefront and I will monitor the bookstores, the print media, the Web media, and e-mail mailing lists for new information, seminars, product demos, the experiences of others, etc. Every month or so, I'll run a search on push to see what's new. And I'll stop by Web sites at Microsoft, Netscape, and the major push vendors to see what's happening.

As the technology changes, should it become more practical and feasible, I will begin recommending it. In the meantime, I can at least discuss it intelligently with clients and those in the industry, and, in the event I have a client who is determined to move forward and try it early, I will be ready to assist them.

I will not significantly alter the direction of my business to actively pursue push projects. However, another business could look at this same situation and decide to abandon other directions and focus solely on finding clients for push projects.

Whether your focus is on Web design and development, programming, or Internet marketing, your first task to is focus on the core services you will offer—and those you won't. Certainly the services you provide will grow naturally from your capabilities, and don't hesitate to draw the line between what you do as, say, a Web developer, and what a Web site promotion firm does, but you must also think through the total mix of Internet services your customers are likely to require. You can extend your service mix by forming strategic partnerships and hiring outside contractors. This is discussed in chapter 4. You also need to be aware of what your competitors are offering. You don't have to match your competitors service for service, but you will want to make sure you cover the main areas and that you are as qualified as or more qualified than competitors in the areas you are focusing on.

All of that said, the main point here is that you must choose what to concentrate on. You cannot be all things to all people (though certainly you must be able to discuss intelligently all *Internet* things to all people). And it must be a choice, your choice. In other words, what you don't want to do is allow the scope of your services be arrived at haphazardly or by accident. It must be a deliberate choice.

ESTABLISHING YOUR COMPETITIVE ADVANTAGE

It is also essential that you determine in which market segments or services you are going to be a leader. Only then will you know how to position yourself or your firm in the client's mind. That's where your competitive advantage comes in.

Let's face it, the Internet field is growing. More and more people and firms are working on Internet projects. That means competition is going to be a significant factor for everyone.

A competitive advantage is a reason why your customer should do business with you versus another firm. It is something which is largely defined by the customer. For instance, you may clearly see some ways in which you far exceed what some firm on the other side of town is doing, but if the customer sees it as a distinction without a difference, it will do little to give you a competitive advantage. Thus, the key here is knowing your customers and knowing your competition. Customers have "hot buttons"—needs and wants—and competitors have strengths and weaknesses.

Some typical customer hot buttons:

Project cost—the lower the better
Turnaround time—the faster the better
Results—the more impressive the better
Professionals—the best at the least cost

Some typical competitor's claims to fame:

Highly knowledgeable about the client's industry
More specialized experience than any other firm
More services included for the same fee
Lower total project costs
Award-winning design
Client roster of Fortune 500 companies
Experts in programming, design, marketing, and so on
Name recognition

Some typical areas where competitors might fall down:

They miss every deadline ever set by the client
They are a bloated overhead billing machine with over-
priced fees to match
They are jacks of all trades and masters of none
Their award-winning design wins beauty contests but does-
n't motivate the client's customers to buy anything
They're cheap and their projects end up looking like it
They are so expert that no one—including the client—
understands what they are talking about
They've been so busy promoting themselves they've fallen
behind and are still selling yesterday's good idea and yesterday's technology

Somewhere along the spectrum of the client's hot buttons
and between the extremes of your competitor's strengths and
weaknesses, you'll find the best positioning for your own firm.
Draw from your own strengths or those of your team. Match those
against what the client is looking for and focus on areas where
there is high value in what you're offering to clients and the results
they can achieve by hiring you, compared to the cost of your fees.

Customer expectations and the competition are subject to
change, of course, so plan to refine your competitive advantages
over time as expectations and market conditions undergo change.

UNDERSTANDING BUSINESS GOALS, STRATEGIES, AND TACTICS

Finally, when thinking about business planning, service mix, and
competitors, and later, when you're down in the trenches slogging
through a hundred project deadlines, it's easy to confuse the three
different types of goals and objectives. However, it is vital that you
are able to distinguish among them.

- A *goal* is the broad concept, the end result.
  Example: *To run a profitable Internet business.*

- A *strategy* further defines what you will achieve and how. Example: *Sell $100,000 of Web consulting services in 1998 and keep total expenses below $80,000.*
- *Tactics* are the steps you take to implement your strategy. Example: *Identify five hundred prospects for Web development services. Call on all five hundred. Sell projects averaging $3,333 each to 30 companies. Refuse to take on unprofitable projects. Increase frequency of reviews of business finances from monthly to weekly, and, if necessary, daily, to keep costs below 80 percent of revenue.*

WHERE TO FIND MORE BUSINESS INFORMATION

AT&T Small Business Administration
www.att.com/small_business

Small Business Administration
www.sbaonline.sba.gov/hotlist

U.S. Treasury Home Page
www.ustreas.gov/browse/

IRS Tax Information for Business
www.irs.ustreas.gov/plain/bus_info

Inc. Magazine
www.inc.com

The Wall Street Journal Interactive Edition
www.wsj.com

American Express Small Business Exchange
americanexpress.com/smallbusiness

Visa Small Business Site
www.visa.com

TIME Vista
www.pathfinder.com/timevista/

Microsoft Smallbiz
www.microsoft.com/smallbiz

Business Plans

Silicon Valley Small Business Development Center
www.siliconvalley-sbdc.org/busplan.html

Khera Communications
www.morebusiness.com/starting

National Consultant Referrals
www.referrals.com/articles/bplan.htm

Writing the Small Business Plan
guide.sbanetweb.com/buspln.html

Inc. Magazine Articles

Venture Capital Express
www.inc.com/incmagazine/archives/11901591.html

The Best Laid Plans
www.inc.com/incmagazine/archives/02870601.html

Garbage In, Garbage Out
www.inc.com/incmagazine/archives/08960411.html

YOU KNOW YOU'RE A GEEK WHEN...

You refer to your spouse as "my domain server."

CHAPTER FOUR

Assembling Your Team

PERSONNEL

Putting together an effective team is the most important responsibility you have in building your business. It doesn't matter whether your team comprises only you and your other partners, or whether they're all your employees, all freelancers and outside contractors, strategic partners, or some combination. Whatever the makeup, it is vital that your team have the ability to sell and service your customers effectively and handle all the necessary administrative tasks your business requires.

Every member of the team must pull her own weight—and then some. Each major area of your business—new business, Web design, programming, Internet marketing, production coordination, administration—must be covered by a top performer, a results-getter who understands the big picture and has enough self-motivation to keep the ball rolling.

As your business grows, the time will come when you have more work than you or your partners can handle by yourselves. Deadlines will start to slip, details will fall through the cracks, and new business efforts will slow down because you are too busy putting out fires in other areas.

Only when you are reasonably certain that your business has grown to the point where you can sustain a sufficient level of work should you consider taking on the additional responsibility of employees. For some, this time may never come and it will make more sense to use only outside help.

SELL FIRST, THEN HIRE

Bring in the revenue first, then hire. Don't try to do it the other way around. Go out and get the business; then, when you have enough projects underway and a steady stream of income, go out and hire. This seems backward to those who can't see how the work will get done without the employees being in place. The solution to this, of course, is to identify freelancers who can do the work until you build the business to the point where you can afford to bring on employees. How much new revenue will you need? Well, at least two and a half times the base pay rate of the employee. In other words, for every $1,000 in salary, you'll need $2,500 in income (see chapter 5).

More Capacity and Control, But More Management Time and Effort Required

You'll need more than additional sales. You'll also need additional time to train, supervise, and coordinate, at least initially. So things will actually get even more hectic when you first bring on a new employee. And you'll need a great deal of patience and understanding as well.

More Personnel Means More Overhead

One inescapable difference between using outsiders and hiring employees: The employees add to your overhead. Unlike a freelancer, who has to be paid only if he works on a project, employees must be paid every week whether you have business coming in or not. That means your overhead goes up when you bring employees on board, and not just for payroll. More employees means more space, more office furniture, and more equipment. This will almost certainly affect your rates, which will have to go up to assure sufficient income during slow periods.

Even when there is more work to do than everyone can handle, you can survive under those conditions for a couple of months with no great harm to the business—in other words, without seriously damaging your relationship with clients. You will inevitably experience peak periods from time to time that stretch the available resources, but those projects will come to completion soon enough and it will be back to business as usual. The situation does not automatically call for bringing on more employees and adding to overhead. In fact, you can experience that cycle many times, and probably will.

USING FREELANCERS AND SUBCONTRACTORS

The simplest way for both the individual and the firm to add additional capabilities is by using freelancers and subcontractors to perform particular functions or handle designated phases of a project. With this arrangement, you hire a business or a self-employed individual on an ad hoc basis. Your client pays you, and you pay the freelancer.

Three characteristics make for a good freelancer or subcontractor. Think of them as the three abilities every freelancer must have:

1. capability
2. availability
3. reliability

Capability

A good freelancer has the talent, skills, and experience required to do the job right the first time. Look for freelancers whose personal and quality standards are higher than your own. For artists and copywriters, a review of their portfolio will indicate what they can produce, although one should not take a portfolio at face value. One must dig a little deeper to determine exactly what contribution the freelancer made to the project. An artist doing Web site design work may show an outstanding site in his portfolio and give the impression that he designed it himself, while in fact it may be that he only converted graphics files of preexisting artwork and credit for the excellent design you are looking at belongs to someone else. Without knowing this, one might be inclined to assume more about the artist's talents than is warranted. So, the rule of thumb here is, as you review each project in the portfolio, ask which portions of the work the freelancer personally handled. Also ask what materials the artist was given to work from and how other portions of the work were handled. This will give you a greater understanding of where the freelancer's responsibilities began and ended and allow you to draw parallels between the way you work and the way the freelancer is accustomed to working. This will give you a good idea of the person's likely fit and suitability for your projects. It will also give you a fair amount of insight into the truth-telling qualities of the individual you are interviewing.

The same is true of programmers. When interviewing, determine the exact point at which they became involved in the project and which portion they were responsible for. It doesn't hurt to ask what the programmer was given to work with by the client and the amount of turnaround time she had to work with. It's also a good idea to ask what whether the programmer's original estimate turned out to be accurate, and, if not, how much additional work was required to bring the project to completion.

Availability

The best freelancer in the world can't help you if he or she is tied up on another project. Rather than pressuring the busy artist or programmer, find someone who is available now. Another aspect of availability: You want someone you can lean on to get you out of the last-minute jams that inevitably seem to arise in any deadline-driven business. This can be a godsend, but be careful. After all, you don't want the freelancer caving into pressure from another client while they are racing to meet deadlines for your last-minute rush project.

Reliability

Internet projects, especially Web development, are a deadline business. Clients expect the work to be completed when promised. So, when turning to outside sources, one must be certain they will deliver their work by the agreed-upon deadline. This is the most common weak area of artists and programmers alike, and their failure can become a major headache for you. The best way to determine reliability is to ask for references of other clients they have worked for and call to see whether deadlines were in fact met. Missing deadlines is rather common, so you may have to adjust your own normal turnaround times if you rely on freelancers or outside contractors. When promising your client to deliver by a certain date, build in a cushion to allow for missed deadlines on the freelancer's part.

WHO TO HIRE FIRST

Probably the first employee you should think about hiring as soon as you can afford to is an administrative assistant who can handle the multiple tasks of receptionist, bookkeeper, and secretary. This person can add tremendously to your productivity and free you from the mundane but nevertheless essential tasks that must be performed if you are to stay in business. With those covered, your time can be better spent on revenue-producing activities and the delivery of high-quality work and service, a winning combination.

You may feel that your first priority is to add a clone of yourself, another salesperson, if that is your main role, or another Web designer or another programmer, if either of those is your primary role. This will work but it will force you to boost your time spent in selling and servicing clients in order to handle the additional overhead, which may be substantial if your clone has experience and capabilities strong enough for you to really lean on. If you go this route, don't do it unless you can also afford to bring on board an administrative assistant at the same time. That is, even if you don't add the administrative help right away, make sure you will be able to afford it immediately when you and your clone soon realize how desperately you need the help (and you will).

Administrative Assistant

Duties: Serve as receptionist for the business, answer phone calls, assist you in coordinating appointment schedules, type proposals and contracts under your direction, handle routine correspondence, organize and schedule paying bills, prepare client invoices, prepare checks for signature, generally keep office running smoothly. May also assist in proofreading of Web pages and other project-related matter and assist from time to time in coordination of project scheduling.

Background and experience: College degree preferred, with one to two years of office experience as an administrative assistant, bookkeeper, secretary, etc. Should have good typing, spelling, and proofreading skills.

Pay rate: Depends on the going rate in your area. Typically $18,000–$25,000 per year.

WHO TO HIRE NEXT

The next critical employee for any firm handling multiple projects at one time is a production coordinator. This person will actually take over and become your boss once the project is started. After setting up a schedule agreeable to the client, you will turn over to the production coordinator the responsibility for meeting deadlines and moving the work forward. Now, instead of spending hours every day assigning work and motivating your team, you can spend an hour in the morning directing your production coordinator and a few minutes at the end of the day to recap. The rest of your day will be free to move on to more important new business tasks and building stronger relationships with your clients. While you're working on that, your production coordinator will be pushing projects forward smoothly, keeping your production team on track. If you hire the right person, this key employee can make your personal productivity—and that of the business—soar.

Production Coordinator

Duties: Keep projects on deadline and moving forward smoothly. Act as a liaison between you and in-house and outside production staff, freeing you up to sell, service, and manage. Coordinate schedules and deadlines for proposals and all project work. May also communicate with clients on an as-needed basis to keep the approval process on schedule. This position is one of coordinating more than doing.

Background and experience: College degree preferred, with one to two years of similar production coordination or customer service experience, ideally in Internet projects or else in an ad agency or similar production environment. Must be detail oriented, be capable of learning your production process, and have respect for the creative process. Should have excellent people skills and be a good team player.

Pay rate: Depends on the going rate in your area. Typically $25,000–$35,000 per year.

STRATEGIC ALLIANCES

Another way to boost the selling and servicing power of your business without adding employees and overhead is by establishing a preferred business relationship, known as an alliance, with strategically selected outside sources.

Typically, in ordinary business dealings, you would treat outside sources as subcontractors and simply dole out the work whenever you needed to. Other than expecting them to perform satisfactorily, you wouldn't expect much else. You might use freelancers only occasionally and go for long periods of time without even communicating with them.

In a strategic alliance, the relationship is much different. By forming an alliance with a subcontractor, you agree to make his business your preferred source for his type of service or area of expertise. You agree to give him a substantial portion of your work, but you don't do so out of the goodness of your heart, only on a win-win basis.

A good strategic partner is someone who has something to offer you in return. That could be any of a number of things, including a lower rate, priority service that puts your jobs ahead of other customers, reduced or eliminated rush charges, consultation and troubleshooting advice, etc.

Another potential strategic ally is a company who hires firms that do what you specialize in. Here, you will seek to take on the role of a preferred subcontractor and your customer will become a key source of business for you. A third category is those companies who are in a good position to refer business to you but not necessarily to hire you.

How You Can Benefit from a Strategic Alliance

Whether you're running a one-person shop or a multiperson firm, with the rapid pace of Web development tools and technology it is doubtful that you or your organization is totally self-sufficient and possesses all of the many skills needed for Internet projects.

You may have a background in graphic design and need HTML coding abilities. Or, you may have CGI scripting or Web hosting capabilities but need copywriting and strong marketing skills. Or, you may be a dynamite salesperson but have no idea how to set up an autoresponder for a client's e-mail account. You may have strengths in all areas of Web development but be asked by clients to handle other types of advertising such as brochures and ad campaigns that are beyond your capabilities or areas you prefer not to handle directly. These are all situations where a strategic partnership comes in handy. Even if you have employees, in the beginning, at least, it is quite possible you still will not have all the talent you need within your organization. Instead, you will turn to outside resources for the skills or services you lack.

With a strategic partnership, you identify another Internet professional or company offering a good complementary relationship between your capabilities and theirs.

How a Strategic Alliance Works

For example, Internet access providers (ISPs) offering dialup accounts are excellent strategic partners for many Web developers. Most dialup providers realize that the Web development business is different from theirs and they prefer to concentrate their resources on the dialup side. However, they may have hundreds or thousands of dialup customers, many of whom will be interested in having a Web site designed, along with the necessary programming and promotion.

One of the issues you will want to address is that of exclusivity. I advise Web developers to consider getting involved only in nonexclusive contracts. This enables you to strike similar deals with other sources of business referrals. The Internet is still quite young and you don't know where your own business or your partner's business will be even six months from now. A nonexclusive strategic alliance gives you the flexibility to grow in whatever direction is best for each of you.

For example, in 1995 Janet Perry formed Vision Interactive, http://visioninteractive.com, as a partnership with several acquaintances who had mutual interests. Janet was no stranger to the Internet, with nine years of experience working for Novell bringing Internet know-how to educational institutions.

Vision Interactive produces and maintains interactive virtual networks for businesses and organizations. Based in the wine-growing Napa Valley, a popular tourist destination, the firm's first project was Napaguide.com, an award-winning network of organizations, schools, content providers, and ISPs. Vision Interactive's LocalPoint community network now produces high-end Web-based virtual communities for other communities and organizations.

During the firm's startup phase in 1995, the partnership had a small amount of capital and did not want to be locked in to server hardware. They considered becoming an ISP but lacked sufficient capital themselves, did not have a financial partner, and did not particularly want one. After considering all their options, they decided to develop an informational resource for their local area. That effort became Napaguide.com—what is today a rich source of information with links to more than eight hundred businesses and organizations in the Napa area.

About a year after Vision was started, Napanet, a local dialup provider, was formed. Initially, Napanet was somewhat of a competitor in that they also wanted to establish a strong identity as a local Internet company. However, Janet's group had a head start and was already getting excellent publicity and recognition for their work in developing a community-based Web resource. Napanet approached Vision Interactive with the idea of teaming up. Vision had the informational resources and Napanet had the connectivity, bandwidth, and server.

The Setup

I interviewed Janet to find out how she went about setting up this alliance. My comments are interwoven with hers.

"Napanet had made a capital investment and our group had made a huge investment of time in developing our community Web resource. Under our agreement, we develop pages for them and they handle billing and receivables. In exchange they get a cut of our Web development fee and we don't need to handle accounting separately or sales. In addition, if we happen to bring in a customer to their dialup business, we get a commission."

The two firms spent a substantial amount of time arriving at their strategic agreement. At first all three partners from Janet's firm met with Napanet's staff, but the meetings became unwieldy. Each firm then selected one representative to meet and hammer out a general agreement. Most of the time spent negotiating was concentrated on fine-tuning an agreement both sides could agree to. The agreement paid off—Napanet provided almost all of Vision's new business for the first six months.

"Basically, Napanet refers anyone to us who says 'Web.' I have been happy with our arrangement and we are considering bringing the companies even closer together. However, I would be cautious about relying on an ISP as your only source of customers. I would also make sure that you both understand and agree on the terms of your noncompetition. For example, our ISP is based in our county. We do not solicit separate business inside the county and neither do they. However, if we get a customer from outside the county, it is entirely our business. By dealing with this issue ahead of time and setting the limits, you prevent conflict over accounts later."

Janet's arrangement serves as an excellent example of how to structure alliances with complementary businesses. ISPs certainly fall into this category and alliances with other types of partners can also be beneficial, filling in whatever gaps you may have in your particular setup, and adding your strengths to businesses who are weak in your strong areas. Examples include ad agencies, graphic design firms, publishers, catalog production companies, printers, marketing consultants, public relations firms, photographers, photo labs, and, in some cases trade associations, chambers of commerce, convention bureaus, industrial development groups, and so on.

As Janet points out, "Another factor in the ISP's decision was that they did not have the internal expertise to do the Web pages. On our side, we needed to have a stronger local presence, and we needed someone to do the initial selling for us."

Janet could not have stated more clearly the excellent potential for teaming up with a local ISP. The fact is, few ISPs will be able to do the dialup side and the Web side and do both well. A strategic alliance makes both partners stronger than if they were not affiliated; that is the power and leverage that such arrangements bring.

Janet also notes, "We are essentially two entirely independent companies." This is a key characteristic of the strategic alliance. It is vital that you retain your independence. That gives you the motivation to grow your business, relying only in part on the work that comes from your strategic partner. You will probably want to have a goal in mind regarding the percentage of your overall revenue that comes from any one source. I recommend no more than 10–25 percent from any one client or strategic alliance partner. At higher percentages, should the relationship deteriorate you will lose a dangerously large chunk of business that will be difficult to replace in a short time frame.

"Pricing services and splitting revenues is another crucial aspect of an alliance. Because there are basic costs associated with doing a Web page, we worked those out and have them as the 'wholesale' cost. These go to us, or through us, to a subcontractor. The remaining component, the profit, is split fifty-fifty between us. So when we invoice, we show the retail price and take off their share of the profit to get our net price."

There are many ways to structure the pricing and profit split. The important thing is to determine in advance who will be billing whom and who will be paid by whom and how much. The challenge is to find a way that works for you, your partner, and the client. And it must be done so as not to create doubt or confusion in the client's mind about who they are doing business with.

In Janet's case, the ISP is handling the sales, so that reduces her costs. With lower selling costs, you can afford to sell at a wholesale level, allowing your partner to price at a profit. Note that this typically won't work the other way around, at least as far as dialup accounts are concerned—the margins just aren't there for the ISP, and the dollar amounts are not high enough to generate any significant revenue for the Web provider. With other types of ISP services, ISDN, leased line connections, virtual hosting services, any associated hardware and software sales, database programming, etc., the margins and price points are higher and there is a better opportunity for you to bring customers to them and get paid for it.

Potential Problems

A possible downside would be where the ISP's pricing is higher than yours for the same services. If they are handling all of the sales, this is not a problem, but if you suddenly have to start selling at a much higher price to align your cost structures, or they have to reduce their costs to match yours, you may have difficulty. This can also happen with any partner where there is some overlap in services offered, and a wide difference in prices.

"Admittedly, the work we do on the Napaguide.com informational hierarchy does take lots of time, and we don't get paid for it. But our partners also are sensitive to this issue and we discuss new branches or projects, and they ask how much we would do on spec and what it would take to make any particular project pay."

By adding spec work to the list of things you bring to the table, you can provide significant added value to your partner's business. But you must be careful here, as Janet indicates. This represents a different kind of cost. It's not so much what it costs you in time to do the work, it's the opportunity cost—that is, the cost of not doing the revenue-producing work you would have been able to do in the same time. So you must budget your spec work carefully and will need an alliance with someone who is willing to understand your side of the equation and be reasonable about making spec work demands. One way is to put the spec work on a budgeted or incentive basis—for example, x amount of hours per week, or x hours of spec work will be performed when x amount of sales have been achieved. (See chapter 5 for more information on handling spec work.)

"However, I think we are particularly lucky in our ISP. I'm not sure all Web designers will be as lucky."

And for that reason, I recommend that Web designers and programmers consider only nonexclusive alliances. You cannot afford to get locked in with another business. Janet is lucky that her business fits well with her ISP. But there are unknowns. Each business can grow at different rates, and one may outgrow the other. Either way, difficult relations can emerge, with one side frustrated at the limitations or demands of the other. At this early stage of the industry's development, there is no telling what will happen in six months or two years, long time frames on the Internet but short periods in your life and the life of your business. One must look to the long term when developing alliances to make sure they will work today and tomorrow, and arrange them with sufficient escape clauses so that you can bail out when necessary and move on.

"One last component I forgot to mention, we have a sort of noncompetition clause. We are free to pursue accounts outside their area, and if they develop a site we have no interest in doing, they will be free to select another HTML house."

Janet's arrangement demonstrates that even with a noncompete agreement, you can have flexibility where one or the other may not be interested in a particular client.

Typically, the first place a dialup customer turns to is his dialup provider when he wants to find out how to get a site designed. Because the dialup provider doesn't do this, it will either have to tell the customer they can't help, or they'll refer the customer to a Web developer. That Web developer could be you.

How an Internet Marketer Uses Strategic Alliances

Webster Group International, `http://www.wgi.com`, is an Internet marketing strategy and Web site promotion firm. Founded by Shari Peterson in early 1995—a time when the idea of promoting Web sites was only just beginning to form even among the most Internet-savvy—Webster is one of the pioneers in the search engine registration and cross-linking business.

To get an edge over other Internet marketing consultants, Shari decided to make promotion Webster's focus. What she did not want to do was become a Web designer. She saw Web designers as potential clients or referral sources and set Webster apart as specializing in Internet marketing strategy and Web site promotion services. Shari sees success on the Internet as one-third design, one-third ISP/technical, and one-third promotion and marketing. "Each one requires specialists," she points out.

Many firms, including Web consultants and designers, offer some version of such a service, but few have achieved anything near Webster's level of expertise. Webster's enviable list of accomplishments include taking The Park, http://the-park.com, already receiving a million visits per day, and doubling its site traffic. Webster also arranges for strategic linking with related sites.

"We always find out what the client is trying to accomplish with its Web site. We see our job as making our client's sites successful. A lot of what we do is an education process." Shari prefers to become involved during the early planning stages of a client's site rather than coming in later to fix things.

Webster also publishes Site Promoter, the only retail software product offering automated search engine registration. "In a sense we're competing with ourselves, but our customized registration services target a different market than our retail product."

Strategic relationships have contributed significantly to Webster's growth. Cross referrals and trade-out of services were important in helping launch the company. Shari traded site promotion for Web hosting and dialup from an ISP and has since worked with a Web design firm on the same basis. "We're careful about selecting the right partners, philosophically and ethically, in their approach to business."

Other Good Candidates for Strategic Partnerships

- ad agencies
- public relations firms
- publishers
- associations

Steps in Setting Up a Strategic Alliance

1. Identify your strong and weak areas.
2. Look for others whose strengths and weaknesses are

the opposite or complement of yours.

3. Use your local contacts to get referrals for potential strategic partners in your area.

4. Go to the business press and trade journals if you're looking for national-level partners. Check out prospective partners by asking around. Interview for information about their industry if you're not familiar with it.

5. Evaluate yourself from the partner's perspective. What will appeal to them? How will it be a good fit? How will it give them a new competitive edge?

6. Formulate preliminary ideas as to how a partnership could work—for both sides. Where is the synergy or leverage? What are the critical details?

7. If you're contacting a large company, determine your initial point of contact. Then be prepared to make your way through the corporate hierarchy to reach someone with the authority and insight you need. Make your pitch brief and to the point—you'll be giving it to busy people.

8. Approach your first potential partner; set up a meeting.

9. Achieve first-meeting objectives:
   • Get acquainted.
   • Share your perspectives; learn theirs.
   • Explore open-ended possibilities .
   • Recap the meeting, thank the other party, and be frank about whether it sounds like there might be a good basis for working together—but don't make any commitments.

10. Think it over. Make a list of questions, relationship details.

11. Identify who should refer work to whom, and when.

12. Assess pricing/discount issues.

13. Firm up your ideas about how the partnership can work for both of you.

14. Decide whether or not you want to pursue discussions.

15. If you do, set up another meeting. If you don't, move on to the next partnership possibility.

Delicate Negotiations

Negotiating a strategic partnership can be a nerve-wracking experience. Because each party to the alliance is an independent business entity, there is little to compel involvement in the alliance. Thus, it usually falls to one party or the other to take charge of the negotiations and steer the effort toward a mutually agreeable arrangement.

When you find yourself in the midst of such negotiations, here are some points to remember.

If you are leading the effort to forge an alliance, you have the double burden of not only representing the interests of your own business but also making an effort to accommodate the desires and needs of another party who may be reluctant to come right out and say what is on his mind. This sometimes requires the patience of a saint and the finesse of a master diplomat. But successful negotiations can be achieved.

You may find yourself dealing with a potential alliance partner who is taking a nonnegotiable, take-it-or-leave-it, my-way-or-the-highway posture. If the demands are not acceptable to the other parties, you will have no choice but to come to the conclusion that the stubborn party must go.

In a multiple party alliance, any of the parties can fall into a nonnegotiable posture at any point in the negotiations, so it is wise to have in mind substitutes for each category of partner involved and, should the time come, be prepared to say good-bye to the one taking an obstinate position.

Keep in mind that negotiations can break down for a variety of reasons. Someone taking what to other parties in the alliance seems like an unreasonable position may be doing so as a result of an unreasonable and unrealistic personality on the part of the individual negotiator. But it may also be a position taken merely due to the demands and restrictions that her business is dictating—it may not be personal at all. Often it will be difficult to tell, and in the end may not make much difference to the outcome of the negotiations. So, keeping in mind what every partner must get out of the deal in order to make it a win-win arrangement can go a long way toward achieving harmonious relations with all parties during and after the negotiations.

The key is to remember that all that is needed is a partner to cover each of the critical areas—it is not important exactly who the partners are, but it is critical that each partner be able to perform his area with expertise. Be flexible and adaptable and keep looking until you find the right mix of agreeable partners.

Try to arrive at agreement through discussion, then draft a document which outlines it all in writing. Circulate the draft among all parties with requests for comments and continue the negotiations.

Make the Alliance Work

- Make the commitment to make it work.
- Be willing to train your partner's staff, especially if they are selling for you.
- Solicit suggestions in your partner's areas of expertise.
- Don't expect to control everything. You can't.
- Build relationships at all levels.
- Give credit where credit is due.
- Reserve time. You personal involvement is needed to make it work.
- End the relationship with a partner when quality, service, and other critical performance areas are unacceptable.

Two Ways to Price Your Services When Selling to or Through a Strategic Partner

To establish a fair basis for compensation when offering your services through a strategic partner, you have an unlimited number of pricing options. However, consider taking one or both of the following positions, once you have established your rate structure. (Don't even think about negotiating until you know exactly what you will charge to clients directly—without the involvement of the partner.)

1. Give the partner a percentage of the deal based on your prices. You recognize that they are incurring the selling cost. With your prices in hand, they recognize the value of your services. Typical percentages will range from 5 to 20 percent. To arrive at the exact percentage, you need to keep in mind the amount of time required on your partner's part to get a sale and the actual dollars that the percentage represents. Be fair to yourself, but be fair to this source of found money and new sales leads.

2. Tell the strategic partner what your rates are and tell her she is free to charge as much additional as she pleases, keeping anything she can get above your rates. This leaves it open to her to determine what the market will bear and gives her an incentive to go out and sell. You don't mind, because these are sales you wouldn't have achieved otherwise, and as long as you are getting your fees, more power to anyone who can get more. If this really takes off and you were to find out that she is charging outrageously high fees, three times as much as your own, then you could give her notice that your rates will be going up in thirty days.

Do not mix these two pricing models with the same strategic partner; it won't work. In other words, what you don't want is for the guy selling your discounted services to also then turn around and sell at whatever rate he wants, keeping the difference. That would leave too much money on the table for him and not enough for you.

So how do you take both positions? By allowing the strategic partner to select the compensation method he prefers. You want him to be motivated, so let him choose.

This same approach works with any strategic partner. And you may have some partners on one form of compensation and some on the other. The most important thing is to go into these deals with your rate structure fully and firmly established.

More information on strategic alliances can be found at: Inc. Magazine Online:

Twenty-eight Steps to Strategic Alliance
www.inc.com/incmagazine/archives/04930961.html

Natural Partners
www.inc.com/incmagazine/archives/06890671.html

Rules of Engagement
www.inc.com/incmagazine/archives/01970481.html

Point of Reference
www.inc.com/incmagazine/archives/06901002.html

YOU KNOW YOU'RE A GEEK WHEN...

*You know Bill Gates' e-mail address but you have
to look up your own phone number.*

Setting Your Rates

Determining your rates is obviously one of the most important decisions you can make. It's uppermost in the minds of every Web developer, programmer, and Internet marketer, and it's a topic that crops up often on Internet discussion lists and newsgroups. In fact, this chapter is based on an FAQ I wrote for the HTML Writer's Guild. That FAQ itself was inspired by a very hotly debated pricing discussion on the HTML Writer's Guild discussion list, www.hwg.org.

Pricing is difficult for industry peers to talk about without running afoul of antitrust laws and the Department of Justice! (For instance, see the HTML Writers Guild Pricing FAQ for an explanation of the legal issues involved with such discussion among members of an industry or profession.) Even an informal survey of what firms are charging makes it clear that rates vary widely. Some firms will charge hundreds of dollars and some will charge hundreds of thousands of dollars for much the same site! Your goal in setting your rates: Be profitable, but be competitive.

Certainly Web development is a new profession, but Web developers are not the first to confront the task of setting rates for the work of creative professionals. Ad agencies long ago figured out how to set profitable rates for work that is in many ways similar, if not identical, to that of Web development. Copywriting, art direction, graphic design, illustration, and related creative problem solving and technical work are services provided by ad agencies and Web developers alike. Indeed, I believe that those involved in developing Internet projects can learn much from ad agencies in many aspects of running a business. Consequently, we will begin by taking a look at how ad agencies go about the task of setting rates.

Of course, when one thinks of hourly rates, many other types of professions come to mind. We will look at some of the ways attorneys, accountants, and others set their rates.

We'll consider too how you might go about determining an hourly rate for your entire business and why you might want to do so. Finally, we'll take a look at how you can figure out just exactly how much your services are really worth!

It is my hope that by understanding the different approaches outlined here, you'll be able to choose the one that is best for your Internet consulting business. This discussion may be the only time you will actually enjoy doing math!

HOW AD AGENCIES SET RATES

Let's begin by looking at the way an ad agency sets rates. Ad agencies long ago solved the problem of setting hourly rates for a variety of creative work. They arrived at a rather simple formula, but you have to understand its components in order to calculate it.

This is the basic formula:

1. Determine the number of *billable hours* per year.
2. Take *annual salary* and add an *overhead* factor.
3. Add a *secret ingredient* many forget to add.
4. Divide *salary + overhead + secret ingredient* by *billable hours*.

We start with a "normal" work week of forty hours, even though you will probably never meet a successful Internet businessperson who works so few hours in a week! However, you must still set your rates based on some semblance of a normal life; otherwise, as you grow and add employees who may not share your workaholic tendencies, you may have trouble keeping them. As a bonus, basing your fees on a normal work week simply means that any additional billable work you complete is just more money coming in the door.

So, we start with the number of billable hours in a year.

normal work week = 40 hours
year = 52 weeks
40 x 52 = 2,080 total hours per year

Now we adjust the total hours to arrive at the billable hours. This compensates for the fact that some of the time we are sick or on vacation or taking the day off for July 4th or Christmas. Naturally, we would still like to be paid for those days, even though we can't bill for them. So we have to look at just the number of billable hours we really have. Traditionally, ad agencies have reduced 2,080 to 1,600 and used that as the standard number of billable hours. So we will use that figure. If you're self-employed and spend a lot of your time selling, then you might want to reduce this further.

And, if you want to get technical about it, we can do that, too. In other words, what percentage of your time is billable? If you can figure that out, then you can use that figure instead of 1,600, but I can already tell you that the industry average is going to be right around 60 percent billable, which is only 1,248 hours, or a little over half of your time. So if you're doing better than that, you're above average. In order to be profitable, however, I recommend that you set a goal of 80 percent which is 1,664 hours, very close to the 1,600 figure from above.

Now we need to take the amount of money you expect to earn this year, whatever you would say is your salary if someone asked you. Let's say it's $10,000, just to make our calculations easy.

Next, we must look at the real cost that you represent to your business. That is, not just your salary, but any associated overhead that the business incurs because you work there. This would include personnel expenses such as employer share of payroll expenses or self-employment tax, health insurance, disability, life insurance, and other nonbillable expenses that are vital to you and unavoidable to your business. Other items in this category might be a car allowance, or typical mileage expenses, the prorated cost of your computer, scanner, desk, chair, and other office equipment and furnishings as well as a prorated cost of your office space. You need to include this even if you are a one-person operation and self-employed, working at home, and living with your parents! Otherwise you stand a very good chance of going broke. And, if you have employees, you will need to add up their contribution to overhead to set their rates.

After many accountants worked long and hard on this in the agency business, a rule of thumb was devised whereby you figure the employee's overhead at 100 percent of the salary amount. In other words, to get salary and overhead, just double the salary. So, in our example, we would double $10,000 and arrive at $20,000.

Finally, we must add one more thing—the secret ingredient. It's the one thing many ad agencies (and possibly Internet consultants) forget: *profit*. Most businesses aim for 20 percent profit and we will do the same. So we must add 20 percent to $20,000, and we arrive at $24,000.

Now we divide $24,000 by 1,600 billable hours and arrive at an hourly rate of $15.00. This works per ten thousand, so, if you make say, $30,000, just multiply by 3 and you'll get the correct figure of $45.00 per hour, or for $100,000 just multiply by 10 to get $150 per hour.

That's the standard ad agency method. It is an excellent method to use and it's the only one you really need to know. But, just to round things out, (and for a little entertainment) we will look at some more exotic methods.

HOW ATTORNEYS SET THEIR RATES, OR, HOW MY ACCOUNTANT SAYS HIS LAWYER DOES IT

When I asked my accountant about setting rates, he told me this story. He was discussing this subject with his attorney, who told him how he does it.

"How much money do you want to make? How many hours do you want to work? Divide. That's your hourly rate."

This is a very simple method, offered somewhat for amusement. Let's see how we would do this if we were attorneys.

Amount to make = $1 million
Hours to work = 1
Rate = $1 million per hour

Right away, we can see why this method appeals to attorneys. But this is actually a quick and dirty way to arrive at a ballpark hourly rate:

1. Figure out how much the job is worth.
2. Figure out how many hours you're going to put into it.
3. Divide.

That's your hourly rate for the job.

This is helpful when dealing with hourly rates on the other side of the coin—when you want to see how the hourly rate you actually earned compares with the rate you think you're charging the client.

HOW MY ACCOUNTANT SETS HIS RATES

What about my accountant? How does he set his own rates for his people? He multiplies what he pays them by 5 to get the rate.

In our example, this would be:

$10,000 / 2,080 = $4.80 per hour
$4.80 x 5 = $24 per hour

This is 1.6 times (or a little more than one and a half times) what we got in the ad agency example. Using a multiple of five is good; you can use it as your method, as long as it does not make your prices uncompetitive. Consider it the upper range for your rates.

HOW YOU CAN SET A RATE FOR YOUR ENTIRE BUSINESS, OR, HOW *I* CALCULATE IT FOR *MY* BUSINESS

In addition to figuring the hourly rate for each employee and each service offered to clients, I also want to know what it costs just to keep the doors open.

In other words, I add up all my costs to operate on an annual basis (remembering to include the secret ingredient). Then I divide by 2,080. This gives me the pay rate for the business itself.

This is very useful. For instance, suppose annual costs are $100,000. That's an hourly rate of $48.08. That means the business is spending, on the average, $48 an hour or $1,900 a week or $8,300 a month, whether there is a lot of work or no work at all. These are very useful figures to have in mind as one is setting sales goals and hourly rates. You might want to calculate the figures for your own business. How much did your business spend? How much did your business bill?

SO YOU THINK YOU'RE WORTH HOW MUCH?

When you go about setting your hourly rate, you'll probably become much more aware of the rates other people are charging for their time. Plumbers, appliance repair people, attorneys, psychiatrists, and photographers are a few who come to mind. Occasionally you'll see hourly rates posted in various businesses or in the media. Here's a way to use those rates to help figure your own.

We all have an idea of how much we think we are worth and how much we think others are worth. Ten years ago, when I discovered this method, the ones that concerned me most were the rates charged by my attorney and my auto mechanic, but you could compare your rates to those of just about any other service business.

My attorney was charging, let's say, $125 an hour. The auto mechanic charged a labor rate of $32.50 an hour. As I got to thinking about it, I figured that, to my clients, my services were worth roughly half what an attorney charges and certainly at least twice what an auto mechanic charges. I decided to calculate a rate based on this, but you could just as easily use the rates of a babysitter or an electrician or whoever, simply adjusting upward or downward based on how much more or less you feel your services are worth in comparison. Here's how I calculated my rate at the time:

Half Attorney Rate: 125 / 2 = $62.50
Twice Auto Mechanic Rate: 2 x 32.50 = $65

Naturally, I rounded up to a bit above the higher of the two calculations. At the time, this represented about a 25 percent increase in my rates. Interestingly, as I eased up my rate over several months, clients did not seem to mind or even notice, probably because I used the rate only to calculate cost estimates by the project.

An added bonus, it proved great protection against inflation. As my benchmarks raised their rates, I raised mine and I had the peace of mind of knowing I could always afford to get my car fixed!

So there you have it, five ways to figure your rates. They have served me well and one of these methods, or some variation, should also work for you.

ANOTHER ASPECT OF YOUR RATES

Graphic designers, programmers, and copywriters each typically have a single hourly rate that they use to estimate project costs or bill on a time basis. However, when you offer a range of Internet services and are more than a one-person shop, you will probably want to establish a matrix of rates that reflects what type of work is being performed, who is doing the work, and how good they are at it.

For instance, you may be outstanding at some things and not as efficient at others. It doesn't seem fair to the client to charge the same rate for things you don't do well. Then again, some of the services you provide simply won't be worth as much as other services. For your own internal management purposes (not for public consumption), you may want to establish a rate grid that takes this into account. For example:

	HTML Coding	Copy-writing	Graphic Design	Program-ming	Account Service	Media Buying	Production Coordination	Admini-stration
Joe	$85	$10	$25	$85	$30	$10	$10	$10
Judd	$85	$10	$85	$10	$10	$10	$10	$10
Jerry	$10	$10	$40	$10	$40	$25	$50	$10
Jessica	$10	$20	$10	$10	$20	$10	$10	$20
Jennifer	$10	$65	$65	$10	$50	$50	$10	$10

Joe is strongest in HTML coding and programming, so-so in account service, and a complete disaster in production coordination and administrative services. He can't write copy, but he can spell and proofread, and although he's not a talented graphic designer, he is pretty good at quickly converting image file formats and doing minor image touchup in Photoshop. He can answer the phone if everyone else is out of the office or on another line.

Judd is good at both HTML coding and programming, but that's it. He belongs chained to his computer, away from the general public and especially away from any clients. He's very good at what he does, and we can charge accordingly, but if we ask him to do other things, it's likely to be a complete disaster and the client may actually send us a bill.

Jessica is strongest at answering the phone and bookkeeping and her rates reflect that. Note that all of her rates are fairly low either because of her skill level or because the market simply will not bear charging any more for the tasks she is performing.

Jennifer, on the other hand, is a top performer in several areas, including copywriting, graphic design, account service, and media buying. She gets along well with clients, thinks well on her feet and is a good brainstormer. While she can write excellent copy, she is not actually a qualified graphic designer, even though we are billing at the same high rate for both services. We can justify the high rate for graphic design in her case because she is very good at quickly coming up with creative concepts that can be executed in detail by Judd.

Here's another way to set up a rate grid. First establish a set range of rates and assign each a letter code. For instance:

A	B	C	D	E
$85	$60	$40	$25	$10

Next assign one of the letter codes to each person based on her individual strengths and weaknesses. This has some advantages in allowing the quick adjustment of rates without redoing the chart. It allows us to rate each employee with an easy-to-understand grade. The hourly rate for any given grade level might change, but the employee's grade code would stay the same as long as his skill level stays the same.

Applying this method to the chart above, we get the following. Note that this new chart also indicates the maximum high and low rates for each service. For instance, the maximum we would ever charge for administration is C, although we are currently charging D. That's because even our best person is only functioning at a D level, though if that changes, so will the rate code.

	HTML Coding	Copy-writing	Graphic Design	Program-ming	Account Service	Media Buying	Production Coordination	Admini-stration
	(A–E)	(A–E)	(A–E)	(A–E)	(B–E)	(B–E)	(B–E)	(C–E)
Joe	A	E	D	A	C	E	E	E
Judd	A	E	A	E	E	E	E	E
Jerry	E	E	C	E	C	D	B	E
Jessica	E	D	E	E	D	E	E	D
Jennifer	E	B	B	E	B	B	C	E

WORKING ON SPEC

Spec work, or work created on speculation—that is, without compensation—is often expected by the client who wants you to prove your capabilities before agreeing to hire you. Spec work is costly and always a gamble. It requires hours of time that could be better spent on paying work. Inevitably, you know very little about the client's real goals and objectives, forcing you to make wild guesses about what is wanted—absurd things like the president's favorite colors and typeface. You're put in the position of being a mind reader—always a risky predicament.

In the ad agency business there is a famous story about an agency guy meeting with a new business prospect. The prospect came to the agency to get the new business pitch for his company's account. The agency guy showed him a number of campaigns created for other clients. The prospect was impressed by the great work and couldn't wait to see what the agency had in mind for his account. Then...

AGENCY GUY: Let's go to lunch
PROSPECT: I thought you were going to give me your pitch for our account before we went to lunch.
AGENCY GUY: I just did.
PROSPECT: But you only showed me campaigns for other companies.
AGENCY GUY: You liked what you saw, didn't you?
PROSPECT: Well, yes.
AGENCY GUY: And we'll develop your campaign with the same high caliber of creativity and marketing expertise that we used to develop those campaigns. Now let's go to lunch.

This anecdote dramatizes the psychology behind selling your creative problem-solving services without giving away the store by working on spec—that is, creating the work, or a good portion of it, for free, in order to woo the client.

- Establish credibility—show only your best work.
- Establish an atmosphere of confidence.
- Begin building a relationship with the client based on trust.

Nevertheless, there will be times when it seems appropriate to do spec work. This is always a judgment call and no one can second-guess your decision. However, there is always the potential, or apparent potential, for getting ripped off. Do not give away your services unless you firmly believe you will benefit.

When you do decide to take on spec work, you end up in a situation where it is easy to sympathize with the music and movie industries and their concerns about digital recording media. The minute you put a spec site on disk and hand it over to a client or give him the URL, you know exactly how the record people feel about pirating.

In the past, spec work meant showing handmade comps (mock-ups) for an ad or brochure, not the final art. While the client could theoretically steal the idea, by itself the idea was not the total solution to their problem—it still had to be implemented. Besides, we all know the typical client doesn't have the foggiest notion of what to do with our ideas anyway. Even if one idea is stolen, we know that we have ten more good ideas where that one came from and a hundred more we didn't have time to think of. That is the creative person's revenge and secret weapon.

Showing a completed Web site is a different ball game. It's easy to duplicate and easy to steal. But there *are* steps you can take to protect yourself.

Five Ways to Handle Spec Work

1. Do not show your site on live media. Use a dead piece of paper that the client can see but not use. Use it as a talking piece and a sales tool, not to do the selling for you. Tell him what happens when you click on the buttons. Tell the client what will be on the other pages. Talk the talk, but don't walk the walk until you get the money.

2. Treat your Web site like a comp—make it a shell of the real thing. Stay in creative control. Gray out the photos, greek in all but the headlines, code only partial pages, partial tables, etc. You should only have to give the client a taste. That's all you want to do anyway. You have to leave him wanting more so he'll sign on. Do not spend more than 10 percent of the total project time doing the comp. Anything more will be unprofitable.

3. Take your cue from the agency story and show only the work of other clients as examples of your capabilities. "We'll use the same

creative problem-solving approach to create a unique site specially designed to meet your needs." Sell your success stories. What
was the problem the client had? How did you solve it?

4.   Make the spec site conditional upon the client's signing an agreement to compensate you if they use the material in any way. The
agreement should state a liquidated damages amount that they will
pay you. Many ad agencies do this. A lawyer should be able to
take your rough draft and make it legal for $150–$200 or less.

5.   In the event of the very-worst-case scenario, what do you do? Add
the site ripped off from you to your portfolio of links. What the
heck, you created it, didn't you?

YOU KNOW YOU'RE A GEEK WHEN...

You look down on people who use low baud rates.

CHAPTER

SIX

What the Client Expects from the Internet and You

Before you even walk in the door your client has been led to expect all sorts of things from the Internet, not the least of which is phenomenal new opportunity and millions and millions of new customers. At the same time, she has a great deal of doubt about whether the Internet will work for her business and probably even more skepticism about whether you can help them.

The fact is, the Internet is many, many things, and you will be expected to be conversant in all of them. Customers looking at the Internet are like the blind men and the elephant—each one typically only sees one facet of the whole and there is absolutely no guarantee that the facet they are seeing is the one they should be seeing! Here are some of the preconceived notions prospects may have and insights that should prove helpful in selling to them anyway.

THE CLIENT THINKS THE INTERNET IS ANOTHER AD MEDIUM

If the client thinks the Internet can help her sell her company's products or services, she's going to see the Internet as a worldwide advertising medium. She's going to see her Web site as a giant ad that reaches millions of customers around the world, and she's going to see you pretty much the way she sees any ad salesperson who walks in the door.

The ad salesperson sells space or time. Similar to a Web hosting service, he does not write copy or design ads or produce commercials. He is interested strictly in selling the space or time to run ads. Unlike a Web hosting service, he has a media kit containing sales copy touting why his magazine or TV station is better than anyone else's, demographic and marketing research information on the people his magazine or TV station reaches, and a rate card and mechanical or technical specifications for preparing the ad or commercial. He has a sales pitch designed to show off his advertising opportunity and an aggressive sales attitude.

Companies have grown accustomed to the typical ad salesperson and if the client has you pegged as one, you will increase her comfort level with the Internet if you come prepared with sales materials that look like a media kit, outlining:

- an introduction to your firm
- statistics on Internet users—how many are online, age, income
- the benefits of being online
- your services
- your rates

THE CLIENT THINKS THE INTERNET IS JUST LIKE DIRECT MAIL

Another twist on the advertising theme is when the client is already in the direct-mail or mail-order business and thinks the Internet is just more of the same. With direct mail, you buy a list of names, offer a good deal on a product, and create a super selling brochure and sales letter and mail it to the list. Then you see how many orders come in and analyze the results. You test different lists, different offers, and different creative approaches until you find the most effective combination. Direct mail is all based on measuring results.

In this case the client will be thinking about response rates—that is, of all those who see his Web site, how many people will actually buy something. He'll also be thinking about sending out millions of e-mails touting his products and he'll be headed directly for the newsgroups to do just that.

Be ready to prepare this type of client for the realities of Internet marketing. I don't recommend that you totally dampen his enthusiasm, but you should be prepared to engage in a frank discussion about the history of netiquette and the possible consequences of spamming. Make sure the client understands that simply having a Web page does not mean millions of people will see it. They won't unless it is promoted.

As for response rates, it is quite possible that, once users reach the client's page, the percentage of those who buy may very well meet or exceed the response rates in direct mail. But the overall numbers are likely to be smaller.

With respect to the controversial subject of bulk e-mail, you might suggest your client read my position in favor of unsolicited bulk e-mail at `http://provider.com/framesbulke.htm`. However, note that even though I am one of the few who dares to publicly make the case for marketing in this manner, I don't advocate doing it— yet. It's still too early. I believe the day will come when bulk e-mail will take its rightful place alongside other Internet marketing methods, but in the meantime, the risk of mail bombs and the accompanying potential legal and financial consequences are real (at best, irritating your ISP and losing your account; at worst, shutting down your ISP's operation and being sued) and should be pondered seriously by anyone contemplating sending out vast amounts (i.e., ten of thousands or millions) of e-mail ads in this manner. You should certainly discuss alternative (albeit slower and more complicated) methods including building a mailing list through a fill-in form on the Web page and rental of lists of users who have expressed an interest in receiving e-mail—yes, there actually are tens of thousands of users who have done just that (e.g., Postmaster Direct, `http://netcreations.com`). Sadly, there are only tens of thousands, which is why opt-in won't succeed as a viable marketing approach overall. But Internet marketers must use what is available and make do.

THE CLIENT THINKS THE INTERNET IS A RETAIL STORE

Having a client who sees the Internet as a store can work for you or against you, depending on what type of company you're dealing with. If the client is already a retailer, you will have a relatively easy sale and should begin discussing shopping carts and the possibility of integrating her existing database, or a subset of it, into a Web site. Other subjects that will crop up in the discussion: secure ordering; secure hosting; forwarding orders from the server to the retailer via a browser, e-mail, fax, etc.; online and offline promotion and cross-promotion techniques. And don't forget that the Web is an excellent merchandising medium. The retailer can bring just about any type of merchandise promotion online that he would use offline: coupons, price-offs, monthly specials, even daily or hourly specials, retail holiday promotions, etc.

THE CLIENT THINKS THE INTERNET IS A CHANNEL CONFLICT

If the client is a manufacturer or distributor, you may run into a mind-set that views a worldwide retail presence as a major problem. For instance he may have divided up the entire world, and possibly much of outer space as well, into exclusive rights territories. His distributors and retailers may be operating under restrictions against selling outside their own territory. Now you walk in to tell him to sell direct to the customer, bypassing the distributor and retailer. He freaks out because, in one fell swoop, this will totally scramble all of the legal and financial framework he's worked long and hard to develop. And, hey, isn't that what the Internet is all about?

After he's finished totally freaking out, you may still be able to sell him an imaginative approach that supports his existing dealer network by getting him to see the Internet as a customer service enhancement and low-cost business-to-business communications medium. He can also take advantage of the Internet as an ad medium by providing a complete description of all of his company's products and services. If you happen to have the name of a top-notch attorney who can help the client rewrite all of his distribution agreements to accommodate life in the Internet fast lane, so much the better (but don't count on it).

THE CLIENT THINKS THE INTERNET IS REALLY AN ONLINE CATALOG

This is a blending of the direct mail and retail store mind-sets.

Catalog companies, especially the midsize outfits with sales between $10 million and $50 million per year, are getting killed on paper, printing, and postage costs. They are one of your prime prospects.

It might cost $250,000 to create the photography, copy, and artwork for a catalog and $1 million or more to print it and mail it out. All this cost just to get some copy and photos of products into the hands of customers. No matter what you charge for an Internet job, it will likely pale by comparison to what these clients are spending on print. So the Internet is perfect for them. Beware, though; they spend big bucks, but they watch every penny and they figure their response rates to the tenth or hundredth of a percent. They will apply the same logic to their Web efforts, and they may not be convinced their customer base is online yet. Convince them with Nieslen Commercenet demographics, http://www.nielsenmedia.com/commercenet (which they've probably already seen, but it doesn't hurt to remind them), showing who's online and how many are buying. Help them think about phasing in their catalog. While an argument can be made that consumers want to see the whole fifty-million-product catalog online right away, the fact is the sales may not support it and the development time frame may be absurdly long (how fast can *you* scan, convert, and resize fifty million products?). Some selling strategies:

- Focus on helping them over the long term.
- Start with their top-selling products and build from there.
- Learn all you can about the back-of-house order fulfillment processes and what form their Web sales data need to be in for compatibility.
- Figure on selling to their team—you may need a team of your own to deal with their product, promotion, accounting and fulfillment departments, all of which are specialized areas.

Topics likely to come up: interfacing Internet orders with their existing order fulfillment process; cross-promotion; banner ads; plus all the topics already outlined under the retail and direct mail concepts.

THE CLIENT THINKS THE INTERNET IS ANOTHER WAY TO PROVIDE CUSTOMER SERVICE AND TECHNICAL SUPPORT

Typically, software publishers fall into this category, and while you might think they all have Web sites by now, you might be surprised at how many still don't and how many who do can't take orders for products and upgrades.

Many companies with large bases of end users will also be thinking along these lines. (The Federal Express site, `http://fedex.com`, is, of course, the classic example.) This will be a good prospect for you because making it easy for the customer to get instant online access to order status information requires a humongous data handling and database integration effort. That means a big project for you, with continual updates and improvements. Try to get the client to think in terms of project phases so that you don't have to bite off more than you can handle at one time.

THE CLIENT THINKS THE INTERNET IS REALLY AN EMPLOYEE NEWSLETTER

In this case you're probably looking at someone who needs a very large Intranet project. Uppermost in her mind will be such in-house items as instantly updating company policies and employee benefits information, training schedules, online training materials, etc. You'll probably be dealing with a committee consisting of human resources, marketing, and management information systems (MIS) people. Your people skills and ability to sit still during what may seem like endless committee meetings will be vitally important, along with a great deal of patience while the corporate beast makes a decision—it could take months or years for it to do so. And don't forget to take your blue suit out of storage—you'll need it.

But once the ball gets rolling, departmental one-upmanship will start to take effect and you could well end up with as many new clients as there are departments in the company, each one clamoring for a better site than the next. And who are you to say that the every-other-weekend janitorial relief crew doesn't need its own Web site?

There are tremendous opportunities to build corporate Intranets. In some ways the Intranet projects are the most enjoyable because you have more control over the technology and you know who will be seeing the pages. You'll have more opportunities for higher-end programming solutions and probably more generous bandwidth for all the streaming goodies. You'll also have lots of database integration opportunities (and cross-platform issues). But you'll have to be prepared to deal with virtually every department in the company, including some extremely bureaucratic ones, and you'll have to dance gingerly to avoid the flying bullets of departmental turf wars—all the stuff you left behind when you formed a firm of your own. The key here is to decide how you want to fit into the Intranet process and find clients whose needs match your preferences. Do you want to design and build and do it all? Or write and design only, program only, or just handle the graphics?

THE CLIENT THINKS THE INTERNET IS AN EXTENSION OF THE PURCHASING DEPARTMENT

This is the newest commerce crossroads of the Internet. Known as an *extranet,* this approach takes a company and its key suppliers and builds an elaborate internal/external information and communications network between them.

According to *Interactive Week* (Oct. 7, 1996), "Extranets represent networks that extend beyond a single company to multiple organizations that must collaborate, communicate and exchange documents in order to achieve joint goals."

Basically, an extranet is a Web site with hooks into the company's purchasing, specifications, and inventory databases for the privileged access of key suppliers. The hooks may also work the other way as well, giving the company access to the online ordering and inventory data of suppliers. Companies are looking to Extranets to accelerate product time to market, improve product and service quality, provide technical solutions to systems interoperability and integration issues, increase awareness of user requirements and acceptance, and enhance exposure to strategic partners, contractors, and customers.

If you're not familiar with extranets, here are three good online starting points:

1. http://www.arraydev.com/commerce/delibadmin/extranet.htm
2. http://haas.berkeley.edu/~citm/supplier-proj.html
3. http://www.niit.org/what/

An extranet can be any semiprivate cooperative joint effort between organizations that must collaborate and share a common set of information. Think of this as intranets taken to the *n*th degree.

THE CLIENT THINKS THE INTERNET IS AN EDITORIAL OR PUBLISHING MEDIUM

Some magazine and newspaper publishers have embraced the Internet. Others have stayed away. Eventually they'll all be there because it is without question the most revolutionary thing to happen in their industry in a long, long time. But the Internet presents problems for publishers perhaps more than any other client you will call on. The very fact that the Internet is a publishing medium scares them to death. And the idea of giving information away for free is enough to give your typical publisher a heart attack.

Magazine publishers make their money by selling ads, selling subscriptions, or both. The major task confronting publishers is how to take their editorial product to the Web in such a way that somebody will pay for it. The odds are against a subscription-based model, despite the efforts of the *Wall Street Journal,* so most publishers are going to have to find revenue from advertising. But that makes them just another Web site trying to sell banner ads and brings into question how they will deal with their existing advertisers.

If magazines and newspapers sell the Web version too hard, the advertisers in their print product might question continuing to advertise at the same levels there. This has the potential of creating a situation where the publisher's Web effort ends up cannibalizing the ad revenue for the print version. As the costs of running a print publication and Web publication can only be more than doing print alone, if the total ad revenue remains flat, the publisher is losing money. On the other hand, sooner or later, publishers know, they're going to have to go to the Web. So they are struggling with the questions of whether to go now or wait, and, if they go, will they attempt to make their Web effort self-supporting at the risk of pulling advertisers away from their print product, or will they, in effect, give away advertising on the Web to keep their print advertisers happy while proving that the publisher is a state-of-the-art kind of guy?

When you show up to have a conversation, the publisher will be negotiating his firm's way through this process. If you can help him think through the business questions, so much the better. If you can't, your best bet is to say so and clearly delineate your role as focusing on the development of the Web site and adding value to their print product electronically by helping create an effective site. That way, you won't be held responsible for areas you don't have expertise in, and you won't be tempted to volunteer your ignorance.

Position your firm as the expert in the Internet, making it clear that you aren't an expert in the publishing business (unless you are, in which case, of course, say so). Show the client how you can help him understand the Internet and reach readers online. Show him how to develop online communities. And show him how he and his advertisers can make the transition to online effortlessly under your guidance.

IF THE CLIENT THINKS THE INTERNET IS A (PEOPLE) NETWORKING OR COMMUNITY-BUILDING MEDIUM

Associations, citizens' groups, social service organizations, and government agencies fall into this category. Though often overlooked in the frenetic Internet gold rush, this other type of networking is in many ways closer to what the Internet is all about—linking people with common interests. You may find these groups have smaller budgets, and in many cases no budgets at all. But building, programming, and promoting their sites, even on a reduced-cost basis, can be productive in at least two ways: The sites will be of natural interest to the media plus these groups have their own built-in constituency and potential referral base. Both can pay off for your business.

THE CLIENT THINKS THE INTERNET IS ALL OF THE ABOVE

Unless you're talking to a competitor in disguise, you have found a really great client, in which case you should find yourself with an opportunity to do your best work and bring on board another success story.

THE CLIENT IS CLUELESS

By now you should have a pretty good idea of the various Internet business models. Find out what the client sells and is trying to accomplish offline and suggest the online Internet model that is most appropriate. Do your homework on the Internet and its benefits and limitations and you will be well on your way to successfully selling one Internet project after another.

What Your Clients Are Wondering: How Does the Internet Fit In?

People and companies are jumping onto the Internet faster than any other communication medium because they realize a successful Web site can:

- Create a leading-edge image.

- Enhance customer communications and service.

- Increase visibility and market expansion.

- Execute online sales and service transactions.

- Provide global information distribution

- Lower communication costs (long-distance phone calls, faxes, and overnight deliveries).

Who's Online?

Tens of thousands of companies—millions of individuals! People are accessing the Internet, hungry for information about every subject imaginable.

How Does the Internet Fit In?

- as an advertising and public relations medium

- as a direct sales medium

- as an Internal communications medium

- as a customer service and technical service delivery medium

- as a direct service delivery medium
- as a collaborative communications medium

As an Advertising and Public Relations Medium

- exposure
- lead generation
- presale and postsale customer service and product information
- investor relations
- presents of a cohesive corporate identity

As a Direct Sales Medium

- online ordering
- one-stop shopping for national/international accounts

As an Internal Communications Medium

- low-cost connection between headquarters and subsidiaries
- reduced cost of leased lines and long-distance calls
- employee to employee communications
- computer to computer communications
- platform for streamlined internal corporate communications
- employees and subsidiary leadership communications

As a Customer Service and Technical Service Delivery Medium

- fast, convenient, affordable information delivery
- instant updates
- lowers expensive 800 number usage and associated labor costs for increased productivity
- satisfies customers' need to know

As a Direct Service Delivery Medium

- suitable where the customer does not have to be present in person to be served (counseline.com psychological services)

- expandable to worldwide market potential

- naturally applicable for information services

As a Collaborative Communications Medium

- Intranets

- Extranets

- online communities

Where Can the Internet Lead You?

- state-of-the-art communications for a state-of-the-art company

- international communications for an international company

- new selling channel—national and international in scope

- added efficiency of ordering process—lets sales reps concentrate on relationships and personal service, not ordering details

- usability by reps to place orders from the field for automated processing

- happy marriage with database technology for easy location of every item in inventory

- maximization of benefits and conquering of HQ/subsidiary organization limitations

- time and space constraints eliminated—plenty of room for all products and sales messages

- reduced reliance on expensive catalog paper, printing, and distribution costs

- full compatibility with existing investment in electronic art

---

YOU KNOW YOU'RE A GEEK WHEN...

Your pet has a Web page.

Finding Customers

For many Internet professionals, Web developers, programmers, and new media people, selling is the hardest part of their jobs. Chances are you would rather do anything than sell. Solving the most difficult technical challenge, hand-coding a twenty-five column HTML table in Notepad, debugging an assembler routine, or frame-by-frame lip-synching for a CD-ROM may be a piece of cake for you compared to picking up the phone or heading out for an appointment to see a new client. If this doesn't sound like you, and sales come easy for you, then consider yourself fortunate and possibly a rare exception in the business.

Regardless of which end of the love-it-or-hate-it spectrum you fall on, the sales tips outlined here will work fine. They're geared for those who are a bit reluctant to tackle sales, and master salespeople will really feel at home. Best of all, these techniques will bring you business.

IDENTIFY YOUR PROSPECTS

Who Is a Qualified Prospect for Internet Projects?

It's a fact of business life that in order to have a business, you must have customers. In order to find them, you will need to identify a pool of prospects to call upon. It's important to have a clear understanding of who your prospects are. Your Web development, Internet programming, or new media business will almost without exception be targeting other businesses. But which ones?

Generally speaking, we can say that a qualified prospect is anyone who wants a Web site or other Internet project and can afford one. That's a great theoretical statement, but as a practical matter, what does it mean?

Internet technology and marketing strategies are applicable in a wide range of businesses. Practically anyone can take advantage of the increased efficiencies in worldwide communication that the Internet represents. But if you've done any selling at all, you know that no matter how useful a product or service may be, only *some* of the prospects you call on will be interested. How do you narrow the field to the most likely buyers? Here are some guidelines for identifying your best prospects.

Primary Prospects

Any company in your local area with annual revenues exceeding a certain amount, typically five hundred to a thousand times your average sale, is a good prospect. Why such a large multiple? The fact is, an Internet project is going to represent only a small part of most businesses' operations or even marketing budgets. Companies will typically spend between 2 and 5 percent of their revenues on marketing and advertising. Many will see their Internet projects coming out of a small percentage of that budget.

Let's say you're a Web developer and your average Web site project is around $3,000 for site development work and another $1,000–$1,500 a year for monthly hosting and site maintenance. A qualified prospect for you would be a company with annual sales of at least $2.5 million. At that level of sales, the company might be spending $50,000 to $125,000 on all its marketing and other communications. Your Web site project will represent anywhere between 4 and 10 percent of their entire ad budget, a significant percentage to devote to one project.

Smaller companies may be otherwise excellent prospects for you, but they probably can't afford your services. Occasionally a smaller business may be able to afford a site and you certainly wouldn't turn away the business, but as a general rule, you'll be looking for larger customers who can easily afford a Web site.

Now let's say your average project fees are closer to $10,000. In that case you would be looking for companies with annual revenues of at least $5 million. The same logic applies. That is, smaller companies may occasionally be able to afford your services and you won't turn down the business, but you'll spend most of your time targeting the larger companies because the odds are better that they can afford you.

Your primary prospects include:

- large companies
- companies selling products and services to other businesses
- companies selling regionally or nationally
- companies selling regionally that want to expand to other areas
- local companies that want to look like state-of-the-art companies
- local companies with more money than they know what do with
- any of the above that have already developed an Internet project but are unhappy with it or with the firm who developed it

Secondary Prospects

Smaller companies with a opportunity to benefit from the Internet that is clear to you or them include:

- some local retailers
- some local service companies
- most local manufacturers, wholesalers, and distributors
- some other local companies selling business to business
- image-conscious companies
- companies that want to look bigger than they really are
- companies with sites that are ready for updating

Who is Not a Qualified Prospect?

Sometimes it is just as useful to know who is not a prospect. If you have some benchmarks to help eliminate prospects who aren't likely to buy, you can focus your energy on your best prospects. Generally speaking, these will make for poor prospects:

- companies that have already selected an Internet firm with which they are happy
- local businesses that serve strictly local customers and have no desire or ability to serve or compete in regional, national, or international markets

- companies that, despite their sincere desire to hire you, cannot afford to

Where Are Your Prospects Located?

It's also vitally important that you decide where your selling efforts will be targeted. By and large, the closer customers are located to you, the less expensive to find them, sell them, and service them. However, if you are targeting specific industries you may be forced to sell nationally in order to find enough customers.

When It Makes Sense to Sell Your Services Locally

- when you're a one-person shop
- when you already have more business from local sources than you can handle
- when you're struggling to get started or need a quick boost in sales

When It Makes Sense to Sell Your Services Nationally

- when selling vertical market solutions (i.e., targeted to a specific industry)
- when your creative, production, and programming resources are top-notch
- when your selling skills and sales personnel are of the highest caliber
- when you have enough other business to afford the long decision-making process—up to a year or more—that is not unusual for large companies

SET THE APPOINTMENT

Establishing Contact

Generally speaking, it's doubtful that clients will hire you without seeing you in person. But does that mean you should just head out in the morning and start visiting businesses in person? Not at all. Literally hitting the pavement and knocking on doors is the most grueling type of cold-call selling. Not only do you probably dread the idea, but in today's business climate, no one has the time to see a salesperson who just dropped in unannounced.

Your goal in establishing contact is to get an appointment, not sell your services over the phone. That's why I recommend establishing the initial contact by phone. Whether you just get on the phone or first send out a letter or fax, ultimately you will be conversing with your prospect by phone and asking for an appointment.

At the appointment you will have an opportunity to meet in person, get acquainted with the client, and listen to her goals and ideas for her Internet project. You'll also have an opportunity to show projects you have already completed or currently have underway.

Of course, before you can set an appointment, you'll have to identify who is the appropriate person within the company. To do that, you'll have to get past any gatekeepers that you meet along the way. Receptionists, secretaries, administrative assistants, and others may intercept your call along the way.

Getting Past the Gatekeeper and Identifying the Decision Maker

Many business owners, executives, and other busy decision makers are guarded by efficient secretaries who help them manage their time effectively. We could all use one of these secretaries ourselves. It is not uncommon to feel like an adversary doing battle with the gatekeepers, but you are far better off seeing them as helpful sources of information about the company.

It is vital that you concentrate your efforts on selling the decision maker. The best sales pitch in the world, the most impressive portfolio of Internet projects, will be wasted on someone who may be ready to sign on the dotted line and hire you but who has no authority to do so. So, when cold calling, your first task is to ascertain who you should be talking to, and you may want to do this without actually talking to them.

The reason you might not want to be put right through is because you need to get the lay of the land before planning your sales attack. You need the first name of the decision maker in order to get past the gatekeeper. This requires doing some advance scouting work to ferret out the information that is vital to establishing contact with the right person. Here's how an initial phone call to a company might go:

RECEPTIONIST: Good morning. XYZ Company.

YOU: Good morning. Who might be in charge of your sales and marketing?

If you're selling Web sites or Internet marketing, I recommend asking who is in charge of their sales and marketing. If you're a programmer, you may prefer to ask who is in charge of the MIS department or possibly operations or finance.

RECEPTIONIST: That would be Mr. Marketing Wiz.

YOU: Is that Jack Marketing Wiz?

RECEPTIONIST: No, that's George Marketing Wiz.

YOU: May I speak with his office? By the way, is that Wiz with one Z or two?

RECEPTIONIST: That's two Zs and they're all out of town at a meeting. Would you like to leave a message?

Remember that you don't actually want to talk to George on this phone call—you're not ready. Rather, your purpose in asking is to find out if there is another gatekeeper in his office. If the receptionist puts you through and he answers the phone, hang up and make a note that he doesn't have a personal gatekeeper.

YOU: When did you say they'll be back in the office?

RECEPTIONIST: I didn't. Next Tuesday.

YOU: Well, I'll be out of town myself for the next few days. I'll try him back next week.

Again, you really don't want to leave a message. That will just start a game of telephone tag. Better to wait until George is in town and you have a better chance of reaching him in one call.
Continuing the conversation...

YOU: By the way, what's George's official title? And does he have an assistant?

RECEPTIONIST: Director of Extra Miscellaneous Marketing Projects and no, but he really could use one. I try to help him out when I can.

Hmm. His title sounds weak. Maybe he is not the ultimate decision maker here.

YOU: Oh, does the company have other executives in charge of marketing?

RECEPTIONIST: Oh, my word, yes. George is one of three, plus the vice president. Who would you like to leave a message for?

YOU: Well, I'll still try George next week. But what did you say the vice president's name is?

RECEPTIONIST: I didn't say.

YOU: That's right. Would you mind?

RECEPTIONIST: Not at all. It's George's brother, Jerry.

YOU: I see. Tell me, which of them might handle Internet projects?

RECEPTIONIST: If you mean computers, that would be Digital Dan our Director of MIS. If you mean advertising, that would be Nancy Dan, Digital's wife.

YOU: Oh I see. You have been very helpful. By the way, what is your name?

RECEPTIONIST: Mary Dan.

YOU: Wow. This is quite a family business. Nice chatting with you, Mary.

As a result of this mind-numbing conversation, you have actually learned quite a bit about this company, and all in one phone call. Everything you learned will be useful in getting the appointment and making the sale. You now know:

- the name of the top decision maker
- the names of the various marketing department decision makers
- the name of the MIS department head
- the name of the person who handles advertising
- the name of the receptionist
- the fact that George Marketing Wizz does not have an assistant

All of this information will come in handy. When the marketing department returns next Tuesday, put a call into George.

RECEPTIONIST: XYZ Company

YOU: Hi, is George in?

Keep it casual. Make it sound like you and George are old buddies. The less information you give to the receptionist, secretary, assistant, or other gatekeeper, the better. Anything you say can and will be held against you!

RECEPTIONIST: One moment please.

SECRETARY: Mr. Marketing Wizz's office.

YOU: Hi, I'm looking for George.

SECRETARY: Who's calling?

YOU: It's Dave Jensen.

Don't volunteer more than you have to. The secretary just might go ahead and put you through, especially if you sound confident and maybe even a tad irritated.

SECRETARY: Hold on.

That might be too easy. What if it goes this way?

SECRETARY: And what's this about?

After years of making cold calls on the phone in the advertising agency business (and more recently in Web development), the absolute best response I have ever found is:

YOU: Helping him increase his sales and profits.

There is no way any secretary is going to argue with that! No one wants to stand in the way of the company making more money. This line of attack works better than any other I have used over the last fifteen years.

Still, every once in a while you'll get hard-boiled-egg types who insist on knowing what color underwear you have on before deciding to put you through. The best approach here is to simply hang up and try back when they're at lunch or after they've gone for the day. Which brings me to the best time to make your calls:

- before 8:30 A.M. (in some cities before 8 A.M.)
- between noon and 1:00 P.M.
- after 5 P.M.

In other words, the best time to get through the gate is when it's not being guarded. Busy executives tend to come in early, work through lunch, and stay late. Why not put their workaholic habits to work for you?

A Surefire Way to Jump-Start Your Sales Effort

In a hurry? There are many ways to go about selling your services. Here is one of the most effective ways to start selling or to pump new blood into your sales efforts today.

Week 1

1.   Get a list of the top fifty privately owned companies in your local area.

2.   Get a list of the top fifty publicly owned companies in your local area.

3.   Get a list of the ad agencies, publishers, and public relations firms.

4.   Get a list of government agencies—city, county, and state—and the weird hybrid public-private partnerships like economic development boards, tourism boards, etc., and the largest associations.

     Where to get these lists: Contact your local newspaper, business journal, chamber of commerce, economic development council, local office of the Small Business Administration, the public library, or state department of commerce.

     These are your suspects. In any city of a million population or greater, you should easily have 150 minimum. If your area is smaller, you will have to cast a wider net geographically and go to neighboring cities and towns.

5.   Now get on the phone. Call every suspect and find out who is doing what with respect to the Internet. Find out who would handle this type of project (president? sales manager? marketing director?). Make good notes and date them. Now rank the leads hot, warm, or cold.

     The hot leads are your prospects. If you don't have at least fifty hot prospects, start with what you've got, but get more lists of local companies, preferably ranked by sales or number of employees. Start with the largest businesses.

6.   Work the hot prospects first. Again, use the phone to contact, but don't sell a Web site or other project over the phone. Your goal is

simply to get an appointment. Schedule yourself for two appointments in the morning and two in the afternoon. Your goal in the beginning is to get out, see, and be seen.

7.   Start a tickler file to call back those who say "Not now. Call me in two months."

Make sure you follow up, and don't wait until the last minute. Call them back one or two weeks or months before they say to.

Week 2

8.   Keep appointments. Show your work. Don't assume clients are online.

Take a laptop or printouts to show them your pages and sites. This is your number-one sales tool. You also need a brief list of services and ideally some package prices you have worked out with optional additional services/additional pages prices. Don't forget to ask for the business—the essential thing most Internet consultants forget to do! "Mr. Prospect, if we can agree on [price or deadline or whatever is bothering him], will you let me handle this project for you?" Always have in your possession a one- or two-page contract that you can fill in and get the client to sign on the spot, should the opportunity present itself.

This is your jump-start plan. It will prime the pump and get the business flowing.

Making the Initial Contact by Phone, Fax, or Letter

How you make your very first contact with your prospects isn't as important as you might think, as long as you end up communicating with them by phone to set an appointment. The most important thing is to contact them by some means. Making the initial contact by phone and setting up the appointment in one call is the simplest, but you may find that one of these other methods works better for you. To find out what works best, conduct a test. Select groups of ten to twenty prospects and contact each group by one of these methods. Keep track of your results.

- Send a letter. Follow up by phone. "Did you receive my letter?"
- Send a fax. Follow up by phone. "Did you receive my fax?"

- Phone. Follow up with fax. "As we discussed on the phone…"

Remember—your main goal is to get an appointment to meet in person.

By the way, don't count on using e-mail to make many of your initial contacts. It won't work. First, it's difficult to get prospects' e-mail addresses. Second, your pitch letter may be mistaken for spam and deleted before it's even read. However, you *may* be able to use it as a last-resort and run around a really tough gatekeeper.

Using an Appointment Setter

Another effective sales technique is to hire someone to do nothing but make appointments for you. That saves you a tremendous amount of time that you can devote to personal selling and other areas of the business.

To make this work, you must find someone who has excellent telemarketing skills. Previous telemarketing experience is important, preferably business-to-business telemarketing, as the person will be talking to top executives and business owners and needs to feel comfortable conversing with individuals at that level. However, she must also understand that her job is not to do your selling for you—it is simply to get the appointment.

This technique works best when you provide your appointment setter with a list of companies that you know are qualified prospects for your services. Don't hand the phone book to the appointment setter or you'll be sorry—if they are good at setting appointments, you'll have plenty to go on, but the odds are that you won't be talking to qualified prospects. Lots of business people have too much time on their hands and would just love to be entertained for a couple of hours at your expense—and they have no ability to afford your services whatsoever.

Pay your appointment setter a small amount for each appointment set, with a larger bonus for each appointment resulting in a sale. That rewards her for getting the appointment and also provides a financial incentive to refer you to qualified prospects—and leads to a win-win arrangement. In the beginning it will take some time for your telemarketer to understand how to recognize a qualified prospect when she talks to one, but with some experience and follow-up and guidance from you, she will be able to set appointments with the right companies 85–95 percent of the time.

Seeking Out New Business

No matter what method you use to find clients, you should devote some time each day to new business. If you don't have enough appointments set up, get on the phone or get your telemarketer cranking. Even when you're busy attending appointments, you should be spending some time each week setting additional appointments.

To avoid a feast-or-famine cycle, remember that even when you are busy, some time, at least a few hours every week, should be devoted to new business sales efforts.

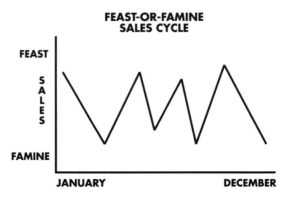

USE REFERRALS AND NETWORKING TO GENERATE STEADY BUSINESS

Referrals and networking can help you smooth out the peaks and valleys in your sales cycle. Your goal is to raise the valleys so that even your slow periods are profitable. All Internet entrepreneurs, but especially the smaller firms and one-person shops, will experience the feast-or-famine phenomenon. There is a natural tendency to not want to devote any time to sales when business is good and deadlines are looming. Then, when projects come to an end, there is a mad scramble to fill the sales pipeline again. That can become an endless cycle, especially because Web sites and programming are often one-shot project deals that don't lead to repeat business.

Fees for Web hosting, site maintenance, and program and database maintenance can offset the one-shot projects, but there will always be a need for new projects and new project income. Referrals and networking are both important contributors to making that happen.

Referrals

By far the most preferred source of new business is referrals. These can come from a variety of sources and should be actively cultivated. The best way to get a referral is to ask for one!

Who to Ask for Referrals

- existing customers—as soon as you've developed a good relationship
- former customers—as long as you parted on good terms
- business acquaintances—let them know you're actively seeking new opportunities
- personal acquaintances—let them know you're an Internet expert
- prospects who it turns out do not have a need for your services—they may know someone who does

When to Ask for Referrals

- just after you have made the sale
- midway in the project when things are on schedule and on budget
- after the project is completed and the client is satisfied

How to Ask for a Referral

Some salespeople use a very aggressive method of obtaining referrals that involves something along the line of asking the customer to visualize how family members, 'friends,' or business acquaintances' faces will look when they see the new Web site or custom programming project you have just completed and then asking the client if any of the acquaintances are interested in having a Web site or programming. Then they write down the names and get the addresses and phone numbers from the client or ask the client to look them up in the phone book if they can't remember. I think that's asking too much of the client, and I don't recommend taking that approach. But here's a slight modification that will enable you to get a referral without literally buttonholing the client.

> YOU: Mr. Magnate, I can tell you're excited about your Web site.

MR. MAGNATE: Yes, the animated logo looks great and we're featuring the site in our next customer newsletter.

YOU: I'll bet a lot of your colleagues in the industry are going to be checking out the site, too.

MR. MAGNATE: Oh, yes, we've already had a number of customers and vendors asking when it will be ready.

YOU: Well, this next month is going to be good time for us to take on new work. I'll bet you can think of quite a few customers and vendors who could really use a Web site, too.

This is a more dignified approach that still gets the client thinking of specific people he can refer. Then you simply jot down their names and phone numbers—but don't make the client look them up. Just make sure you get the correct spelling of contact names and their company name. You'll be able to take over from there and look up the phone numbers yourself if necessary. The result: hot leads from a satisfied customer—the best kind of lead.

Networking

Networking is another good way to acquire new business over a period of time. There are many ways to engage in developing a network of referral sources and you should participate in at least one of them to maximize your sales potential. Local chambers of commerce, fraternal organizations, and industry associations can be productive sources of business over the long term. Join these groups, attend their meetings, and get acquainted with the other members. It won't happen overnight, but as you know and become known, you'll find the broad circle of acquaintances will bring you business.

But there is another type of organization that can be even more productive. Networking clubs or leads clubs bring together companies representing a wide variety of local businesses. With proper organization and careful selection of members, such groups can be extremely effective in bring businesses to your attention.

How an Effective Leads Group Works

The most effective group of this type that I have ever participated in had sixty members. Meetings were held at 7:30 A.M. each

Tuesday. All members were required to attend every week or send an alternate representative. In addition, only CEOs and business owners were permitted to join the organization. There could be only one business in each category, so no member ever had to be concerned about communicating openly for fear that a competitor was listening. More important, every member was required to supply a fresh lead each week. A secretarial service typed up the leads after each meeting and mailed them to each member.

Each lead had to meet certain requirements and the group was very strict about members following the rules. Penalties were assessed for incomplete leads and failing to furnish a lead resulted in a $10 fine. This group had learned that following up on a poorly documented lead is a waste of time. For instance, each lead listing was required to include the name of a contact person, the business name, complete street address (including zip code), and telephone number. A lead could fall into one of several categories including business moving to a new location, business expanding to a new location, and completely new business. Other acceptable lead categories included those where one member of the group had done business with another member of the group for the first time. And, a lead could also be a direct lead for another designated member, or it could be a general lead for use by all members. Each member also indicated whether his name could be used when following up on the lead or whether it had to be kept confidential.

The result was a weekly list of sixty companies with complete contact information, ready for quick use in new business efforts. That was sixty leads a week, 240 leads a month, and almost three thousand leads a year, not to mention the opportunity to do business directly with fifty-nine other members of the group.

I've also been a member of leads groups that were pretty pathetic by comparison. Only three or four members showed up at one group that supposedly had thirty-five. Or plenty of members would show up to eat breakfast but "forgot" to bring a lead with them. Those are groups you can do without. Before joining a group, ask to attend one or two meetings as a guest. Find out what kind of leads the group is looking for and offer to bring one with you, even though you're attending as a guest.

Where to find groups: Many local newspapers carry a listing of business networking groups. Or try your local chamber of commerce or local library.

Cyber Networking—The Basics

Just in case you need a reminder, the Internet can also be a source of business, though not a likely source of local business and I don't recommend trying to depend on it as a sole or even primary source of new business—you're much better off using the old technology to sell the new.

Nevertheless, the Internet obviously offers tremendous opportunities to tap into key industry discussions through magazine and association sites, newsgroups, online forums, and e-mail discussion lists. And you may as well practice what you preach. An hour a day is about all it will take to keep tabs on specific industries, jump into discussion threads, and monitor the latest industry developments and leading edge opinions—and offer your own leading-edge opinions and observations.

Just to put this in terms of the kind of advice you should be giving your clients: Networking and prospecting on the Internet is an excellent enhancement to traditional cold-call selling. It gives you a ready-made opportunity to reach a targeted audience, demonstrate your knowledge and expertise, and do so in a way that will be welcome. In fact, you should network online just to prove to yourself that it does work. If you believe in the Internet, you'll do a much better job of persuading your clients to believe in it, too. Get an e-mail program like Eudora Pro that allows you to set up filters and organize your e-mail. That will go a long way to making this effort productive.

Of course, e-mail is just the beginning. But then, I really don't need to tell you how to develop and promote your Web site, create an online community, and extend your reach back to your customers and prospects with autoresponders and your own e-mail lists now, do I?

Offbeat, Guerrilla-Style Methods

When all else fails, you might consider taking a more offbeat approach to scouring the countryside for customers. Here are two approaches in this vein.

1. Think about your suppliers and the businesses you do business with. Often overlooked by consultants, that pile of bills that comes in every month contains a wealth of potential business. Any company that thinks enough of

you to have you as a customer might just be willing to become your customer in turn. The phone company, electric company, your landlord, insurance company, bank, credit card company, travel agency, car rental company, car dealer, office supply store, computer store, etc. are all possibilities. And if they don't pan out, well, start calling their competitors.

2. Look for patterns or reasons why a company could justify wanting a Web site. For example, you might conclude that any company with a display ad in the yellow pages is a good candidate for a Web site based on their apparent understanding of the value of advertising. And, because the annual cost of a Web site could be less than they're spending in the phone book, you might conclude they can easily afford it. This particular example may or may not hold true, but it should give you an idea of how this works.

Online Networking Jump-Start Plan

1. Go to Altavista or Dejanews and search on keywords pertaining to the industry you're targeting.

2. Make a note of the newsgroups that show up most frequently, sampling some of the messages to verify relevant discussion.

3. Log on to each of the online services (CompuServe, America Online, Prodigy, Microsoft Network) and use their search function to locate forums and bulletin boards targeting the desired industry.

4. Newsgroups tend to be informal, online service forums a bit more formal in user behavior standards and rules. So don't worry about posting an introductory message in most newsgroups, but consider posting one to the appropriate topic area in the online forums.

5. Depending on your level of experience in posting messages and participating in online discussions, look for ongoing discussions you can jump in and contribute to (less experience) or consider priming the pump with interesting new topics (more experience). Avoid spamming and cross-posting to multiple lists, forums, and forum topics with the same post.

6. Your goal is basically to become known as a reliable and knowledgeable source of information. Over time, your prospects will raise their hands and say, "Here I am. Sell me something." When

they do, make sure you take the discussion to private e-mail. Hey, you don't hang your dirty laundry out for everyone to see. Why conduct business out in the open?

7.   A word of caution: You are unlikely to find much local business through online marketing. For your local market, hit the phones and work your local contacts for referrals.

HELPFUL SALES FORM

To convert this to computer format, simply treat each entry and column heading as a database or form field.

PROSPECT LEAD TRACKING FORM

CONTACT NAME_____ PHONE _____ FAX _____

TITLE_____ SECRETARY/ASSISTANT_____

COMPANY _____

ADDRESS _____ CITY _____ STATE _____ ZIP _____

REFERRED BY _____ COLD CALL (LIST SOURCE) _____

ADDITIONAL INFORMATION _____

DATE	PHONE/FAX LETTER/E-MAIL	RESULTS/DISCUSSION	FOLLOW-UP

YOU KNOW YOU'RE A GEEK WHEN...

You start tilting your head sideways to smile.

Planning the Presentation

OK. You've got some appointments lined up with hot prospects. That was the whole idea of getting on the phone. But are you prepared to walk in and make your sales pitch?

Your goal so far was to get the appointment. Now that you've accomplished that, your next goal is to get the *business.*

In order to do that, you will have to use your appointment to find out what's really motivating the client to take on an Internet project, whether he can afford to hire you, and whether he's ready and willing to hire you *now.* But are you ready to meet? Here are some essentials to keep in mind prior to your presentation.

WHERE TO MEET—YOUR PLACE OR MINE?

You're probably better off seeing the prospect on their turf for the initial meeting—because that's more convenient for the client. If yours is a virtual organization, you'll have little choice, unless you have alternative meeting space available.

If you have a laptop, it will be easy to show examples of your work. If you don't, but your office is fully equipped, you may prefer to have the meeting on your turf. Depending on the client's computer is dangerous and not recommended. Even if a client assures you she has a connection to the Internet or a machine with a suitable video monitor, it is wise to take along your own equipment just in case. Too many have been burned trying to count on the client's equipment. The client's machine may be underpowered or in need of repair, or, worse, contain a virus. Better to steer clear of these problems during the sales presentation. You can always deal with them later, *after* you've sold the project.

That said, some Web developers find it difficult to show sites on a computer without losing the client's attention. They prefer using paper printouts of Web pages, finding that approach more techno-friendly to clients accustomed to seeing things in print. My advice: If you go in with paper, it's better to be prepared to show the site on computer as well. And any time you show a site, expect to deal with a few newbie questions about browsers and navigation. A few extra minutes spent giving your prospects a larger peek into the Internet window can pay off with a perception that you are an expert and one who is down-to-earth enough to share the wisdom. That can do wonders in helping build your reputation.

A lunch meeting allows you to use a casual and personal approach than presenting to a group of managers in their office, which would call for a more formal approach. One disadvantage of a restaurant is that you'll find it awkward to show your sites on a laptop. Don't! Plan on using the lunch as an opportunity to get acquainted. When you set up the meeting, let the client know you'd like to return to his office after lunch for a ten- to fifteen-minute review of some of your work. You can have the client look at your sites online, but you'll be more in control if you lead him through in person.

WHO WILL BE AT THE MEETING?

Whether you present by yourself or take along other members of your team will not be critical to most new business presentations. In some ways it is far easier to handle a client on a one-to-one basis, and it's expensive to utilize the time of several team members for new business.

Generally, you should reserve a team sell for second meetings where the client has a committee of people that are eager to hear what you have to say. At that point, the key will be prior coordination and rehearsal between you and your team members covering the order of the presentation and the points to be brought out. Someone must be the team leader and lead presenter who takes charge of the presentation, introducing team members to present their particular area of expertise. The team leader must be prepared to show off each team member's strengths, but arrange a signal to give if someone starts getting bogged down in boring details or areas that are way over the client's head.

WHEN WILL THE MEETING TAKE PLACE?

You're in control. If you have more energy first thing in the morning, schedule your new business calls for that hour and go directly from home to your first appointment. If you need a few hours to wake up or clear a few items off your to-do list before feeling ready to tackle new business, set your appointments for 10:30 or 11 A.M.

For lunch appointments, whether you meet the client at his office or connect at the restaurant, try to set it up at 11:30 A.M. in order to avoid the rush. You'll appreciate the quieter environment.

If you like to cap the day with a final challenge, make your appointments for late afternoon or after hours.

Where to Find the Latest Demographics

The demographics of the Internet—that is, the description of who is online—is undergoing constant change and will continue to do so for some time. To keep up with the latest data, go to these sites:

- CommerceNet/Nielsen Study,
  http://www.commerce.net/nielsen/

- FIND/SVP, http://etrg.findsvp.com/index.html

- Hermes Study of Commercial Use of the Internet,
  http://www-personal.umich.edu/~sgupta/hermes/

- Georgia Institute of Technology's Graphic, Visualization & Usability Center's WWW User Surveys,
  http://www.cc.gatech.edu/gvu/user_surveys/

WHAT TO WEAR

This may seem obvious, but it doesn't hurt to point out that one is often judged by appearance. To the extent that you feel comfortable in normal business dress, it is almost always safe to assume that's what you should wear. The definition of *normal* will vary from one city to another and from one type of client to another. In some parts of the country it's acceptable to wear "professional casual" (dark slacks and golf shirt or dress shirt for men, pantsuit or skirt and blouse for women). In other areas it's strictly business suits all around. If you're located on a tropical island you may be able to do fine in an airbrushed T-shirt and cut offs, but everywhere else you should aim to look like you mean business—meaning that if a casual bystander happened to see you in the client's office, they might be willing to believe that you are one of the key people who works there.

Some graphic designers feel they must look artsy and dress in unusual or attention-getting clothing styles. The truth is, a little goes a long way. If your personality is as outgoing as your clothing and a wild style works for you, by all means wear it. But if you're a bit on the introverted side, you're better off sticking to more conservative styles. Otherwise, your clothes are likely to draw more attention than you feel comfortable handling.

Some technical people rarely see the light of day, what with their long hours and dedication. They also are known to skip shaving and haircuts, even showers when on a mission to solve an important technical problem. Everyone is grateful they have so much dedication and don't let life's little necessities get in the way, but don't let anyone in that condition get anywhere near a prospective client—even if the client is Geek of the Year.

LAST-MINUTE DETAILS

If your presentation is in the client's office, plan on having everything you need to set up your laptop, including the A/C adapter, a fully charged battery, and if they make an adapter that plugs into a cigarette lighter, get one of those, too.

If you're going to log in to a dialup account, make sure all Web sites you'll be showing the client have been fully copied to the hard drive, a floppy, or a zip drive, and that all pages and graphics load properly. Be prepared to explain away any that don't work. And if you're going to log into an account that others have access to, make sure they aren't going to be online during your appointment. If possible, have a backup account on another ISP that you can use in case of busy signals, line noise, or a slow Internet connection.

Pre-Presentation Checklist

Prospective Client _____

Company _____

Phone _____

When

Date _____

Time _____

Where

Your Office _____

Client Office _____

Restaurant _____

Reservations Needed? _____

Who

❑ Solo or ❑ Group

If group, who is the leader? _____

Person   Area to be Presented

_____   _____

_____   _____

_____   _____

_____   _____

_____   _____

Rehearsal Needed? _____

To Take

❑ notes on the client made while setting the appointment
❑ brochure
❑ bullet Sheets
❑ handouts on Internet demographics, etc. (see box)
❑ business cards
❑ notepad
❑ pen
❑ laptop and accessories
❑ disks if needed
❑ printouts of work in progress

REHEARSE—OR WING IT?

There are two schools of thought on rehearsal. One believes you can't rehearse enough; the other believes that too much rehearsal can make your presentation come off as tired and uninspiring.

When You're First Starting Out

When you first begin selling, it is inevitable that you'll make some mistakes. That can't be avoided. In fact, it should be expected and understood as a natural part of gaining sales experience. In a way, rehearsing your presentation at this stage is of limited value— there's no point rehearsing something that may not work, and, although it is often said that practice makes perfect, it is also true that practice makes *permanent*—it is often more difficult to *un*learn than it is to learn.

Nevertheless, much is to be gained from rehearsing your presentations until you know them forward and backward. For example, you will gain self-confidence from knowing your material inside and out. You'll come across as more polished and professional when you can easily and effortlessly communicate what you have to offer and why it is better than your competitors,' anticipating what prospects will say and how you will respond.

> PROSPECT: Why should I hire you to do my Web site for $500 per page when I can get a kid in my neighborhood to the same job for $50 a page?

> YOU: There is no question that all kinds of people are going into the Web design business, and we encourage them to do so. However, as I'm sure is true in your industry, quality varies from company to company and product to product. It's no different in the Web development business. So, to answer your question, if the only services we offered were in the areas of Web design, you might do just as well with a teenager. But keep in mind, design is only one part of the development of a successful Web site. Marketing expertise is even more important than design and we have more than ten years of experience working with companies in your industry. If your Web site is to be successful and achieve your sales goals, it's imperative that it perform at maximum capacity. Would you turn any other area of your business over to teenagers?

PROSPECT: Why should I hire you to develop a database for my Web site when I can use Microsoft Access and do it myself?

YOU: Well, we develop Access databases, too, and of course there is no reason why you couldn't develop one your-selves if you're familiar with the program. We have found there are some significant limitations to Access. Even though it is a very good program, we also develop in three other programs that work better in many applica-tions, including the Internet.

PROSPECT: Why should I hire you? You're just a teenager. What do you know about my business?

YOU: We don't claim to be experts in your business. We expect that our clients will always know more about their business than we do. Our expertise is the Internet. Now you can certainly hire an expensive consultant with a lot of business experience and pay her $100 an hour to study the Internet for a couple of months. But we already understand it and we're ready to develop your site in just a few weeks. One of the great things about the Internet is how economical it is to make revisions and fine-tune things as needed. For just a few thousand dollars you can try all kinds of ideas out in the Internet marketplace—far less than you'd pay a consultant who will only produce a study. You'll still have to develop a site and then you'd probably be locked into the initial design or face more expensive fees. So we offer you the best of both worlds. Your site will be up and running quickly and our afford-able rates make it easy to test new ideas and make changes as you go.

When You Have Experience

No amount of preparation can substitute fully for the learning that comes only from experience. The more selling you do, the less rehearsal you will need. After you've heard the same questions asked in a variety of ways, you will be able to answer without think-ing, and rehearsal will not be necessary. Eventually you can walk in totally unprepared and wing it.

In sales there is always something new to learn. You'll come across a client in an industry you've never dealt with before, or find an opportunity to sell a new type of project you've never worked on before, or you may raise your rates, change your terms and conditions, or offer a host of new services to stay ahead of the competition. In these cases, it's back to the basics of memorizing the pertinent details and anticipating questions the client will have about them.

What about becoming stale? When you repeat the same material over and over, day after day, let's face it—it's a bore. If you think so, your clients will too. So, occasionally, mix things up a bit. Don't be reluctant to change the order of your presentation now and then. Sometimes use handouts, other times leave them out. Leave all your materials in the car once and see what happens. You can always fall back on the tried and true if you get into trouble.

So, should you rehearse or not? Are you just starting out? Then rehearse, rehearse, rehearse! Already have plenty of experience under your belt and getting bored giving the same old pitch? Try winging it, but if that doesn't meet with equal success, be prepared to go back to the reliable old methods (even though you may find them boring).

WHAT YOU SHOULD KNOW LIKE THE BACK OF YOUR HAND FROM DAY ONE

- *All the ways the Internet fits in* (see chapter 6)
- *The major benefit you offer your clients.* Examples: your expertise, your ability to achieve results in the marketplace, your quick turnaround time, your affordable rates, your award-winning designs.
- *Your rates.* You should have your entire rate structure memorized so that you don't have to read off a rate sheet. After all, if you're not sure of these vital details, how can the client be confident that you know the details about anything else?
- *Your most significant accomplishments to date*—your success stories, your most impressive clients. When you're just starting out, of course, you may not have much in this category. But you must make do and use what you do have in order to gain additional experience. And if you

have absolutely nothing, say so, but be prepared to offer your services at terms and rates so attractive the client can't say no. Then use those projects as your success stories to justify higher rates.

Try to think through what questions clients will have for you and prepare answers. Try your sales pitch out on friends and others you know and note the questions they raise. Then develop the necessary answers.

YOU KNOW YOU'RE A GEEK WHEN...

You can read binary code fluently.

CHAPTER

NINE

Making the Presentation

Let's review some of the material covered earlier:

Marketing Your Services as a Professional

- Be a professional who can sell, not a professional sales-person.
- Minimize uncertainty.
- Understand the client's problems.
- Achieve credibility.

Typical Client Expectations

- The client thinks the Internet is another ad medium.
- The client thinks the Internet is just like direct mail.
- The client thinks the Internet is a retail store.
- The client thinks the Internet is a channel conflict.
- The client thinks the Internet is really an online catalog.
- The client thinks the Internet is another way to provide customer service and technical support.
- The client thinks the Internet is really an employee newsletter.
- The client thinks the Internet is an editorial or publishing medium.
- The client thinks the Internet is a (people) networking or community-building medium.
- The client thinks the Internet is all of the above.

APPROACHES TO THE INITIAL PRESENTATION

What Works

The Consultative Sell: Conduct an examination of the client's situation by listening to what the client has to say and responding with information about how your capabilities in those areas can help the client.

What Doesn't

The Hard Sell: Show your product and try to sell it to a client who may or may not need it. Ignore the fact that you may be putting a square peg into a round hole. Just sell whatever you have available and assume it makes sense for the client. This approach is suitable only for products like automobiles, photocopiers, and computers, and a few services such as pest control. The focus is not on how you can help them, but rather on the features of the product: "The model GQZWV-2 prints 25,000 copies per minute and is powered by the Super Duper Nuker with Plutonium 2000." For professional services, however, the hard sell will turn off prospects and cast doubt on your ability to advise them.

Taking Orders: The opposite of the Hard Sell; say little, allow the client to dominate by telling you how to handle his project, and act like an order taker, doing whatever the client tells you to do. This role makes you look extremely weak and will cause the client to question your capabilities. Sometimes, despite your best efforts, a client will put you in the position of being an order taker. In those cases, you will have to decide whether to accept the job anyway and take full direction from the client, or whether to say no, thank you, and walk away from the project.

Of the three approaches, the Consultative Sell is by far the strongest and really the only effective one for Internet projects.

THE CONSULTATIVE SELL

Everything I've covered so far has been designed to prepare you for selling on a consultative basis. This is your best approach for the vast majority of Internet and new media projects. Basically, it boils down to this:

1. Meet the client and establish rapport.
2. Find out what's most important to the client. Establish your credibility in those areas.
3. Discuss fees.
4. Ask for the business.

Too simple? Perhaps, but these brief steps are the essence of your initial sales presentation. How you implement them will depend on a number of factors, and flexibility is the key here. Unless you specialize in selling only to certain industries or sell only certain narrowly defined types of projects, you are likely to find yourself walking into ten appointments with ten different clients and end up making ten presentations, no two of which are alike.

WHAT DO YOU SAY AFTER YOU SAY HELLO?

For that matter, how do you say hello? For those who are extro-verted, this is not a problem. Those who are naturally outgoing always seem to know exactly what to say to start a conversation and keep it going. However, much Internet-related work is best per-formed by introverts—those who can work by themselves for long periods of time with little or no contact with others. That kind of work will quickly drain the energy of the accomplished conversa-tionalist, but introverts thrive on the isolation and do their best work under those conditions. Of course, what is a strength in the production area can be a limitation in the sales area, but it doesn't have to be. Both introverts and extroverts can learn to sell equally well, though with much different styles.

The key to breaking the ice is to be yourself. You probably can't make radical changes in your personality, even if you wanted to. On the other hand, it's important to recognize what people like in other people and strive to meet those expectations. According to Robert W. Bly, author of *Selling Your Services,* people like people who are friendly, warm, polite, courteous, respectful, and on time. They like people who like them, who share their interests, and who listen to them. And they like people who treat them well and help them. We all have these traits in us—some more than others, per-haps, but these characteristics are within everyone's reach.

Think of the sales call as a conversation. Start by greeting the client with a firm handshake, a big smile, and by making good eye contact. And that's a FIRM handshake and a really BIG smile. Show those pearly whites and you'll fill the room with friendly enthusiasm. There's nothing worse than a limp, wimpy handshake, so make sure yours isn't. This is not an arm wrestling contest, so if you're not strong, try simply extending your hand and holding it fairly stiff and rigid. That will cause most people to grip your hand and they'll do the gripping. On the other hand, if you are of above-average strength, go easy on the little lady—grip, but don't crush.

YOU (smiling widely, hand extended for a firm shake):
Hello, John. I've been looking forward to meeting you.

Arm yourself with subject matter to keep the conversation rolling; take advantage of time spent waiting in the lobby before the appointment to glance through the company's brochures or annual reports. Look for interesting facts about the company that you can mention later. This also helps avoid the cliché about how beautiful the client's offices are. Ideally, you can find something that will help turn the conversation toward the Internet. You can say something like, "By the way, I noticed you have an office in Europe. Are you enjoying good success there?" That will get the client talking about her international business and you can easily bring up the Internet.

Establish Rapport and Be Yourself

We're talking personalities here—yours and the client's and how they mix. If you have an outgoing personality, find it easy to get along with others, have no problem talking about yourself, and have a natural interest in others, you've got a head start on selling yourself and developing good personal chemistry with the client.

If you tend to be more introverted, you may find it difficult and uncomfortable to meet new people and talk about yourself. The best thing to do in this case is to use your introversion as a strength and keep the focus on the client rather than yourself. Use your work as another focal point. You may find it much easier to talk about what you've done than about who you are. The main thing is to get an understanding of what the client wants or needs, and focus on the areas of your work and experience that are most relevant.

Knowing your own personality and how others see you is helpful in understanding and interpreting client reactions during the sales process. If you've never taken a personality profile test, you might want to try one online. The Myers-Briggs Personality Inventory is well known and an excellent tool to help team members better understand and appreciate each other's personality characteristics (OK, in some cases, "quirks."). And knowing your own profile can be helpful in anticipating how you come across to others.

Two sites featuring personality profile tests are:

1. The Keirsey Temperament Sorter,
   `http://www.keirsey.com/cgi-bin/keirsey/newkts.cgi`
2. A similar but slightly different version of the test can be found here:
   `http://sunsite.unc.edu:80/personality/keirsey.html`

Focus on the Other Person

People love to talk about themselves, so let them. If the client brings up football and you're a fan, you'll have a lot to talk about. If you can't remember the last time you even thought about football but you remember checking out ESPN's Web site, ask if he's seen it. If you can't think of anything to say, be honest. "Gee, I have to confess I've never really been much of a sports fan, but your enthusiasm is becoming contagious."

In general, then, always be on the lookout for interests you have in common with the prospect.

Listen More Than You Speak

The key to getting the information you need to do an effective job for the client is to be an active listener. Look interested in what the client has to say. Acknowledge the points the client is making by nodding your head, saying "I see," "I didn't realize that," "That's something I'm making a note of," etc.

Ask Questions

Use questions to stay in control. Just because the client is doing most of the talking doesn't mean you're not in control. Direct the

conversation the way you want it to go by asking for the information you need and use questions to clarify the vague statements
clients tend to make sometimes.

> YOU: You say you probably would like to have online
> ordering capabilities. Is that something that we should
> address from the beginning or should we figure on that
> coming in a later phase?

You're actually helping the client by asking these questions.
You have an agenda for the meeting. You know what you're trying
to achieve: Get to know the client, qualify him, and close a deal.
The prospect you're talking to, however, very likely has a much
looser agenda and may not be at all organized in thinking about an
Internet project. So your questions serve a vital role in assisting the
client in thinking through his Internet plans. Don't be afraid to ask
them.

Relate to the Client as an Equal

You're there to see what you can do to help the client with her
Internet project. Her company has needs; you have the capability
to meet those needs. That doesn't make the client superior nor
does it make you inferior. The client needs you every bit as much
as you need the client. Treat this strictly as a conversation between
adults of equal stature.

How Listening Paid Off for One Web Developer

In 1993, after seventeen years serving in top marketing positions
for major companies including Seiko, Epson, and Mattel, George
Rasher left the corporate world to strike out on his own. He began
by starting Cabrillo East, http://cabrillo.com, a multimedia publishing company, a "junior Electronic Arts Publishing," with the goal
of developing successful retail CD-ROMS. He felt well equipped to
do so because throughout his career his key responsibilities had
been in the areas of planning and launching new products and
new business units. So the idea of forming a new business was not
a formidable one.

George put together a business plan and sought venture funding. Just as he was getting very close to securing investment he
began meeting many people who were working on Web design

projects. They encouraged him to focus his business plan on the emerging Web medium.

A few months after founding the multimedia business, George concluded that he should indeed give serious consideration to the opportunities arising from the Internet. He realized that in order to be effective, he would need to get a better understanding of the Web. So he devoted the better part of the next three months to studying Internet technology, TCP/IP protocols, HTML coding, etc. In early 1995 he made the transition away from CD-ROM development to focus on Web development.

"It meant that instead of selling clients on commercial sponsorship or underwriting of CD-ROM infotainment with an underlying corporate message, we were selling the same thing on a Web platform, but with a significantly lower cost structure," Rasher says. Today, 85 percent of Cabrillo's revenue comes from Web development projects.

This wasn't all the result of a savvy and deliberate business strategy. "It was reality. We moved to the Web just to keep the doors open. We had developed some prototype CD-ROM projects in order to give potential clients an idea of what our capabilities were, but we did not have any completed work to show. We also didn't have any Web sites to show, not even a site of our own. We were out cold calling customers and promoting the World Wide Web itself more than anything. I positioned our firm as an interactive marketing company. In effect, our portfolio was my accomplishments with multinational companies. Our first clients were buying me."

What Makes Cabrillo East Different

Simply put, George's ability to talk the language of his clients, many of whom are top managers and marketing managers in large companies. That makes a big difference and clearly positions him well against other Web developers.

Listen yourself as George explains. "Other developers talk about their catalog engine or their servers or some other gee-whiz technology. I engage the client in a conversation about their business. I spend a lot of time listening. I might talk about how the company can properly position and price their products and services when bringing them to the Web. Or I might discuss channel conflict, which is a common problem for companies selling through established product distribution channels. A manufacturer's Web site can wreak havoc even with carefully thought out distribution agreements with wholesalers, distributors, and retailers. I am extremely comfortable discussing these areas with a client because I dealt with the same problems for years in the corporate arena. They are areas in which the client is seeking knowledgeable input and we position ourselves as adding value to the Web."

Those abilities enable George to form a relationship with a prospect and establish a comfort level that makes him a natural choice among competing Web developers. "As opposed to discussing technical issues, we focus the discussion on strictly marketing-based areas. That clearly sets us apart. We offer strong technical expertise, of course, but today the technical issues are pretty much settled. The technology works. Now it's a question of what do we do with the technology, how do we put it to good business purpose."

George continues, "Putting up a Web site often becomes a litmus test for companies. It causes them to rethink fundamental issues about their business. The process of thinking through what they want to accomplish on the Internet gives them an opportunity to test their assumptions about how they position and sell their products, the message they are sending to consumers to do so, the tone, and so on. Often we hear them saying, 'We never did like that,' or 'No one really knows why we do it that way.'

"For many companies, the Web becomes a cross-departmental effort. When you look at the Web not only as an advertising medium but also as a customer service medium, it crosses over boundaries and gets people talking around a table who would not ordinarily talk to each other.

"Because the Internet is in the news, it has the attention of top management. They're interested in what we're doing. You can end up with many masters," George points out.

TYPICAL CLIENT SITUATIONS

Selling effectively under a variety of conditions means being able to apply general rules and think on your feet to address whatever specifics are relevant. After you've been on a dozen appointments, you'll know exactly the types of clients you'll run into. Of course, there will always be new variations and the occasional client who throws you a curve ball, but that helps keep you sharp and prevents boredom from setting in. In the meantime, here is an overview of client situations you're likely to run into.

How Familiar with the Internet is the Client?

- Is the client online?
- Are they newbies or power users or somewhere in between?

These are among the first points you'll want to find out in your discussions with a prospective client. It's a lot easier to sell someone who has some appreciation for the Internet, who uses e-mail and has done some surfing on the Web. Those that haven't can still be sold, but you'll have to do a lot of explaining or demonstrating of what the Internet is, how it works, what the benefits are. Trying to find someone in the client's organization who is Internet savvy is one possibility, but the approach can backfire if the decision maker does not consider the person's opinion important.

How Far Along is the Client in Thinking About His Internet Project?

Not far at all. In fact, he really hadn't considered it until you called.

This is probably a long shot, but he could be an excellent client if you can show him where the opportunities are for his company— but before you can determine that, you'll have to do some probing. Probably the best thing to do with this client is quickly show him some of your work and then bring up the subject of budgets and fees.

If getting something for nothing is more what he had in mind, then you'll know it's time to move on. If he has a sufficient budget, then it may be worth developing a working relationship and steering him in the right direction. Your first project should probably focus on some planning steps. You may as well get paid to educate this type of client.

He has some unrealistic ideas about it.

Probably of the get-rich-quick kind. You'll have to tread carefully around this one. You don't want to dampen his enthusiasm for what could turn out to be a lucrative project, but you want to be cautiously enthusiastic about the potential. If you totally feed his unrealistic fantasies, you can be sure they'll come right back at you when money does not fall out of the sky. It's better to begin lowering expectations from the beginning.

He has the right goals but hasn't a clue how to get there.

Now we're talking. Listen carefully and the client will tell you exactly what he wants to accomplish. It will be up to you to explain how you can help him get there. But be careful. It is easy to end up giving away your knowledge. Keep the focus on examples of other projects you have handled.

If you're just starting out and don't have a lot of experience, try illustrating with projects you know of that had similar goals. Don't present them as your own work if they're not, but don't hesitate to use the work of others as examples to focus discussion with the client.

He has a plan worked out and needs help implementing it.

This client has made it one step farther. You may feel you're jumping in midstream. You may wish perhaps he hadn't proceeded this far without your involvement. Be patient; listen carefully. By encouraging the idea of bringing you on as a member of his team you can develop the type of relationship that will ultimately allow you to make whatever suggestions you believe are appropriate.

The midlevel people are well informed, but the decision maker/boss doesn't have a clue.

They need your help in convincing the boss. Good news or bad? That will depend on their boss. As soon as you recognize this situation, be looking for an opportunity to meet directly with the decision maker, and the sooner the better. You really haven't begun to sell until you do. Be prepared to discuss the benefits of your Internet project. Will it lead to increased sales? Will it improve customer service? Will it enhance the image of the company? Will it provide convenient, low-cost communications with branch offices, customers, and suppliers? When you get to the decision maker, use whatever you have learned along the way about the company's goals and any information you may have about the decision maker. For example, if the company wants to sell products on the Web and you know the owner thinks Java is really cool and you have Java capabilities, by all means discuss the idea of writing the shopping cart in Java.

He's been called by every Internet company in town, but for some reason you're the first person he decided to talk to.

Congratulations! If you can find out why he agreed to see you when he hasn't seen anyone else, you'll have a good idea of how you are being perceived by your customers. Of course, it could simply be that you happened to call at the right time. In any case, you'll still have to identify which of the other situations this client falls into and sell accordingly. Act quickly and you may get him to commit without shopping around.

He is interviewing several firms.

This will become more the norm as the industry develops. The more knowledgeable you are about the Internet and Internet marketing in general, the stronger you will look. Bring out all the ammunition for this client, including references or testimonials from other clients, and decide early on whether you will need to make an investment in spec work.

He has drafted a Request for Proposal and wants you to submit a competitive bid.

You will find this typically only with government agencies and possibly some trade associations. Find out whether the project *must* go to the lowest bidder or your contact has discretion over who is selected. Regardless, treat this like any other client—establish rapport with the key people. If the decision will be handled by a committee, watch out. Selling to a committee is one of the most difficult sells there is and requires more time than any other client situation. If you don't already know some of the key people on the client side, you may decide it's not worth the time and effort to submit a proposal.

He's already interviewed everybody else in town and is really going out of his way and doing you a big favor by seeing you, so whatever you have to say better be really good.

Don't even think about walking into this situation without first getting back on the phone with the client and probing for information about who and what you're up against. Who are the strongest firms he's seen so far? Perhaps there aren't any and the job is easy pickings for you. What are the goals for the project? The client should have them pretty well thought out by now—he's had to explain them to every other firm in town. If you have experience or expertise in similar projects, consider going for it. But no one will fault you for passing on this one if you decide conditions are not friendly.

He's been burned by another firm and is looking for someone he can trust.

There are several variations on this theme. The original firm could be his ad agency, his ISP, his brother-in-law, a former employee, even a current employee. This client expects the worst and is really hurting. His bank account may also be hurting if he paid big bucks for a Web site or program that isn't working, so you'll want to address the subject of fees early on in your discussions—and the client will be eager for you to do so. Your biggest obstacle with this type of client is overcoming the bad feelings he has toward the other firm. Figure on a lot of hand-holding sessions and take everything slowly, spell out everything in advance, go overboard with status reports and updates, build in extra steps for approvals, and use progressive billing throughout the project. If you can develop a positive relationship with this client, you may have a customer for life.

On the other hand, sometimes it is the client who burns the firm and then acts like it was the other way around—so be careful. Get details on what went wrong. What exactly was it that the other firm did that has the client upset? If it turns out to be something very minor, something you might very well have done yourself, watch out. The client may have extremely unrealistic expectations.

He's looking for a Fortune 500 company that also happens to do Internet projects.

For some clients, only the biggest and best will do. If you fall into this category, no problem. If you don't, don't give up. You may be able to deliver faster and more economically than a hundred-person firm. Do some probing over the phone about the client's goals. If you have strengths in those areas, say so. If it turns out that the project is so huge that you couldn't handle it yourself anyway, consider finding out which firms he's looking at and calling on them to see if you can handle parts of the project.

He's ready for a redesign because last year's model is starting to look and feel out of date.

The Internet moves at a fast pace. Times change. Design trends change. New looks come into fashion. Yesterday's Web design is yesterday's news. Database interfaces need updating, just as Web pages do. The effectiveness of marketing approaches fades over time. Yesterday's Phase One Web site is now ready for Phase Two,

complete with chat rooms, database connections, automated transactions, and personification, etc., all of which makes for great sales
potential. But be careful not to harp on the negatives, even when
invited to do so. Give the client input on what is good and should
be salvaged as well as what should be changed, added, or expanded. Make the company and its products and services the hero. Your
job is to sell the client on your ability to show his company in the
best possible light and take his Internet project to the next level—
and beyond.

JUST TO RECAP

1. Meet the client, listen as he tells you what he'd like to
   achieve on the Internet, and in the process attempt to
   establish rapport and identify what he perceives his company's greatest needs to be.
2. Establish credibility and minimize uncertainty by introducing your services and showing the prospective client
   examples of your previous work, especially sites or projects that solved similar problems or challenges. Discuss
   your design, programming, or multimedia philosophy and
   how it enables you to successfully approach a wide range
   of Internet, programming, or new media projects (or how
   it enables you to achieve a high degree of expertise in
   focused areas, if you are specializing in certain types of
   projects or particular industries or audiences).
3. Discuss the subject of fees to confirm that the client can
   afford your services.
4. Ask for the business. Close the sale on the spot, if possible, without doing a proposal, by getting a commitment to
   move forward.

Do You Hate the Idea of Selling? Here's One Way to Stay Psychologically on Top

A large part of successful selling deals with psychology. For professionals who sell, a large part of the psychology is involved with keeping one's
motivation level high. There are probably a million and one other things
you would rather be doing than going out and selling. So, right away,
you have a motivation problem.

You may be much more comfortable working with computers than
with people. Unfortunately, you won't have many projects to work on if

you don't bring in the business. This can quickly become a game of Spy vs. Spy, or you against your brain, leading to confusion and exhaustion just from thinking about selling.

Accountant Allan Boress, author of *The I Hate Selling Book,* compares the sales presentation to an audit or an examination by a doctor. Taking this approach puts you in control, much like a doctor examining a patient, and gives you the opportunity to obtain the information you need about the client's situation without feeling like you are selling. Boress lists the following steps in a sales examination:

Step 1: Test for personal chemistry.

> This involves assessing whether or not prospective clients feel at ease with you (one indication that they do is that you feel comfortable with them).

Step 2: Test for emotional needs, wants, desires, or musts.

> If your prospective clients don't have these underlying aches, they're not going to buy anything from you.

Step 3: Test for commitment to action.

> Your prospective buyers must have aches, but if you want to make a sale, they must also be committed to doing something to cure them.

Step 4: Test for ability and desire to pay.

> Even if your prospects have many problems *and* want to fix them, you must also make sure they have the money to pay your fees. If not, you're out of there.

Step 5: Test for knowledge of the decision-making process and the ability to influence that process.

> After you've found aches, commitment, and money, you still need to find out exactly who will make the decision to hire you and then do your best to contact the decision makers and control the process.

Step 6: Test to see if a presentation or a proposal is necessary, and determine what it should look like.

> Sometimes presentations and proposals are necessary. If so, you must have the prospect tell you exactly what these items should look like in order for you to get the sale.

If you are able to reach Step 6, you can then choose to proceed to the final two steps:

Step 7: Prepare a custom-designed presentation and/or proposal.

If you have successfully taken the prospect through the first six steps and she wants a presentation or proposal, you must now create a custom-designed price—if you want the business.

Step 8: Finalize the agreement.

In this last step, you need to resolve all the relevant issues, such as when the work will begin, payment schedule, and so on.

By advocating a set procedure that involves thinking about the sales call as a series of tests that must be passed by the prospect, Boress creates a psychology that puts you in control, rather than the buyer, thereby taking away some of your sales pressure. The sales presentation becomes a consultation or an interview and an opportunity to find out whether the prospect really will make a good client, one you will enjoy working with and who truly needs your services and can afford you. You can use the Boress approach to keep yourself on top psychologically and feel more like you're helping the client and less like you're selling the client something she may not really need.

HANDOUTS

Helpful Sales Tools

Do you need handouts? It's unlikely you will actually lose any sales because of your sales materials and even the best materials are no substitute for an effective sales presentation on your part. If you're planning to take a laptop to demonstrate sites or programs, you may not need handouts to make the sale. At the very minimum, though, you will need a business card to leave behind with the prospect.

I have successfully sold advertising, public relations, and Web development services with and without handout materials, with equal results. However, a more professional image will be conveyed if you have well-designed materials promoting your business and outlining the services you offer. In addition, handouts can be a lifesaving crutch for the inexperienced professional who may feel awkward in a selling situation during the first couple of months. Handouts at least give the sales newbie a selling tool—something to hold and something to use to focus the clients attention while building sales experience. The danger here, of course, is that the new salesperson will forget that the client is buying the professional—you—not your brochure!

What to Include in Your Handouts

Descriptive sales copy—several paragraphs describing and positioning your firm and the areas you specialize in. This copy should cover:

- your experience and background and that of the other principal partners or employees in the firm
- a list of the exact services you are offering
- the types of companies you are targeting or specializing in serving
- the benefits of using your firm
- testimonials from satisfied customers (can be added later)
- if relevant, screen shots of your Web pages or program GUI
- contact information

Ideally, the copy for your handouts should be written by an experienced advertising copywriter. However, if you prefer to do this yourself, your best bet is to obtain samples of other companies' sales kits to get ideas for the appropriate tone of the copy. Just remember that your materials must properly convey what your business is all about.

A Low-Budget Solution

A very attractive, serviceable, and economical way to package your handouts is in the form of a sales kit folder with inserts. You can obtain plain 9x12 pocket folders in solid glossy colors at any office supply store. Simply prepare your inserts on standard letter-size paper and insert in the folder's pockets. The kits will cost less than $2.00 each. They won't have your company name printed on them, but if you use a distinguishing color, that alone can serve as an identity for you, at least temporarily. This type of kit can be produced in a day or two and updated just as quickly. That's important if you're eager to get your sales effort moving forward without delay. Indeed, I know of more than one Fortune 500 company that used just such presentation folders for their initial sales efforts. An easy step up is to apply an inexpensive custom label printed with your logo to the covers of ready-made pocket folders.

A More Elaborate, More Costly Solution

A more professional approach, but more costly, is to design a custom sales kit folder and have it printed and die-cut by a local commercial printer. This allows you to print photos on the cover, or to put your logo in gold foil, for example, to make a more impressive printed piece. The same applies to inserts, which can be as elaborate as your budget permits. Finished kit cost at this level: typically $2.50 to $4.00 each, depending on quantity printed (higher quantities result in a lower unit cost).

When To Distribute

In most cases, distribute your handouts after you have made your presentation. Otherwise, most clients will read through them instead of listening to what you're saying—and selling. Handouts are best used as leave-behind materials the client can refer to later.

Visual Aids

Sales books, flip charts, and overheads are the traditional sales tools used for group presentations. Consider using a laptop instead, at least for one-on-one and small-group presentations, and you can avoid the additional expense and time of producing these materials. A quality sales book can be produced in PowerPoint or other presentation software, printed out on a color inkjet printer, and put in vinyl sleeves in a three-ring binder, but think of this as a poor man's laptop. A real laptop will have a much more computer-savvy impact.

PUTTING IT ALL TOGETHER

Now let's walk through a typical presentation. We'll look at a Web development presentation to a business interested in a basic Web site, but the same overall approach applies to the presentation of any Internet service.

John, the owner of a Web development firm, has an appointment to see Walter, a business owner. Prior to calling on the company, John knew only that the company had sales of approximately $4 million per year; he had read this in the local paper. Before learning that Walter was the key decision maker, John had first called and spoken with the receptionist to find out what the company sold.

The receptionist, who was new, did not know, and referred him to the sales department. John asked basic questions about what the company sold and was told by the sales rep that they sell specialty aluminum products. They import some of their materials from other countries, but most of their suppliers are in the United States. Similarly, their customers are located throughout the Midwest, but they do have some customers in other parts of the country and overseas. John also asked whether all of their sales are to other businesses or whether they also sell to consumers. The sales rep indicated that while they get calls all the time from consumers who need a specially machined piece of aluminum for their boat or their mobile home, the company considers these nuisance calls and is not interested in that business.

The sales rep became curious about whether John might be in the market for aluminum products at which point John candidly revealed that he was in the Internet business and was wondering if the company had a Web site. The sales rep told him they did not and John asked who within the company might be in charge of such a project if they decided to develop a site. The sales rep said all computer matters are handled by their network guy. John asked who handles marketing and advertising decisions and was told that would be Walter, the owner of the company.

Ask the Right Questions

In the first of two conversations with Walter prior to the appointment, John inquired about the company's interest in having a Web site and set the appointment to see him. On learning that the company was interested but did not yet have a site, John asked additional questions to determine whether or not the company could likely benefit from a site. In order to do this, he asked Walter to confirm the approximate annual revenues of the company. He then asked Walter whether the company sold regionally, nationally, or internationally and how important to the company those markets were.

During the initial call, Walter explained that his company's sales were primarily focused in the Midwest, but a significant portion came from other parts of the country. International sales, he said, were a small but growing part of the company's business and clearly an area he planned to pursue. John also asked if the company spends a significant amount on long-distance calls and long-distance and international faxes. Walter indicated that phone bills had become "astronomical" over the past two years, in part because the company acts as a matchmaker and value-added processor between a large Brazilian supplier and several customers in Argentina. He said these customers were always asking for Walter's e-mail address, but he didn't have one.

This conversation told John that the company had sufficient revenues to pay for a site, that they had significant long-distance communications with customers and suppliers, and that there would be immediate benefits to the company from being online by replacing at least some international faxes with e-mail. John indicated as much to Walter, who said he had no idea all that was possible, but wanted to know how much it would cost to save money and whether the company could really benefit from a Web site. John said he felt there really were substantial benefits for the company and that he would be happy to explain in more detail in person. He indicated that he had developed Web sites for as little as $2,000. This did not seem to faze Walter, so John asked him when it would be convenient to stop by and discuss this further. They set an appointment for the following week.

On the day before the meeting, John called Walter's office to confirm the appointment. Walter himself took the call, so John took advantage of the opportunity and inquired how the company goes about marketing itself. Walter indicated that little is done other than to place classified ads in trade publications; the company doesn't even have an up-to-date brochure. He indicated that he's been after his sales manager for months to come up with copy for a new brochure. This told John that developing a site, would involve a significant amount of creative work, as apparently there were no substantial marketing materials to base it on.

Finally, John remembered that he had forgotten to ask whether customer service before, during, and after the sale was a critical area to the company. Walter indicated that his sales reps, some of whom were employed by the company and some of whom were independent manufacturers' reps, handled customer service, but that he had recently added a customer service department because the reps were too busy handling growing sales to new customers to properly service existing accounts. John mentioned that a Web site could play an important role in customer service, especially where technical information had to be conveyed and when knowing the status of orders was important to the customer. Walter also mentioned that technical drawings come in by the truckload. His U.S. customers send CAD drawings and his international customers send blueprints. They all ask if they can modem files to the company.

With the appointment confirmed, that night John hit the search engines to see what he could turn up in the way of sites by competitors of Walter's company. He found plenty of companies selling aluminum products of various kinds and printed out the home pages of several of the largest. But he wasn't sure if he had identified any of Walter's direct competitors. He did a quick check of the newsgroups through Altavista to see if anyone was talking about Walter's company, but this search did not turn up any results.

John made sure that his best sites were properly loaded and viewable from the browser on his laptop, both with and without an online connection. And he assembled three of his handout packages, not knowing who else might be at the meeting in addition to Walter.

At the designated time, John arrived at the company. The receptionist called Walter's office to announce John's arrival and Walter's secretary took John to the conference room and told him that Walter was finishing up a meeting. John took advantage of the delay to quickly fire up the laptop and load the first site he planned to show Walter.

Walter arrived a minute later, catching John somewhat off guard, but he recovered and immediately smiled and extended his hand for a firm handshake. "It's a pleasure to meet you, Walter."

Walter noticed the laptop and seemed impressed. "I see you've come prepared."

> JOHN: Yes, I have some things I'd like to show you which I'll cover shortly.

> WALTER: Great. Let's get started.

> JOHN: Walter, just to recap what I've learned so far about your company through our phone conversations—you manufacture specialty aluminum products, you sell to companies primarily in the Midwest, but you also sell nationally and internationally.

WALTER: So far, so good. The bulk of our business really is within the region. How many people are really using the Internet?

JOHN: Approximately thirty million users worldwide, about ten to fifteen million use the World Wide Web, which is where your site would be located.

As John moved the laptop around so both could see it, he continued. "Let's take a look at one of the sites we've done for another company selling to other businesses."

At this point, John showed Walter a site for a manufacturer of medical equipment. "This is what users see when they come to a Web page. This is known as a browser and it allows you to move from page to page. Right now we're looking at the home page for this medical equipment company. As you can see, the company sells wheelchairs and other equipment to local dealers. Over on the left we have a separate area of the page with pictures that are actively linked to various parts of the site. You see, if I move the mouse pointer over to the picture of the wheelchair and then click the mouse button like this, here's what happens. As you can see, we are now looking at a page devoted to information about their wheelchair products."

WALTER: How about that.

JOHN: Notice that the area on the left is also on this page. That allows the user to always find his way around the site. Users are accustomed to navigating in this way. Notice too, that although we refer to these as *pages* they are really files stored on a special computer called a Web server. When a user visits a site the files are transferred to the user's computer so that they can be viewed on their computer.

Now also notice that at the bottom of every page we have complete contact information for this company. We make it a point to include the options for the customer to communicate however she wishes, whether by e-mail, phone, or fax.

WALTER: How many people use e-mail and how many just pick up the phone? I'd probably just pick up the phone.

JOHN: You're not alone in that regard. But many do use
e-mail because it's quick and convenient. Let me show
you how it works. To send an e-mail message to this company, all we have to do is move the mouse over this
underlined text. This is known as a hot link. When I click
the mouse, like this, it will open up a special window
where we can easily write a message to this company. I'll
just write a quick note saying hello to my client."

John typed a quick greeting. "Notice that the e-mail
address is already entered in for us right here. Now we're
ready to send the e-mail message. If we were online, we
would simply click here and the message would be on its
way. So you see how easy it is."

WALTER: Well, you make it look easy, but I wouldn't have
any idea how to do what you just did.

JOHN: I understand. It really is quite easy to learn and the
important point here is that many of your customers no
doubt already know how to use e-mail.

WALTER: Yes, we get inquiries frequently, as we discussed.

JOHN: Now let me show you another site. This one we
developed for a company that sells a specialty architectur-
al product used to create permanent borders in land-
scapes. Notice that, again, we show the company's products front and center on the very first page you see, and
that we also have convenient links to the other parts of
the site. In this case, the links are at the bottom of every
page.

WALTER: You can send e-mail to this company also, I suppose?

JOHN: Yes, and as you can see, these sites have the kind of
information you might put in a brochure—some background information on the company and products, some
sell copy covering the advantages of doing business, and
contact information. But on this site, there's something
else I'd like to show you. This company's products are
engineered to specific dimensions and landscape archi-
tects must know what those dimensions are in order to
produce their landscape designs. So for this company, we

created a page that shows small pictures of the various designs. Now an architect can easily come to this page and download over the Internet a file with CAD drawings which he can incorporate or modify. Perhaps you have engineers who would like to come to your site and do something similar.

WALTER: I think they have been asking for that, or at least the ability to send by modem, which we're just experimenting with.

JOHN: Walter, let's talk about what we might be able to do with your Web site. Tell me about the products your company sells.

WALTER: Well, we have a product line with three products. That is what we have built the company on. We sell them to original equipment manufacturers who incorporate them into their own products, and we sell replacement parts.

JOHN: It sounds like that should be a major focus of your Web site.

WALTER: Well, certainly if we were talking about a company brochure, I would say so, but I am really relying on you to provide guidance as to what we should do on the Internet.

JOHN: "I understand. Let me ask you this: Do you sell your products strictly as is, or do you get involved in customizing?"

WALTER: We're known for our custom services. Each of our manufacturer customers has its own engineering for the part, mainly where it connects to other parts of the product. Then, we also do quite a bit of custom surface finishing.

JOHN: Well, Walter, I think you have a pretty good idea of how the Web works now. And I've got a good idea of what we'll need to include in your Web site, so perhaps this is a good time to discuss our fees.

Reaching for a handout package and opening it up to show Walter, John continued, "We have three packages of services that I'd like to discuss with you. Each package has a different number of pages, but of course we can develop a site with however many pages are appropriate. Just to give you an idea, our smallest package includes five pages and is priced at two thousand dollars. Our largest package includes fifteen pages and is goes for a little under forty-nine hundred. Would you say that's in the range of what you might expect to pay to develop other types of promotional projects, such as a company brochure?

WALTER: That sounds about right, though I doubt that would cover the printing or photography.

JOHN: Well, of course with the Internet we don't have any printing costs and we can certainly incorporate any existing photography you already have. If we need new photography, it certainly won't cost any more than it would for a brochure and you can use the same photos in both.

WALTER: I see. Well, our photography is fine. Our products really haven't changed. So those are the only costs, then?

JOHN: There is also a monthly hosting fee that covers the cost of maintaining your site on our server and making it available to Internet users. That runs about one hundred dollars per month.

WALTER: Well, what's this going to cost me on an annual basis?

JOHN: That's a very good question. And we have all of that information covered in our handouts, which I will leave with you. But just to give you an idea, the first year costs for our smallest site are four thousand, not a huge sum by any means and probably less than you would spend to run an ad in a trade publication once or twice a year.

Walter: I never thought of it like that. Of course, we do almost no advertising that way.

JOHN: Well, perhaps you can advance to the next level and take advantage of the Internet to get the word out about your company.

WALTER: Well, what did you say our site would cost, then?

JOHN: Well, based on what you've told me about your company and products, I believe we'll need ten pages to properly present your company on the Web. That would be right at thirty-five hundred. Is this an expenditure you could handle within the next month?

WALTER: Well, our cash is pretty tight right now. Is that the best you can do?

JOHN: Well, of course our services are ultimately based on the amount of time it takes to develop a quality site. We'd rather see you have a quality site from the beginning rather than have you get involved with extra expenses later on. Let me ask you this, Walter: If we can agree on price, and I'm certain we're not very far apart here, would you be interested in having us develop a Web site for your company?"

WALTER: Well, if you can deliver within the prices you've discussed, I think so. But I'd like to have some of this in writing before going any further.

JOHN: I can fax a confirming proposal to you tomorrow morning and follow up with you by phone to answer any questions you may have. Would that work for you?

WALTER: That would be fine.

JOHN: Great. Well, Walter, it's certainly been a pleasure meeting with you this morning. I think the Internet has a lot to offer your company and I look forward to developing your Web site.

Notice how John moved the presentation forward but used a conversational approach with the client to do so. Neither John nor Walter spoke from a position of superiority over the other. Rather, both came to the table as equals and engaged in a frank discussion. That is the most effective way I know of to make a presentation.

John used prior work as a selling tool to demonstrate features and functions that he suspected would be of interest to Walter, and he did it in a way that accommodated Walter's lack of knowledge about the Internet. Walter learned something and John made the sale. John was prepared to use a laptop effectively and had extra sets of handouts available in case Walter had invited some of his staff to join the meeting. John also turned to the handouts only when needed, rather than using them automatically as a crutch, and mostly did so only to show the client where the information could be found. Every presentation will vary, but this example contains all the components of a good presentation by any Internet professional for any Internet service.

John attempted at several points during the presentation to get Walter to state that he was interested in having a site, wanted John's firm to develop it, and was willing to pay for it—three conditions that must exist in order for the sale to take place.

Note that John did not hesitate to bring up the subject of fees as soon as he had established the capabilities of his firm and did some probing of the client to determine what the site would have to include. With some quick calculation, John was able to arrive at a price to discuss with Walter.

Walter, who typifies the client who does not have much familiarity with the Internet, was willing to accept John's professional recommendations about the site. But the same probing process works with any client, no matter how knowledgeable they are. In fact, a more knowledgeable client will allow you to cover the vital points more quickly.

YOU KNOW YOU'RE A GEEK WHEN...

You no longer ask, "What's your sign?" You ask, "What's your URL?"

Writing the Proposal and Contract

Once you obtain agreement with a client regarding your services, your next task is to present the necessary written documents in order to sign and seal the deal. However, few clients buy the proposal. They're buying *you*. So we have to put proposals in their rightful place and not allow them to dominate the sales process.

Most Internet projects are not rocket science. Unless the project is more than $20,000 or $30,000, you should be able to prepare a proposal in fewer than five pages that simply outlines the project and the services you will be performing, terms and conditions, payment requirements, and ongoing hosting or maintenance arrangements that will be involved. Smaller projects can be proposed in two or three pages, and for those ripe, opportune sales moments when you can close in one call, you should carry with you a one-page fill-in-the-blank version along with a separate sheet of terms and conditions that can be filled out, reviewed with the client, and signed on the spot before a good deal gets away.

If you prepare separate documents for a proposal and a contract, these documents should closely follow each other. Whatever you develop in the way of a price list, hourly rate sheet, or package pricing should be laid out consistently with a logical flow and an easy-to-follow connection between your proposal and contract documents. This will not only make it easier for the client to understand how you arrived at the contract you are asking them to sign, it will make it far easier for you to draft these documents quickly and painlessly and make revisions later.

What a Proposal Is Not

A proposal is not a lengthy educational document created to teach the client about your services and the Internet.

THE AGONY OF PROPOSALS

Proposals are part of the reality of the business. However, if you're in a major selling mode and making a lot of sales calls, nothing is more tedious than having to drop everything and prepare *another* proposal. Proposals can become major time sink and the bane of the Internet professional. In the very worst case, they take weeks to write and are allowed to become a prerequisite to closing every deal. Which means if you close one out of five prospects, 80 percent of your time invested in proposal preparation is down the tubes.

Here are some tips to maintain control over the proposal process:

- *Make an effort to fully qualify prospects before offering to do a proposal.* At a minimum, make sure they're a good match for the services and types of projects you're looking for. Can they afford you? Is there good rapport? Don't get in the habit of ending every sales call with, "Well, would you like to see a proposal on this?" Instead, say, "I think we have a good understanding of the services you need. If we can agree on prices and terms, can we handle this for you?" If the client says "yes," then you're ready to write the proposal.
- *Don't send in a 200 MHz Dual Pentium Processor when an 33 MHz 486 will do.* No doubt you are a dedicated, serious-minded individual who would like to give the client good value for your fees. That's why you prepare detailed proposals. However, if you're calling on non-technical people, and most business executives fall in this category, probably the last thing in the world they want to do is read a twenty-page proposal. Keep your proposal short. (That doesn't mean print it out in 8-point type to keep the page count down. Give the reader a break, especially if they're older than forty, and print it out in at least

12-point type.) Use lists and bullet points to get ideas
across succinctly.

- *Avoid doing proposals when possible, but don't avoid
making the sale.* If you suspect the only thing standing
between you and the sale is a proposal, don't hesitate to
do what it takes to get the sale.
- *Use a format that includes the proposal and contract in
a single document.* In other words, make the proposal
serve double duty to avoid spending even more time
drafting a contract after the client accepts the proposal.
The proposal example below shows how this can be
done.

Listening Pays Off

The proposal stage is where all that time you spent listening to the
client will really be an asset. Basically, all the significant points that
came out of your discussion with the client about her business and
goals should go right into your proposal.

In the preceding chapter, John agreed to fax Walter a proposal. But recall that John referred to this as a "confirming" proposal. At
this stage, John wants to avoid going back to square one and having to renegotiate everything after Walter sees the proposal. There
is no guarantee this won't happen, but John took a presumptive
approach with Walter and continued it with his fax.

A CONFIRMING PROPOSAL

Via Fax

From: John

To: Walter

Subject: Web Site Cost Estimate Confirmation

To recap our meeting yesterday, we will develop a Web site for your
company consisting of the following components:

- ten Web pages
- all necessary copy based on your existing brochure
- all necessary graphic design and HTML coding

- all necessary scans of up to five photos/logos per page

- all photography to be supplied by you

- e-mail response capability for customer inquiries via the site

- registration of the site with six major search engines

Cost: $3,500.00

Fifty percent due in advance. Balance due upon completion.
Delivery: Approximately three to four weeks from receipt of payment deposit.

I've included a separate page that spells out all the details of our agreement terms. I'll be happy to review those with you at our next meeting; feel free to call me before that to discuss. If everything looks in order, please sign where indicated on this page and the terms page and fax back to me.

Walter, it's going to be a personal pleasure for me to work on this project and I look forward to developing a successful Web site for your company!

(John's signature)   (date)

_____   _____
John   Date

_____   _____
Walter   Date

This approach is short, sweet, and highly effective. In most cases it's all you'll need to take care of the contractual details of your project.

TERMS AND CONDITIONS

The proposal and contract outlined above is easy to set up as a template for quick editing to turn out proposals as fast as you need them. The proposal section will change substantially from one client to another. Your terms and conditions, if properly thought through and carefully drafted, will not need to be changed much from client to client. You may want to separate the two, putting your terms and conditions on an additional page or two, to make the proposal preparation process even simpler.

A wide variety of areas should be covered by your terms and conditions, including copyright and intellectual property rights, payment terms and conditions, client penalties for failing to make timely payments, the ability to have or be given credit for your work on the project, noncompete and confidentiality clauses, and other language designed to protect your interests.

In fact, the list continues to grow and promises to become overwhelming for Internet professionals to sell and clients to understand. This does not bode well for the industry, yet there seems to be little anyone can do about it. Other businesses have an equally long list of fine-print items, but because the Internet is so new, the associated terms and conditions for Internet projects require a clear explanation for client understanding.

Everyone enters into a project hoping it will go well and have a satisfactory outcome. Thus, the need for clear understanding by both the client and the Internet professional is at the project outset quite clear—otherwise you won't end up with a signed contract—but the client may still be thinking one thing will happen and you something different. It is therefore equally important that a clear understanding occur later on, perhaps well after all of your work on the project is completed, should there ever be a disagreement over what was meant. To avoid misunderstandings before and after the contract is signed, it is essential that this portion of your proposal and contract be written in the clearest nonlegalese and, where possible, the least technical contract language possible.

Which is not to say that you don't need to have an attorney review or even draft this section—you do. In fact, while what is presented here is a review of the more important items, it is not by any means exhaustive, and it does not in any way constitute legal advice. Rather, in each area discussed below, instead of attempting to provide language that can be picked up wholesale, I have indicated the more practical business aspects of what you will want to achieve in the language that is drafted (or, at least reviewed) by your attorney. Your legal advisor will no doubt have opinions of her own, so consider this discussion a starting point for your own individual efforts at thinking through the important business issues involved in your relationship with clients.

With your proposal and terms and conditions in hand, you'll be well equipped to sign all the deals you can generate.

Time Frame/Schedule

You should clearly indicate a time frame or schedule for completion of your services and delivery of the finished project. This can be written as a single deadline for the completion of the entire project, as a schedule of phases with a final deadline only, or with deadlines for each phase. You can also describe the typical turnaround for the entire project or each phase. If you plan to include this information in the main part of your proposal, then you can simply indicate that here.

Deliverables

This covers the physical form or format of your finished work when the project is turned over to the client. For Web sites, deliverables are typically a printout of each page for reference, probably in color, and a copy on disk of all finished graphics files, HTML files, CGI scripts, etc. It is also helpful to provide the client with a summary page listing the file names and a schematic outline of the site organization.

Clear Statement of Who Owns the Completed Site

As a general rule, I recommend that Web developers sell complete rights to all site creative materials. The client will expect it, though probably will not say so before the issue comes up, and it often won't come up until long after the project is completed.

To the extent you are dealing with clients who are knowledgeable about advertising and graphic design, you will get along with them much better if your terms and conditions closely parallel typical *small* ad agency and designer terms and conditions. That means giving the client all rights so they feel comfortable knowing that their costs are predictable and fixed. Nothing upsets a small-business owner more than finding out that a minor change in how he uses something he thinks he's already paid for could end up costing big bucks. His response is to moan, groan, whine, complain, and hassle you to death. This tends to turn an otherwise satisfied customer into a dissatisfied one and the time you take to deal with all the fussing is time you could be using to profitably sell another satisfied client and add another Internet project to your portfolio.

I therefore recommend that your terms specifically state that upon receiving final payment for the project, you give the client all rights to all Web site copywriting, illustrations, buttons, banners, logos, and other artwork you created for the site. The cleaner and neater the deal, the fewer headaches you will have down the road.

Terms along these lines, combined with appropriate "hold harmless" contract language, will protect the client and protect you by eliminating a tremendous amount of irritation and time spent being hassled by clients months or years after you have moved on to other projects—not to mention the record keeping you'll have to do to keep track of who bought what from whom when.

If you are not going to give the client all rights, then you need to carefully describe those rights you will retain and outline a procedure to be followed by the client should she desire to obtain rights for additional uses, such as brochures, trade show displays, advertising, etc.

Copyrights

In keeping with the idea of giving the client ownership of the creative materials on her site, your proposal and contract should indicate that you are the original creator or have obtained the right to use all copy and graphics appearing on the site with the exception of materials furnished by the client, thus indicating that you have the right to transfer ownership to the client.

Just as your proposal and contract should give the client assurances that you are the original creator of your work or that you have the right to use work created by others that is included in the site, you should also include a statement from the client to the effect that he owns the rights to use any of the copy, graphics, and other materials he is furnishing you for use on his site. Your goal here is to avoid having a third party come forward later, say a photographer, illustrator, or copywriter, to claim that you used their material in a way that goes beyond the limitations of the rights she granted to the client. Your proposal and contract should make it clear that your prices are based on the idea that getting this permission is the client's responsibility, not yours. You should ask the client to hold you harmless from any claims that are made by third parties for materials furnished by the client.

Licensing of Program Code

If program code is included in the project, you will need to clearly state what rights you are giving to the client. This applies to code developed by third parties as well as code that you create. If the code is crucial to the operation of the Web site, as in the case of a search engine or shopping cart, then you should provide for the possibility that you and the client may one day part ways. Should that happen, you will want certain protections relating to the client's use of the code, such as prohibiting her from copying and reselling it, and the client will want certain protections, such as her right to continue using it, the right to modify it, and perhaps access to the original source code. All of these issues must be thought through with the assistance of a capable intellectual property attorney.

Client Responsibility for Changes After Approval

It's a good idea to include in the proposal a schedule of work showing client approval as a scheduled step, just like all the other steps in the production process. When the client signs the proposal and contract, she is agreeing to the schedule and her role in approving work. Your contract should have a statement to the effect that any changes to portions of the project previously approved by the client will be made at additional cost to the client. That protects you from endless changes and locks the client in to whatever work has already been performed and approved so you can move the production process forward. Now, I'm not suggesting that you be entirely rigid and inflexible about this, merely that your terms should contain language to protect you.

Noncompete and Confidential Information

Because you may become privy to confidential information about the client company, you may be asked to sign a confidentiality agreement that prohibits you from disclosing information about the company to others. These are always tricky in the area of advertising and marketing, which Web sites, Internet marketing, and some other Internet projects typically are considered. Bottom line, the purpose of having a Web site is to promote, to give people information. But the client may feel you are exposed to confidential information in the course of developing the site. One counterpoint in your favor: The client is only, in effect, "renting" your time. He doesn't "own" you, as in an employer-employee relationship. His main protection from your unauthorized disclosure? Your professional reputation. If you are known to let secrets out, you won't have much future in the business.

You probably aren't giving up much by signing a nondisclosure agreement. After all, who did you plan to tell, anyway? But, watch out for noncompete agreements the client may ask you to sign. Why should you sign a noncompete agreement when you're in a completely different business than he is? It most cases it won't make sense to agree to what was surely drafted to apply to his employees, not an outside third party supplier or consultant. The advice of an attorney is extremely helpful here and may be necessary if the client is adamant. Or you may prefer to pass on the project, unless it is huge. In any case, carefully think through all of the requirements these agreements entail—for instance, what further agreements must you then have with any of your employees, freelancers, subcontractors, and suppliers who may be required to be privy to the same confidential information?

Specific Services that You Will Not be Providing

Don't leave this ambiguous with the client. Because the Internet is still new to many clients and they are not experienced or familiar with the range and scope of Internet projects, it is common for Internet consultants, Web developers, and programmers to run through a long list of possible ways to promote a business on the Internet and end up handling only one or a few areas initially. To avoid a situation where you think you were hired to do one thing and the client thinks she hired you to do something else, you should spell out services that came up in a conversation but that are not included in your project, as far as you are concerned.

For instance, if you are not providing Internet marketing services (and even if you are), you might want to specify that you are not responsible for any particular number of users coming to the site or viewing any particular page. Nor would you want to be responsible for the number of sales that result from the site.

Hosting

If Web hosting will be part of the project, you'll need additional terms and conditions pertaining to those services. You might want to break these out into a separate agreement. If the client is controlling where the site will be hosted, you will want to state the extent of your responsibility for making the pages operate correctly on their server.

Another hosting-related areas you'll want to cover is domain name registration procedures. As in the copyright area, I recommend that it be clearly stated who owns rights to the domain name.

Should you register any name on the client's behalf, of course, the name should belong to the client. One exception: so-called vanity domains as in `http://clientname.yourfirmname.com`, where the client's name is appended to the left of a domain name you own. Obviously you would not want to give the client the right to your domain in that case! She would have to seek another vanity domain from her new hosting service. However, you might want to agree to maintain a redirect page for a certain amount of time.

Another objective here is to get yourself off the hook should any trademark infringement issues come up with respect to the client's domain name. Why should you be caught in the middle of that? Aim for language that makes it clear that any domain name registration you perform on the client's behalf is indeed being done on the client's behalf. Be careful about naming anyone other than the client as the administrative and billing contact, and if you will be the technical contact, you might want to state what the limits of that role are.

Client's Right to Move Site

Another issue that arises when hosting is the client's right to move the site. If his bills are paid in full, let him go and state that you will cooperate in the transfer of the domain name to another name server.

Site Updates, Backup, and Maintenance

If you are offering to perform any of these services, you should be clear about when they will be performed and, in the case of updates, place some limits on how much work can be performed (perhaps a stated number of hours of staff time or a certain amount of words, etc.). Don't leave this open-ended or it could come back to haunt you.

Project Performance and Limits of Responsibility

If project performance is an important issue for the client, or if you hold yourself out as a firm that prides itself on fast-loading Web pages and graphics, bug-free code, or top placement in the search engines, you should include in your terms the particular performance criteria you are agreeing to and the areas you are not agreeing to. For instance, you might want to specify that the maximum load times for the site's home page or main section pages does not exceed a certain amount of time, or you might want to specify that graphics files will not exceed a certain file size. And you might want to specify the browser software and versions you are agreeing to make your pages viewable on.

You might even want to define a Web page and specify its length in some convenient terms. For example, you might want to limit a page to the equivalent of an 8½x11 page, or perhaps somewhat larger, say legal size, when printed out, or limit it to a maximum of a certain number of words in the copy visible to the user. That would protect you from the client that wants a home page with ten pages of information crammed in at no additional fee.

Unsophisticated clients can have some extremely sophisticated expectations—unrealistic and unwarranted expectations. You may find it necessary to specify what you are *not* responsible for.

Portfolio Credits

I recommend you have a clause that gives you the right to either place a small logo and link to your firm's site on the client's home page (or separate credits page, if that is how the site is set up) as well as the right to mention the client's site on your site and in the sales presentation of your work to prospective clients, in any publicity about your firm, and the right to submit the site in design competitions and for industry awards.

Prohibiting the Client from Hiring Your Employees

This may be a concern when dealing with large projects for large companies. With small clients this will not be as likely a problem, though some may try an end-run around you to do business directly with an employee or a subcontractor.

Limitations of Liability and Client Hold Harmless Agreement

This is an area to discuss with your attorney. You'll need to address business liability issues as well as publisher's and advertising liability issues including libel, defamation, and false advertising. It should be clear which of these liabilities are assumed by you, if any, and which by the client. And if by you, make sure you have the right and ability to access the site (meaning access to passwords,

whether hosted by you or not) and to change any offending matter. If the client is providing you with copy and product photos, or
if the client is approving your work at every stage, it will be fully
justifiable for you to hold the client responsible for these liabilities.

Designated Locality for Legal Purposes

This is a customary clause indicating where any legal action arising
from the agreement will be filed. It is to your benefit to designate
the city or county where you are located, especially if your client
is located in another state. It will be more convenient for you to
appear in court and your legal expenses will likely be lower dealing with a local attorney.

Payment—By Whom, How Much, and When

This covers your payment terms—whether the client will pay a
deposit and when the balance will be due. Whenever possible, I
recommend a no receivables approach whereby you receive 30–50
percent in advance and the balance upon completion.

Availability for Approvals and Sign-Offs

Sometimes things can be going quite well in dealing with a client
right up to the time when the project is completed and you are
ready for the client's final sign-off and approval. You will occasionally find a client who is suddenly unavailable to see you or who
says he will get back to you but never does. Your final payment may
be hanging in the balance while the client does a disappearing act.
Your contract should contain language to the effect that the client
will have a certain amount of time to review your work and indicate approval or any desired corrections, and should the client fail
to do so within the indicated time frame, you may assume that your
work is satisfactory and the client is obligated to pay you as if
approval had been given.

Ordinarily, establishing a set period of time (typically a few
days) for the client to review or test your finished work and report
any problems is all that will be needed to tidy up any loose ends at
the end of the project development cycle.

Right-to-Terminate Agreement

Many Internet projects can be considered one-shot deals where you will not have an ongoing relationship with the client beyond a several-week time period. But in those instances where you and the client will be dealing with each other over several months or possibly several years a client may be reluctant to begin working with you without assurance that there is a mechanism for parting ways prior to the expected termination date.

Things do not always go as planned. Business priorities can change on the client's part, companies can be bought and sold, the personal chemistry may sour between you and the client, etc. Similarly, the client may become unprofitable for you to continue servicing. It is wise to anticipate these situations and clearly indicate in your contract who may terminate whom, when, and how.

A typical arrangement includes both parties' right to terminate the contract with a specified period of advance notice (usually by giving thirty or sixty days' written notice to the other). Annual contracts usually contain language to the effect that the contract will be automatically renewed at the end of the contract period unless written notice of termination has been given.

Procedure for Early Termination

What if things do not go well? Occasionally projects will be plagued by unfortunate circumstances despite everyone's best efforts. Deadlines may be missed. Your relationship with the client may deteriorate. The client may not fulfill his payment obligations. It is wise to include a procedure spelling out how payment and transfer of ownership of work completed to date and work in progress will be handled in the event of early termination of the project by either party.

A MORE DETAILED PROPOSAL

The simple approach won't always do. Sometimes you'll need a more elaborate proposal. Perhaps the sales presentation did not go quite the way you planned and you weren't able to cover all of your points and obtain a commitment from the client. Or you may be calling on a large corporation where executive decisions cannot be made as quickly or easily as they can by the owner of a smaller business. A big company turns slowly, like a battleship. A small company turns like a speedboat. Or your prospect may be soliciting several proposals before you even have an opportunity to meet with the decision makers. In these cases you will not be able to rely on the short agreement just presented. Here, then, is an example of a longer proposal and contract. Again, the terms section is not included in the example, though it is a vital part of the document. All of the terms and conditioning just presented should, of course, be included in a more detailed proposal.

The Client Who Requires a Longer Proposal

John has been busy making sales calls and has already met with Ted, the owner of Fly-by-Night, on three occasions. Fly-by-Night is a travel agent specializing in selling unsold seats on red-eye flights—you know, the ones that leave between 1:00 A.M. and 5:00 A.M.

Ted has had an America Online account for years and is very comfortable using the Internet. He is eager to get his travel agency online and at each meeting he increases the number of features he would like to have in his site. John has just about given up trying to close this deal. Twice already he has faxed over one-page confirming faxes similar to the fax he sent Walter. Walter had no problem signing and getting things started. Ted is a different story. Not only can he not decide whether it's more important to get a basic site up quickly and then add to it or to take more time and develop a site with all the bells and whistles from the start, he also put half of his twenty-person staff on a committee in charge of planning the Internet effort. Not to mention that his budget is limited.

In order to address all of the directions Ted wants to go while zeroing in with something less complicated to get things moving, John prepared the following proposal. The work is divided into stages or phases to keep things manageable and within Ted's budget.

A Traditional Proposal
[cover page not shown]

I. Goals
National Web will assist Fly-by-Night Travel Services in developing and implementing Internet marketing strategies that capitalize on the company's inherent strengths and economical evening air travel reservation services.

The ultimate goal, of course, is to use the Internet as a tool to build a positive image, optimum visibility, credibility, and name recognition for Fly-by-Night so as to enhance the convenience and desirability of choosing the company when making arrangements via the Internet for evening air travel.

We know that by increasing the awareness, acceptance, and preference for your services on the Internet, sales will follow.

II. Objectives

The most effective way to achieve all of the goals Fly-by-Night has established for its multifaceted Internet marketing program is to break down the total list of objectives into phases that allow you to proceed in manageable steps. Based on our understanding of your goals, we propose the following phases of implementation.

Phase I

Fast track creative development of a get-started Web site that projects a market-leading image and properly conveys the major benefits of Fly-by-Night services. This phase will primarily promote Fly-by-Night's top ten best-selling travel packages.

In addition, the Phase I effort will take into account and be compatible with the near-term and longer-term goals and objectives for the company's future Internet involvement.

Phase II

Expand the Phase I site to include all Fly-by-Night travel services, including reservation services for travel during daylight hours as the company adds that capability. Other possible Phase II services:

- convenient Web-based access for Fly-by-Night customers to personalized itineraries for easy updating from anywhere in the world

- Red-Eye Travel Club Discussion Forum for agency staff and customer-to-customer communications about travel tips and travel experiences

- additional services to be determined

Phase III

Use Internet-based services as a revenue-generating value-added component of Fly-by-Night's overall service mix. Possible revenue-generating Internet services include:

- automated online reservations and payment over a secure Internet connection

- Travel Club membership registration and renewal

- sale of flight insurance and trip cancellation insurance

Phase IV

Use the Internet to enhance internal company communications between Fly-by-Night's planned offices. Possible goals for this phase include:

- development of a secure employee-only Intranet consisting of e-mail, Web page information, database access, and conferencing, including possible video conferencing

- other components to be determined

III. Services Outline

This proposal is limited to Phase I services to be provided by National Web. The following services are included:

- Internet marketing consultation pertinent to Web site development

- Web site creative concepts and production, including:
  - design of overall site organization and information flow
  - creative direction
  - copy editing
  - art direction
  - account service and production coordination
  - all necessary Web page graphic design
  - all necessary HTML coding
  - three to five color scans/logo conversions (per page)
  - one image map for use on multiple pages for easy navigation throughout the site
  - up to three reply/response forms
  - automated registration of site with one hundred search engines for up to five keywords

- Pages and Site Content

  We believe we have acquired a good understanding of the services Fly-by-Night offers its clients. Based on our knowledge of your company thus far, we believe the following information should be included in your Phase I site:

- introductory home page with links to additional pages
- Fly-by-Night company overview
- top-selling travel packages
- the Fly-by-Night Service Pledge
- Fly-by-Night travel services staff
- week's special offer/response form
- last-minute deals/response form
- frequently asked questions (FAQ)
- how to contact us/e-mail response form
- Red-Eye Travel Club sign-up form

IV. Cost of Services

Recognizing that part of our services will consist of site design, we believe that the outline offered above should be considered a starting point. Additional pages not listed in the above outline may be mutually agreed upon between us for inclusion in the site. Similarly, during the design phase, we may determine that some pages can be combined to achieve improved navigation or clearer communications. However, for purposes of pricing this proposal, we are estimating that the Phase I site will consist of a maximum of ten pages in order to convey the above outlined content.

Development of Ten Page Site $2,850.00
Plus applicable state sales tax.

Monthly Maintenance $350.00
Includes:

- one hour of Internet marketing consultation/creative direction

- two hours of account service/production coordination

- two hours of HTML coding/graphics

Additional services shall be cost estimated in advance for client approval prior to proceeding with work.

V. Optional Additional Services

We offer a wide variety of additional Internet marketing and traditional advertising and public relations services. For purposes of this proposal, the following optional services will be most appropriate to Fly-by-Night.

- stock photography (Cost varies widely. Approximately $300 per photo.)

- copywriting (approximately $150–$200 per Web page)

A complete services rate schedule is attached.

VI. Timetable

Goal: Have site up and running within six weeks of the signing of this proposal.

From receipt of all site background and source materials:

Site Concepts, Site Architecture	4 days
Approval	2 days
Initial Copy Editing and Rough Page Layouts	4 days
Approval	2 days
Final Graphics	1 week
Approval	3 days
Preliminary HTML Coding	3 days
Approval	2 days
Final HTML Coding	2 days
Final Approval	1 day
Delivery of site on disk or installation on server	2 days

VII. Terms
[See discussion earlier in this chapter.]

ACCEPTED

Fly-by-Night Travel

_____

Printed Name of Authorized Representative

_____   _____

Authorized Signature   Date

National Web

_____   _____

John, President   Date

_____

YOU KNOW YOU'RE A GEEK WHEN...

You have pictures of all your computers in your wallet.

Organizing and Managing the Web Development Process

With a signed contract in hand, you are ready to proceed with the development stage of the project. Getting the sale presented one set of challenges. Now you are faced with another: creating a top-quality project that lives up to your personal and professional standards and the expectations of the client.

DOES THE CLIENT THINK SHE HIRED YOU OR AN AD AGENCY?

Clients clearly expect Web developers, Web designers, programmers, and Internet marketers alike to have complete mastery over all of the technical details pertaining to the project; they also expect a good understanding of and appreciation for their marketing goals, quite similar to the expectations client shave of their ad agency. Even those companies that have never worked with an agency—indeed, especially those—will rely on Internet professionals for Internet marketing advice.

In other words, most clients assume that a Web developer will be as accomplished at selling products and services via the Internet as an ad agency is adept at selling through other media. Your ability to live up to that expectation will be put to the test during the creative and production phase.

In fact, it is already clear that the playing field is quickly being divided between those who can communicate persuasively with

Internet users on behalf of clients and those who can't. Persuasive communications is the business of advertising, but it is also unavoidably becoming the business of Web development and Internet marketing, and the same process that enables ad agencies to create effective, persuasive advertising is ideally suited to the development and design of Web sites.

You may have observed or suspected that having the skills to design sites, code pages, and write programs for the Internet is often no longer enough. Perhaps you realize that in order to offer clients an Internet project that solves a marketing problem or achieves a marketing goal requires insight into advertising creative and production procedures. If so, the development process presented here, well-honed by the advertising profession, should be of particular value to you. The large agencies established the key components of the model and raised it to a high art. Smaller agencies adapted the model to make it practical on a smaller scale—one that is well suited to Web developers, who also typically have small staffs.

KNOW THY ENEMY

Within a few years, it is quite possible that most ad agencies—large and small—will have complete Web development capabilities in-house. They probably won't be hosting sites in-house, they won't be handling all of the programming tasks in-house, and they won't be developing the best Web sites, as a general rule, but they won't be creating the worst ones either. If your Web development team can function at an agency level, you'll be able to compete successfully against any ad agency your client may be considering. If you're not ready to compete with the agencies, well, you can always end up working for them—just like yesterday's desktop publisher.

Indeed, we need look back just a decade to when desktop publishing (DTP) was at its heyday to see a dark parallel to the Web development business. Another personal computer–enabled technology, DTP blossomed forth, championed by many pioneers who overcame almost insurmountable obstacles in the form of really weak initial software and hardware capabilities. They stretched the technology to the limit and built the necessary know-how only to see lower costs and improvements in technology pull the rug out from under their investment in equipment and learning.

Today one can hardly find a desktop publishing firm anywhere. What began as an outsource business turned into an inhouse profession, and, worse, it was a function that soon became split across several professions—graphic artist, illustrator, production artist—rather than a profession in its own right. Whose inhouse office did most of these positions end up in? Some ended up at publishers, some fed at the corporate trough, but the vast majority ended up working for the ad agency as either employees or freelancers. Why? Because few desktop publishers were capable of seeing the big picture. They were not able to assist their clients with good marketing, only good production skills. The very same thing could easily happen with Internet projects unless Web developers, programmers, and marketers learn the lesson of desktop publishing (which the ad agencies ignored for years until they suddenly swallowed it up): Know thy enemy or he will soon become your employer.

Is the ad agency indeed the enemy of the Internet professional? Not really. As a potential strategic partner, the right ad agency is a potential ally. However, looking industrywide, agencies, though slow to recognize the value of the Internet and slow to seek an understanding of it are indeed the one force on the horizon that potentially threatens to replace many of those now working independently on Internet projects. If you don't want to join 'em, make sure you can beat 'em.

Bottom line, certainly in the client's mind, if not in actuality, Web developers and other Internet professionals will often be competing against ad agencies and therefore need to know what such competitors have to offer clients and how they approach the creative and production process. Savvy Web developers and all Internet consultants, including programmers, will take the best from the ad world and apply it to the Internet, beating the agencies at their own game.

TAKING THE CLIENT TO A HIGHER LEVEL

The fact that the Web offers low-cost reproduction means that what would otherwise require prohibitive printing or advertising media costs are not a factor and quality design, including color photography, is now within reach of companies that would not otherwise be able to afford them. This is something that the desktop publishing revolution promised but could never deliver, because it was wedded to the print medium, but the Internet can.

As clients come to understand the beneficial price-value relationship of a Web presence, the result is often that they expect the Web developer to fulfill the task of creating a national level image for the company—from scratch.

Let us not forget what is now an old saw about how the Internet enables small companies to compete on a level playing field with big companies. This was certainly perceived as the case in 1994 and 1995 when the idea first became widespread. A lot has happened since then, and some have questioned how feasible it really is, but the fact is, it is still a largely correct fundamental observation and assumption. You will often find clients who see the chance for a small company to leap nationally or internationally solely via the Internet and appear, often for the first time, like a big company. Hence, the burden—and opportunity—of leading the client in the proper marketing direction with your Internet project.

Unless you're working alone, presumably you have assembled a team or at least identified who you will bring on board to work on the project. A team needs a creative leader, a team needs a coordinator, and a team also needs a system. This chapter will present a Web site creative and production system that I have used successfully in a leadership role in the development of more than forty Web sites. It is designed to take the best of the ad agency creative process and apply it directly to the Web site development process.

One chapter, one book even, cannot cover everything required to be accomplished in these areas. However, an overview of the essential steps involved can be presented. Nothing here is intended to be the only way to go about these tasks. Every professional, every firm, has an individual approach, and while most may find that the procedures presented here work for them, it is recognized that there is more than one way to skin a cat. Results, and results alone, are the determining factor. However, any process, in order to be effective, must cover the following areas, one way or another.

AD AGENCIES AND WHAT THEY CAN TELL US ABOUT THE WEB SITE CREATIVE PROCESS

Most ad agencies haven't got a clue about the Internet. A few savvy ones do, but they are still the exception. But they can easily learn the Web development, programming, and marketing business if they really want to because they've already mastered the art and science of effective communications and the creative production process in many other media. For them, the Web is just another communications medium.

The Web site creative and production process is much like the advertising and editorial creative and production processes—it is a marriage of copy and graphics to achieve the larger goal of communications. In the case of advertising, the communications goal is one of persuasion. In the case of editorial, the focus is based on presenting information from a particular point of view.

To the extent that ad agencies and Web developers and designers both typically create projects on behalf of clients, whereas most editorial production efforts take place within a company—there generally isn't a "client" in the editorial process; it all happens on an in-house basis—the ad agency comes closer to describing the production process applicable to Internet projects.

Granted, a Web site is not like any advertising that has gone before it. It's not really quite an ad. It's not quite a brochure. It's not quite a magazine. It's not quite a video or CD-ROM presentation. And yet it is all of these and more. But any Web developer, new media professional, or Internet marketer faced with the task of creating a compelling banner ad expected as a matter of course to achieve more in four square inches than any similar size ad has ever achieved in the entire history of advertising will certainly be interested in the process ad agencies go through to create effective advertising.

George Rasher of Cabrillo East, `http://cabrillo.com`, clearly sees the similarities between Web developers and ad agencies. "For a brief time I owned a small ad agency. I also supervised the work of agencies on multimillion dollar ad budgets throughout my corporate career. I definitely see the parallels between the ad agency business and the Web development business. I also see the large agencies increasingly developing internal departments to handle interactive projects and Web development. Web developers need to take note." George points out that large agencies provide many services to their clients, services that go beyond "content creation" of ads and commercials—or Web sites—and beyond the "technical services" of film editing and media buying—or Web site database programming. "Agencies look at a client's positioning in the market, they look at brand personality, they conduct market research, they handle product merchandising. There is no reason why Web developers can't offer the same services."

THE AD AGENCY CREATIVE AND PRODUCTION MODEL

When an ad agency sets out to develop advertising materials, whether an ad campaign, a brochure, or direct mail, the following process is utilized to organize the creative efforts. We will look at the more elaborate process followed by large ad agencies to see the full picture and then examine how the small ad agency and Web developer typically implement the various steps. And, by the way, the exact nature of the process, the names of the steps, the order of the steps, etc., may vary from one agency to another, but all agencies follow some version of this process. The outline shown here was inspired by the Advertising Development Process used by Hill, Holiday, a leading national agency, and described at their site at `http://newmedia.hhcc.com/process.html`. However, the description, comments and analysis are based on my own two decades of experience in advertising, three years in Web development, and six years of online and Internet marketing experience.

Boiled down, the process is one of learning what you can about the client's business, industry, products, services, customers, and competitors; developing a strategy that puts strong, memorable, persuasive messages and pleasing, evocative visual design in front of carefully selected audiences full of good prospects; and measuring the results, keeping what works, modifying what doesn't and measuring it again.

Three views of the process are presented. Each differs slightly in the details, but all are designed to achieve the same end result: a Web site that succeeds in communicating effectively and persuasively.

The Big Agency Model and the Web Developer

The following ten steps illustrate how the big agency model can fit the Web developer:

1. background information on the client's products and services

 2. gathering information on the client's markets and
    industry
 3. interviewing owners/top managers
 4. performing independent market research/customer
    research
 5. developing advertising strategy
 6. developing creative platform/competitive
    positioning/brand identity
 7. generating rough creative concepts
 8. presenting final creative
 9. producing final creative
 10. measuring results

Background Information on the Client's Products and Services

This step typically features a client presentation of the company's story, or explanation of what its all about, its products, its position in the marketplace vs. the competition, customer attitudes toward the company and its products, etc. The client presentation may be made by a top executive or by a midlevel marketing manager. The agency may also interview the client to bring out any additional information needed to develop the ad campaign.

The Web developer and small agency generally perform this step before and during the sales calls that lead up to the client agreeing to do business. It happens naturally and rather informally in most cases. However, if you have a sales staff, on occasion you may find yourself in a situation where you have signed the client but no one has more than a vague idea what the client's business is all about or how the company makes money. In that case, it is a simple matter to call the client or schedule an appointment to find out.

Get your facts straight; understand the complete range of the client's products, services, and office locations, even if you will only be involved in some of them. You want to get the big picture. Ask for copies of brochures, catalogs, and other promotional material, ads, and press releases the client may have, even though it may not all be directly relevant to the project you're working on. The more knowledgeable you are about your client's business and products, the more on target your efforts will be. This also lets the client know you are genuinely interested in their business and not just moving in to make a quick buck.

The key here is to be a quick study. Learn to skim over the materials to pull out the key concepts on what the company stands for, the benefits of their products and services, who can benefit, their unique advantages, and why they are better than the competition. Look, too, for the key selling themes, slogans, and headlines the company is using to promote itself. It's amazing how often clients leave out the best sales copy when handing over Web site materials to the developer. For example, it seems inevitable that midway through the project you realize you are without the details on a key division or product and the client casually mentions, "Oh, haven't you seen our such-and-such brochure?" which of course you haven't. Or you may be down to an approval stage and the client gets extremely agitated because he doesn't see some vital information. Of course the reason he doesn't see it is because he never provided you with it. So it pays to really probe at the beginning. No harm at all if you end up with more than you need.

The proper spelling of names, proper titles, and location of key client personnel who will be involved in the project is vital. This saves you from making embarrassing mistakes later on when dealing with the client and assures that you have the right information to use when listing company personnel on the site.

Gathering Information on the Client's Markets and industry

The agency uses its own resources to research all available information on the company, its markets, and its industry. Much of this may come from the client, but many other sources are consulted as well. Key agency employees who have expertise in the industry are identified at this stage as well.

A formal process for the big agency, this step is handled informally by the small agency and Web developer and at a much reduced scope. It may involve a few phone calls or one or two meetings.

While the agency looks to published statistics on market research and requests demographics and industry data from relevant media, the Web developer typically turns to the Internet to see what sites are already up and running in the industry, especially those of the client's competitors. The developer also takes a quick look around to find sites that might be suitable for banner swapping and paid banner advertising. A sweep through the newsgroups via Altavista or Dejanews is also be advisable, along with a look to see what turns up in a search of the Web on related keywords, including any of the client's brand names that may have been registered on the search engines by competitors. A look at Internic's Whois service to see whether or not the company's name is available as a domain name is also advisable at this stage if the client does not already have one.

When reviewing related sites, make a note of the scope and format of each one (general information, online brochure, online sales, accessible database of product information, customer service support, brand/image building, entertainment, attempt to be the dominant site for the industry, etc.). Use this information to develop a better site for your client and as ammunition and support when persuading the client that your approach is the one to take. Focus on how it will help position your client against the competition.

Interviewing Owners/Top Managers

In the big agency, key agency personnel schedule interviews with the client's top managers, product/brand/marketing managers, etc.

The Web developer also wants to hear it straight from the horse's mouth. What does the company stand for? What makes it stand out from its competitors? Where is the company headed? How did it get where it is today? How will it get where it wants to be tomorrow? What are the critical marketing challenges facing the company?

Again, much of this will come out during the initial sales calls, but if not, make sure you understand where the company is ranked in its industry. Is it the dominant leader? One of several dominant leaders? Aspiring to be a leader? Or is it content to be profitable without attaining dominance or the highest revenues?

Leaders, naturally, should look like leaders. But, those who aspire to be leaders will seek to look as good as larger competitors in the eyes of their customers, if only in certain industry or product segments. That will affect the design and functional purpose of the Web site—whether online "brochure," shopping cart, investor relations, or customer service. And it will determine how aggressive the company's Internet presence should be and how receptive the client will be to your promotional ideas.

Interviews with the top people (or the uppermost level you can reach—you won't always get the very top management) can also put a personal spin on what the company stands for. Listen for the attitudes and beliefs that come from these key people. They are imbued with the corporate culture. Even a small business owner personifies a business culture no less characteristic, even if less sophisticated.

Performing Independent Market Research/Customer Research

The big agency conducts interviews with customers, undertakes market research in the form of focus groups and surveys, spends a day in the field with some of the client's salespeople, and gets an understanding of the sales process to learn how and why the client's customers choose to buy the client's products or services. The insights gained from this step pay off in a stronger, more focused ad strategy and more persuasive creative, particularly in the form of stronger ad copy.

A small agency typically pays no more than lip service to these areas. The most aggressive interview customers, but almost none spend their own money to do anything other than the most preliminary types of original market research. Salespeople can be interviewed by phone (with good results) and, along with interviews with others in the company, the industry, and the media, the small agency attempts to get at least some familiarity with the industry, the sales process, and the client's customers. Where the small agency already has experience in the industry based on experience serving other clients, perhaps from having worked with the current client's competitors at some point in the not-too-distant past, the amount of time invested and the learning curve is reduced substantially. Again, the goal is to gain the background necessary to understand the psychology of the buyer and his reasons for buying, all of which goes into the finished ad.

The Web developer most likely is not able to invest more than half a day in these activities, if that, for any given project. Many Web developers never perform any of the activities in this step. As long as the client is supplying the Web site copy, and it often seems to be the case for clients to do so, the Web developer is largely let off the hook with respect to becoming knowledgeable about the industry. But where the Web developer is responsible for the copy, it is advisable to spend some time performing the same tasks as the small agency. This pays off in more effective Web copywriting, a more efficient production and client approval process, a more satisfied client, and a more effective Web site.

Developing Advertising Strategy

In this step the agency prepares its overall ad strategy, the big idea behind its campaign—in other words, how the client should be uniquely positioned in the marketplace, the key benefit of the company or its product, or what problem it solves for the consumer.

The smaller team typically arrives at this intuitively based on what is known about the client's situation in the marketplace and the client's goals.

While ad agencies develop new promotional strategies for the client, the Web developer often inherits the client's existing strategy or defines a separate Internet-only strategy in terms of how the Web site will benefit the client's customers—online access to company information, enhanced customer service, convenient communication with the company, round-the-clock ability to purchase the company's products, etc.

However, the Web developer may be expected to address how the client's existing advertising strategy should be adapted to appeal to Internet users. And when developing banner ads for the Web site itself, the Internet marketer also needs to develop proper positioning and a strong benefit in order to get users to click through.

Developing Creative Platform/Competitive Positioning/Brand Identity

The advertising strategy is now boiled down to a one-page written summary. This briefly outlines the advertising objective, key facts about the company or product to be addressed in the advertising, the key selling points that must be communicated by the ad, competitive aspects, consumer benefits, and the reasons why the consumer should be convinced to purchase. The purpose of this document is to guide the creative effort in creating an ad that is on target and persuasive from the standpoint of the intended audience. Its purpose is to guide the creative effort, but it doesn't tell the copywriter and designer *how* to get the points across. It's their job to figure that out.

The large agency with a large staff needs a formally developed creative platform because one group of personnel may develop the strategy while another group may do the actual ad creation. The formal decision-making process within the agency and on the client side also dictate a formal statement.

Though it doesn't hurt to do so, the small agency often doesn't formalize this process because the strategy development and creative are generally performed by the same people. This is also true of most Web developers, though any time the creative staff has little direct contact with the client, it's a good idea to write down a summary of the Web site objectives and creative goals for the Web team and client alike.

Generating Rough Creative Concepts

At this stage ad concepts and rough ideas begin to take shape through brainstorming sessions and a lot of interaction between the creative team members. The client may also be a part of this process to help generate the widest possible range of creative solutions.

For the small agency and the Web developer, the process is the same, though on a smaller scale. Assuming the client was given a preliminary cost estimate and preliminary schedule when the contract was signed, a revised schedule and budget, if needed, will be presented at this time. The client may or may not be shown rough concepts and layouts, depending on the nature of the relationship. The stronger the relationship of trust with the client and the more sophisticated or experienced he is at understanding rough concepts, the more comfortable the creative team will feel in bringing him into the process early.

A strong agency and strong Web developer uses the rough concepts as a tool in building a stronger bond with the client. However, this is a process that must be handled carefully. The danger is that an unsophisticated client will think he is being shown finished art and will question the credibility of the creative team.

A lot of advance explanation, proper setup of the situation, telling the client what you're going to tell them before you tell them, and being prepared for some hand-holding is called for here. It's worth it whenever you believe there is an opportunity to build a long-term relationship with the client. If it's a one-shot deal, you are probably better off showing them your work after completion of the next step. Brand-new clients and those who appear less familiar with the creative process should probably only see more finished work to help them visualize the end result and give you the necessary approval to move on to the next phase.

This is a balancing act. You don't want to show work that is so rough that only someone with an advanced degree in graphic design or an extremely lively imagination will get it, yet you also don't want to invest too much time in finished art at this point because the client may not approve of the basic concept, in which case you will have to abandon your initial efforts and start over.

A Web developer may present a preliminary site schematic showing a home page and all major links from the home page to other main subsection pages. This can be as simple as a visual treatment or rough illustration of all the copy, design, and navigational elements on the home page, along with enough roughs of subsection pages to give the client a feeling for the overall visual look of the site and how it is navigated. Roughs are typically shown in pencil, colored pencil, or marker rather than electronic form, though electronic art with similar colors, textures, and other effects may also be shown to indicate how the finished electronic art will look. Some may prefer to show all copy in place, already formatted in HTML, and to show empty ruled boxes for logos and other design elements. Or, Photoshop and Illustrator art for major logos, photos, and other main design elements may be shown in nearly finished form either onscreen or as printouts.

CGI scripts, Java, and other code probably will not be very far along at this stage, but the location on the page of forms and other programming-dependent, code-specific items that will be visible on the finished page should also be clearly indicated. The client should be walked through and talked through the interactive aspects of the site and how they will function when complete.

When banner ads or other forms of Internet promotion are a part of the project, a preliminary media plan and budget are also presented at this stage.

Client approval is the ultimate goal of this step. Getting the client to buy into the creative concepts as early as possible is crucial because it will make life easier throughout the rest of the project and may very well dictate whether the project ends up being profitable. Nothing is more costly than having to redo finished copy, art, or code.

Presenting Final Creative

The big agency presents its final recommendations for the advertising creative and all other elements of the communications plan including media, public relations, promotions, merchandising, trade shows, direct mail, special events, etc.

The same goes for the small agency, though the client's overall advertising plan may feature fewer components.

The Web developer shows completed HTML pages with graphics in place and at least some links to other pages actually functioning. CGI scripts and other program code is probably still in development at this stage, but all program functions and capabilities should be well established and known by now so that final coding can be done after client approval is obtained.

Producing Final Creative

At the big agency for, say, a print ad, this means developing a schedule for production and approvals and a budget. Completed advertising materials are forwarded to the appropriate media to run in accordance with the media plan.

The small agency and the Web developer probably introduced the schedule and budget earlier in the process.

For the small agency, the focus now is on the preparation of final copy, necessary photography, final illustrations, typesetting, final film, and proofs—everything required for reproduction of the ad in a magazine or newspaper.

The Web developer moves ahead with final HTML, production of final graphics files, and completion of final program code. Proofreading, testing and debugging of links and operation of forms, installation on the server and debugging of programming-dependent components is also performed at this stage. Final client approval is sought for additional bug fixes or changes (hopefully minor). Preparation of final deliverables for handoff to the client is also performed at this stage.

Measuring Results

The big agency undertakes a variety of studies and measurements to determine the effectiveness of the advertising creative and the media plan. Ad readership, increased awareness, increased sales, and copy testing may be measured to ascertain campaign effectiveness.

The small agency likely does not have a budget for this and few of their clients have the budget to pay for it either. Cruder methods of measurement are used, such as tracking increases in sales or sales leads. Seat-of-the-pants measures may also be relied on, such as how many customers make favorable mention of the ad to the client. This is a treacherous method that can give the agency a fit, but it's a typical predicament for the small agency.

The Web developer's client looks at hits, or, if more knowledgeable, the number of visitors to the site. The Web developer may or may not be held accountable for this, depending on whether site promotion is part of the services included in the project. Often basic registration with a few search engines is thrown in for free. This can cause problems if the client thinks all thirty-two million

Internet users will visit the site in the first week (not all that unusual an expectation!) and no other promotion or cross-promotion is being done.

Internet marketers launching a banner ad campaign have an easier time of obtaining meaningful measurements for the client. That doesn't mean, however, that client expectations will be met any more than with search engine registration. But banner advertising does provide more control, and poorly performing banners can be tested to see whether the problem is with the banner copy, banner design, or site placement.

PROCESS FLOW

The outline above may be difficult to visualize. The following flow chart should help. It boils the process down to a kind of shorthand. The steps presented here were originally developed for a thirty-person Web development firm specializing in the production and promotion of shopping cart sites of five to fifteen pages. It is designed for a high-volume production team handling the development of dozens of sites at one time but illustrates a process that can be used equally well in whole or in part by a lone freelancer or multiple-person firm of any size. All steps of the ad agency process are covered in the flow chart except for Step 10, Measuring Results.

Turnaround Time

Note the turnaround times indicated for each step. The times shown are based on "normal" turnaround time. Normal turnaround time is defined as the amount of time it takes for the development team or firm to complete the work. It is arrived at based on the following assumptions:

> all personnel are working on more than one project at a
> time
> there is no overtime involved
> no rush charges will be paid by the firm or charged by the
> firm to its clients

Turnaround time indicates how long it takes to complete the step, not the number of manhours required to perform the step.

KEY TO STEPS IN THE AD AGENCY PROCESS

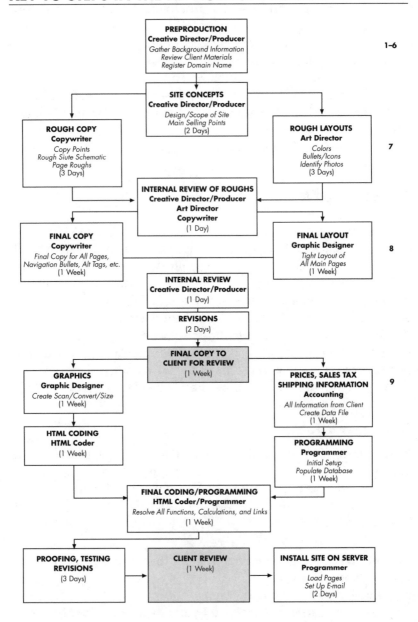

Turnaround time might be indicated as one day, but actual staff time may only be an hour or two. That difference provides the necessary time for internal review and approval and allows personnel to work on more than one project at a time, leave work on time at the end of the day, and enables the firm to avoid paying or charging rush fees.

To gain control over your production process, it is essential that you establish normal turnaround times for each of the steps involved. Each Web developer will establish his own norms which may differ substantially from those of another firm. That's fine. What's important is for everyone in your firm—from the owner and salespeople to the production coordinator and production team right on down to the receptionist—to understand the concept of normal turnaround time and be familiar with the times that have been established for the most frequently performed steps (or overall project completion). When everyone sings off the same songsheet, internal communications improve and so does communications with the client.

A Word About Sales While We're Talking About the Production Process

The secret to achieving a steady stream of business lies in seeing sales as a vital part of the production process. Sales is something that must be attended to on an ongoing basis under conditions of both feast and famine. That is the only way to achieve a smooth, consistent, and profitable business operation.

Even during the absolutely busiest periods, at least thirty minutes a day should be invested in new business, *every day,* or two to three hours per week, *every week.* This chapter addresses the production process and won't have much else to say about sales. But scheduling time for sales must not be forgotten in the heat of production.

EIGHTY-EIGHT-STEP WEB SITE DEVELOPMENT PRODUCTION PROCESS

Every firm has its own methods of creating sites. The exact order may vary slightly from one firm to another. It is a useful exercise to document the work flow that you have arrived at, and these charts and outlines are essential tools in getting everyone on the team (including the client) thinking along the same lines. Confusion is the enemy of efficient production and you can go a long way toward clarifying who is supposed to do what when by using a flow chart and a written description of each step.

Here is a detailed outline of the steps I use to develop sites; who does what is specified. Note that while this process differs somewhat from the flow chart and the agency process previously presented, the overall approach is very much the same. There is, after all, more than one way to skin a cat.

Producer/Account Executive

Preproduction Phase

Client Background:

1. Gather client literature, industry information, notes from sales meetings, interviews with client personnel.

Domain Name Development:

2. Brainstorm name ideas.
3. Hand off to Production Coordinator for research of available names.
4. Review available names with client to select desired name.
5. Hand off selected name to Production Coordinator for registration of name.

Production Phase

6. Review notes from client meetings and project proposal.
7. If necessary, meet with or call client to further discuss goals and scope of site.
8. Determine main points to be communicated, intended audience, key selling points, main transactions to be performed by user, information to be captured, etc.
9. Determine appropriate visual theme concepts and tone of site creative, interactive components. and balance of sales/entertainment/information influences and flow.
10. Prepare overall site concepts statement or rough outline of overall site organization indicating informational and navigational flows.
11. Discuss overall site concepts and theme concepts with client.
12. Chair initial creative meeting attended by Account Executive, Copywriter, HTML Coder, Internet Marketer, Programmer. Present overall site concepts.

13. Chair second creative meeting. Resolve creative differences among team members.
14. Review copy and design roughs.
15. Review page roughs.
16. Present page roughs to client in person, via fax, or online and discuss to obtain approval. Revise as necessary and hand off to Production Coordinator.
17. Review finished site. Hand off revisions to Production Coordinator for revision by appropriate team member.

Copywriter

18. Review material supplied by client.
19. Review Producer/Account Executive's notes.
20. Contact the client if additional background information is needed.
21. Attend initial creative meeting.
22. Develop headlines, bullet points following Producer's site concepts.
23. Attend second creative meeting to review copy and design roughs.
24. Prepare revised rough copy if necessary.
25. Hand off to Production Coordinator for approval by Producer/Account Executive.
26. Prepare copy for each individual page in site.
27. Hand off page roughs to Production Coordinator for review by Producer/Account Executive and client approval.
28. Upon client approval of page roughs, prepare final copy.
29. Meet with Internet Marketer to coordinate marketing/search engine requirements for opening paragraphs of copy on home page and no-frames tags.
30. Hand off to Production Coordinator for incorporation in site by HTML Coder/Designer.
31. Upon completion of HTML coding, proof site pages for fidelity with original copy as well as final check of spelling and punctuation details.
32. Hand off corrected pages to Production Coordinator for final HTML changes.
33. Upon completion of final changes, review finished site in temporary online location. Report errors to Production Coordinator.

HTML Coder Graphic Designer

34. Review materials supplied by client.
35. Review Producer/Account Executive's notes.
36. Attend initial creative meeting.
37. Following Producer's concepts, develop rough layout of home page and main section pages showing all design and navigational elements.
38. Attend second creative meeting to review copy and design roughs.
39. Prepare revised layouts if necessary.
40. Begin scanning of photos and logos.
41. Upon receipt of final copy, prepare all finished art for logos, photos, illustrations, buttons, image maps.
42. Prepare rough HTML coding for each page.
43. Hand off page roughs to Production Coordinator for review by Producer/Account Executive and client approval.
44. Meet with HTML coder to incorporate alt tag copy.
45. Prepare final HTML except for programming elements.
46. Meet with Programmer to coordinate HTML code and hooks to program code for forms and other program elements. Revise final HTML as necessary to conform.
47. Mount finished pages at protected server location and hand off to Production Coordinator for reviews and testing.
48. Revise graphics and code as necessary.
49. Mount approved site at appropriate server location.

Programmer

50. Attend initial creative meeting.
51. Attend second creative meeting.
52. Attend meeting with HTML Coder/Designer to coordinate HTML code with program code and establish program parameters and specifications pertaining to forms, scripts, databases, password-protected access, redirection, secure server functions, automated transaction processing, and creation of pages on the fly.
53. Prepare and debug scripts and code to support all necessary functions and navigation.

54. Coordinate with HTML Coder for incorporation of program calls in HTML and HTML fragments for incorporation in scripts.
55. Test and debug final HTML pages on server.

Internet Marketer

56. Review material supplied by client.
57. Review Producer/Account Executive's notes.
58. Attend initial creative meeting.
59. Attend second creative meeting.
60. Create temporary placeholder home page with meta tags for keywords and description to enable initial search engine registration while site is under development.
61. Meet with Copywriter and coordinate marketing/search engine requirements for opening paragraphs of copy on home page and no-frames tags.
62. Write alt tag copy for all graphics files to increase keyword count for search engines. Prepare all other search engine–oriented copy requiring incorporation in HTML code. Meet with HTML Coder to incorporate alt tags and other additions.
63. Research relevant newsgroups, Web forums, commercial online service forums, and e-mail discussion groups for site announcements and ongoing participation.
64. Write site announcements for release to relevant newsgroups and media.
65. Prepare banner ad campaign creative.
66. Research compatible candidate sites for complementary link swaps.
67. Research banner ad media for relevant topic areas and keywords.
68. Prepare media plan, schedule and budget indicating selected locations for banner ads.
69. Negotiate rates and buy.
70. Prepare all necessary insertion orders.
71. Track impressions/visitors/transactions.

Production Coordinator

72. Review information supplied by client.

73. Review Producer's notes.
74. Attend initial creative meeting. Take minutes.
75. Prepare production schedule.
76. Attend second creative meeting. Present production schedule. Take minutes.
77. Hand off completed phases of project to team departments and client as appropriate.
78. Meet daily with all team members to keep project on time and on budget. Bring production bottlenecks to the attention of Producer.
79. Identify budget overruns before they occur and bring to the attention of Producer.
80. Communicate with client as needed to expedite production flow.
81. Proofread final copy.
82. Verify that photos, illustrations, logos are correctly selected and placed.
83. Test all links on completed HTML pages and image maps.
84. Check all page load times and graphics file sizes.
85. Test all forms for proper function and data handling.
86. Test all mailto: links.
87. Expedite signoffs by Producer and client.
88. At completion of project, prepare project recap for Producer highlighting lessons learned and recommendations for improvements in production process.

NOW HERE'S A CONCEPT

A mistake often made by computer-savvy professionals is to fall into the trap of showing only finished copy, art, design, and programs for client approval. Just because technically it can be done that way does not mean it is good business to do so. In fact, usually it is not and you should not feel compelled to show only completed work or hesitate to show partially completed work during the production process. It won't reflect negatively on your professionalism. Far from it. Instead, it will allow you to be seen as someone who is in command of the project and strengthen your relationship with your client .

Certainly the client will understand the finished product better. Unfortunately, the client may not agree on the creative direction or implementation, in which case all of the time invested in bringing the concept to completion is wasted. Some of this can be avoided simply by doing your homework on the client's business and selling strategy. But without involving the client throughout the decision-making phases of the development process, you are gambling on your ability to read the client's mind—never a good position to be in.

It is far more efficient and economical to present rough concepts and use the very fact of their roughness to open discussion with the client and secure endorsement of the direction you are headed in than it is to incur the expense and time of showing only finished product. The idea is to not allow the client to summarily reject the entire concept simply because of some petty concern, usually akin to your failing to pick their favorite color of the month, or because you made their logo too large or too small—things you know can easily be changed in an instant but that the client can't get past in order to give you the approval you need to move the project forward.

More fundamental errors can also be made, such as developing the entire project around a feature of the company's product you heard the sales manager speak about eloquently at length, only to discover that while you were hard at work on your end, that very feature was engineered out of the next version, which the Web site is designed to promote. These errors can be avoided by using partially developed work product as a communications tool to keep the client apprised of your progress and as a reality check against the client's changing business agenda and preconceived notions about the project.

Of course, the Internet is the ideal medium to use for this. Sometimes you'll need to show the client something so vague you can drive a Mack truck through it. Other times you'll want to show something that leaves only a few details left to the imagination, such as colors or minor body copy in the text. Either way, it is amazingly simple to put together concept pages in HTML and Photoshop to give a feeling for a Web site without filling in all the details or retouching all the photos. It's also just as easy to do it the old-fashioned way if your client is not online—print out your rough pages or sketch them out in markers or pencil and fax them over or take them to a meeting. Programs and scripts can be handled in much the same way, showing rough ideas of screen layouts, input forms, etc., and rough flow charts outlining functions and data flow. Banner ads, full-page transitional and interstitial Web ads can also easily be presented in conceptual form in the same way.

Using Concepts as a Management Tool

Concepts are useful as an internal management tool and an aid to communicating with your own team. Use them during the design phase to clarify ideas and obtain agreement among team members. Work out as many bugs and difficulties as possible during the conceptual stage, thinking through what will be entailed to make the concept a reality. You can also use concepts to aid in staying on time and on budget; obtain estimates of how long it will take to implement various concepts under consideration and weed out the ones that take too long or will be too expensive.

Concepts are ideal tools for overcoming client waffling and indecision over project details. By getting the client to buy in at the conceptual level, when you go back and show the finished product it is usually a simple matter to convince the client that it follows naturally from the concept he previously approved.

How to Present Concepts

The key to presenting concepts convincingly: Have a reason for everything. Walk the client through the concept, one step at a time, from top to bottom. Explain what each part represents, describe what it will become in the finished product, and discuss the directions you could take—in other words, what it is, what it will be, what it could be. Encourage the client to not get hung up on the details. Instead, focus on the goals of the project and how the conceptual elements are designed to reflect them or implement them.

If you are the creator, it will be a simple matter to explain how you arrived at the ideas you're presenting. If you are presenting the work of others—a designer, programmer, or HTML coder, for example—make sure you are briefed by the creator firsthand before attempting to discuss it with the client. A good understanding of the thinking process behind the ideas is essential to explaining it to others.

Of course, problems the client has with what he's looking at must be dealt with. Here are three basic approaches you can take:

1. *Agree to do it the client's way.* Worry about winning the war, not each and every battle. A word here, a color there, and other minor details are not worth getting bogged down in. Be gracious and defer to the client's preferences on the small items. But don't leave the meeting without

confirming that, other than those details, which you will
be happy to address, the client is in agreement with the
overall direction you are headed in.

2. *Postpone the client decision.* When the client completely
rejects the entire creative direction or some other fundamental aspect of the concept, be glad you invested only
in a concept! You have several choices here—depending
on how you read the client and what you think is nego-
tiable. Some clients may simply need time to think things
over in order to warm up to the idea you have presented.
If so, giving the idea time to grow on them often eliminates their objections. This is a strategy worth trying
when you know your approach is a good one but is a few
steps ahead of conventional thinking. You can also offer to
develop additional concepts, which you should be able to
do quickly, as a matter of course, and without additional
cost. You'll have to draw the line somewhere, of course,
and it's not at all unreasonable to show two or three concepts at once, have the client choose elements from each,
and end up doing a third or fourth that the client accepts.

   Sometimes the client is in sync with your overall direction but you have difficulty getting approval on one or
more significant portions. You may have to come back
with those areas developed more fully or develop new
concepts for them. Let the client know you can see that
you'll need to rethink your approach; point out that this is
a team effort between your firm and her company and
that her input is exactly what you were looking for at this
stage. Indeed, this really is a normal situation you will face
with many clients.

   Assure the client that you understand her concerns (it's
not always necessary to mention that you don't agree)
and that you fully intend to address them in the next
phase of the project.

3. *Come back with a tighter version.* For the client who
just can't get it, who gets bogged down in minutiae when
you want him to see the big picture, or who cannot visualize what you are trying to do, it's especially important
that you let him know you can understand and appreciate
how he feels about it. In this case, it's appropriate to apol-
ogize for the inconvenience of showing them only a

rough execution so far. Try to focus the client instead on the overall direction you are headed in. Promise that the next version they see will be clearer and easier to understand. Emphasize that you feel it's important to have client input throughout the design and production process and even though it may be difficult for him to know exactly where you're going on the project based on the rough concept, his comments at this stage are extremely helpful and will enable you to reach the next level more quickly. Then make sure you follow through with a tighter version that leaves less to the imagination.

YOU KNOW YOU'RE A GEEK WHEN...

For fun you think up funny domain names (www.dot.com. Get it? Dot-dot-dot-com.)

Billing and Budgeting

In chapters 2 and 7, I mentioned the dislike many creative people have for the notion of selling—a feeling that may extend to other business tasks and responsibilities. As an accountant friend whose clients include Web designers and other Internet professionals recently observed: "Creative types tend to be bright, but they're basket cases when it comes to dealing with numbers."

For better or worse, my friend's point contains more than a grain of truth. Indeed, the unwillingness to deal with certain financial and business realities can undermine your best creative efforts.

Don't worry. It's not my intention to turn you into some kind of pseudo-accountant or financial wiz. I realize that one of the most appealing aspects of being in business for yourself is spending most of your time doing what you do best. For most of us, that probably does not include these tasks:

1. collecting overdue fees from clients
2. organizing a budget
3. thinking about insurance
4. dealing with taxes
5. asking for loans

While I can empathize with this view, my primary objective in writing this book is to give you the tools to run a successful Internet business. Unfortunately, unless you are willing to devote some time and energy to these admittedly tedious matters, your company's long-range outlook will not be bright.

What follows are some relatively simple concepts and techniques designed to make these tasks more manageable if not more enjoyable. Who knows? You may find that you have quite a knack for handling these critical facets of your business.

BILLING: THE DELICATE ART OF GETTING PAID

I believe that by the time you fulfill your contractual obligations to a client you are entitled to receive payment in full. I know this is not how many Internet professionals and other consultants handle their billing. In my opinion, they are making a big mistake.

I am going to show you a simple and effective way to set up your billing. This is a *no-receivables* approach. You receive a percentage of your fee in advance and the balance in installments as specified portions of the project are completed. This approach is a variation on what is sometimes referred to as *progress billing,* but there are important advantages to no-receivables billing.

With traditional progress billing, you bill the client according to the progress you are making. As it turns out, though, most progress billing entails waiting for the client to pay the invoice long after you have completed the contracted portion of the work.

Assume, for example, that your progress billing arrangement calls for a 25 percent payment upon client approval of the concept and design for a Web site. You complete that phase of the project and invoice the client. Now the waiting begins. Your invoice specifies that payment is due within 30 days—which would be fine if you could be assured of payment within that time frame. Unfortunately, the trend today is to stretch out payables from 30 to 60, 90, or 120 days.

Now what are you supposed to do while you're waiting for the overdue check to arrive?

There are two choices—neither one very attractive. You can either hold up further work on the delinquent client's project and risk not being able to meet future deadlines. Or, you can keep on working without compensation. That's never a good idea, even if you feel confident that the client will eventually pay the full amount due. Knowing that your check is in the mail is nice, but it doesn't pay your bills.

Internet professionals, Web developers, programmers, and Internet marketers may have lower overhead than entrepreneurs in other fields. Still, no business can survive long without cash flow.

A no-receivables approach solves this problem before it starts. A no-receivables payment policy means that you will promptly receive a check for payment as soon as you complete a contracted portion of the assignment. When the work is completed in full, you will be paid in full.

No-receivables billing means that clients are required to pay you *as soon as* you deliver a previously agreed-upon portion of the work. This method provides predictable cash flow while greatly reducing paperwork and eliminates worries about collecting overdue fees.

Traditional Progress Billing versus No-Receivables Billing

	PROGRESS BILLING	NO-RECEIVABLES BILLING
Time of Payment	*Typical Amount*	*Typical Activity*
At signing of contract	None	Check for 25–30%
Upon approval of rough concepts/design	Invoice for 25–30%	Check for 25–30%
Upon final approval of project	Invoice for 25–30%	Check for 25–30%
Upon client receipt of deliverables	Invoice for Balance	Check for Balance

Handling Clients' Objections

You can count on some clients objecting to your no-receivables payment terms "on principle." Please don't be fooled. The only principle is the desire to hold onto your money as long as possible. Be courteous in fielding objections, but be firm in explaining that no-receivables billing is how you do business.

- Point out that your company is not in a position to finance your clients' Internet projects.
- Demonstrate that progressive payments upon delivery is the fairest method to both you and your clients.
- Explain that a no-receivables policy allows you to devote your energies to working on the client's project instead of collecting overdue fees from other clients.

The best way to avoid problems is to establish the ground rules early in the selling process. By setting up your proposals and contracts to reflect the kind of no-receivables payment structure described here, collecting fees in a timely fashion will rarely be a problem.

Should a client continue to balk at this perfectly reasonable billing policy, you may need to reconsider whether she is someone you want to work with. Clients who want and can afford your services should be willing to pay on time.

Three Timely Tips for Successful Billing

1. *Don't wait to bill.* Regardless of what billing system you use, it's essential that you bill the client as soon as work is completed. Send out the bill immediately, while the value of your service is fresh in the client's mind. Your best chance of collecting payment is in the first 30 days. After that, things tend to become far more difficult.
2. *Make sure your invoices are accurate and complete.* Errors on an invoice give clients an excuse to delay payment, and they don't always call you to say there's a problem with the bill. When an invoice isn't paid promptly, follow up with a phone call. Ask if the bill was received and if everything is in order. Ask why the bill hasn't yet been paid.

    It is also a good idea to provide a full description of the completed work right on the invoice. See the sample invoice from National WebSite.
3. *Use a personal touch.* Even with a carefully planned no-receivables billing policy, you can still occasionally run into problems collecting. Say that your Web design company has completed a project and your final 25 percent payment is now due. You invoice the client, reminding him that payment is due immediately. Thirty days go by and you still haven't been paid.

Should a bill become even slightly overdue, it's a good idea to call the client as a follow-up to the written invoice. People often respond more quickly to a personal request than a printed one. Be friendly but firm in your inquiry, and make sure that you are speaking to the person who handles accounts payable for the client's company.

National WebSite
P.O. Box 9999 Orlando FL 32899

PLEASE MAKE CHECKS PAYABLE TO: NATIONAL WEBSITE

Invoice
Terms: Due Upon Receipt

January 16, 1997

To: Acme Industries
       80586 Cyber Street
       Cybercity NY 10101

For: Acme Industries Web Site

Creative and Production Services per signed contract	$3,000.00
Less Payment Received	($1,000.00)
Balance Due	$2,000.00
	No Tax.

Thank you. We appreciate your business!

Note: Invoices more than 30 days past due subject to interest charges at the rate of 1.5% per month.

Handling Seriously Overdue Bills

Unfortunately, there are a few deadbeats out there who will try to cheat you out of your money. But if you are diligent in checking out your clients before signing contracts, you will have a much better chance of collecting what you're owed—eventually.

One measure you might consider is to charge interest should payment not be rendered within thirty days. Such a policy can encourage clients to pay on time and serve to remind them that it costs you money to carry their overdue accounts.

BUDGETS: WHY DO YOU NEED THEM?

Okay, it's Monday morning and the mail has just arrived. What do you know? You find a long-overdue check from a client whose project you finished two months ago and an initial payment for a project you've just taken on.

There you sit, money in hand. No doubt about it—collecting fees is one of the great parts of being in business. Life is good.

But wait, the rent on your office is due, and so are the phone and electric bills. Then there's that new 2400-dpi laser printer you've been planning to buy, not to mention your quarterly tax bill that's due in three weeks. Worse, your financial advisor called to say that you don't have enough fire and theft insurance on your office. He also recommended buying some disability insurance, in case you suddenly became too sick to work for an extended period.

Suddenly those two checks that just arrived aren't looking quite so fat. After a few rough calculations, you realize that your earnings are barely keeping pace with your expenses. At this rate, you will soon be operating at a loss. The solution? Budgeting. A process that can ultimately help you contain costs and maximize profits.

A budget is a prediction of income and expense. It deals with the future as opposed to an accountant's financial reports which only deal with the past.

The coming boom in Web site development projects has been predicted by Forrester Research, `http://www.forrester.com/pressrel/970205IT.htm`, to be a $10 billion business worldwide by the year 2000 (that is outsourcing of Web site production and programming.) Of course, we have to keep in mind here that this prediction is by the same outfit that says a typical Web site costs $250,000. But even if Forrester is off by a factor of 10, the Web development business will still be a $1 billion industry, not an insignificant figure.

Unfortunately, there is not much information available about the expenses of Internet development firms, so we really don't know what the industry averages are. However, we can look to the small ad agency business, those with total billings under $1 million, for a rough comparison. This will at least give a general idea of what a budget should contain and some percentages that can be used for comparison. A sample annual budget appears later in this chapter.

Taking Stock: A Critical First Step in the Budgeting Process

The first step in mastering budgeting is to write down your *income* (how much money comes in) and your *expenses* (how much money goes out) for a given period of time. Chapter 13 shows how this information can be expanded into a formal income, or profit and loss, statement. For now my objective is to help you gain some objectivity on how you are controlling your money.

Once you develop the habit of getting your finances out of your head and onto paper, your thinking begins to shift from a vague somehow-I'll-manage-to-stay-in-business to a firm this-is-what-I-need-to-do-to-succeed-in-business.

In order to take stock of your current financial situation, start keeping a written record of the following:

- **Expenses**
  - Fixed expenses (expenses that must be paid periodically): rent, utilities, insurance, mortgage, taxes, employee salaries, loans, and credit card payments.
  - Variable expenses: office supplies, equipment repairs, new business equipment, software, travel, entertainment, and out-of-pocket expenses.
- **Income**
  - fees
  - interest
  - dividends

Some people are surprised by what this simple exercise reveals. Others are relieved to find that they are doing better than they anticipated. Once things are written down in black and white, almost everyone finds room for improvement. Which raises an interesting question.

Which Is More Important: Earning More or Spending Less?

Quite naturally, most professionals want to generate as much income as possible. Many of the necessary selling skills for doing so have already been covered. The other side of the profit equation is to contain costs and reduce overhead whenever possible—without sacrificing quality, customer service, and long-range business objectives. This is an important part of a process I call *dynamic budgeting*.

Professionals who work on Internet projects need to create budgets for individual assignments as well as for long-term growth. The goal in the short run is to design a budget that will help you maintain positive cash flow while meeting your obligations to clients, suppliers, and employees. For a small business, that usually means playing it close to the vest—especially at the beginning.

As your business begins to prosper, you may want to hire more employees, or move into larger offices, or purchase state-of-the-art equipment that will help you gain a competitive edge. But however profitable your company becomes, you never want to abandon sound cost-containment policies. Keeping expenses down will speed your growth in good times while allowing you to stay afloat when business is slow. In the long run, it may well prove to be more important than increasing your income.

Designing a Dynamic Budget

A dynamic budget is a set of numbers that reflects a well-conceived plan of action. It helps you establish your objectives and develop plans to achieve them—while providing a structure for periodically evaluating how your business is doing.

As you look over the sample budget on page 191, keep in mind that mere numbers never reveal if a particular budget is dynamic. That can only be determined by the way any long- or short-term budget fits into the total business picture.

There are many advantages to establishing budgets that truly reflect what is going on in your business. Such budgets are useful tools for analyzing day-to-day expenses. This kind of monitoring forces you to think through each purchase before you write a check and gives you profit targets to shoot for. Some factors to consider in plotting future revenues and budget goals include:

- your clients' buying habits
- anticipated actions of your competitors
- trends that pertain to your industry
- short- and long-term economic conditions
- your company's past sales figures
- seasonal factors in your business

If you're concerned about the mechanics of setting up a budget, you'll be happy to know that a number of good programs on the market simplify the process. These include Quikbooks, M.Y.O.B., Peachtree Accounting, and Up Your Cash Flow.

Typical Budget

1998 Budget

		Percent
Net Income before taxes	$9950	**6.6%**

Income

Web development fees	105,000	
Programming fees	30,000	
Web site promotion fees	15,000	
Interest, etc.	1,000	
Total	**$151,000**	**100.0%**

Expenses

Accounting/Legal	2000	1.3%
Advertising	5500	3.6%
Auto expense	3000	2.0%
Computer equipment	3500	2.3%
Contributions	200	0.1%
Delivery expense	500	0.3%
Dues & Subscriptions	1000	0.7%
Insurance	4500	3.0%
Interest expense	100	0.1%
Miscellaneous	1500	1.0%
Office supplies	1500	1.0%
Outside programmer	3000	2.0%
Payroll tax	8500	5.6%
Postage	750	0.5%
Rent	10,000	6.6%
Repairs/Maintenance	400	0.3%
Salaries	88,000	58.3%
Software	4000	2.6%
Taxes/Licenses	300	0.2%
Telephone	2800	1.9%
Travel/Entertainment	900	0.6%
Total Expenses	**$141,050**	**93.4%**

Remember, the true measure of any budget depends on whether it enhances your ability to realize your business goals and remain profitable. Here are eight suggestions for designing this kind of dynamic budget:

1. **Budget for profit first.** In order to end up with a profit at the end of every project, at the end of every month, and at the end of every year, you must start with the resolve that you will make a profit. You must also budget for profit first, then budget for expenses. That is the only way I know of assuring you will end up with a profit.

2. **Don't rely on project budgets alone to assure the financial health of your business.** Project budgets tend to include only those costs directly associated with the project. They don't include the costs that aren't specific to any project—overhead costs such as rent and telephone don't show up in a project budget. While you may build in plenty of padding and overhead into your project fees, those reserves are the first to go when projects run over budget and exceed deadlines. It is a simple matter for all of the cushion you built into the project budget to evaporate by the time the project is complete. To counter this, you must also have an annual budget for the business. Use the annual budget to measure your progress on a monthly or project by project basis. If pricing adjustments or cost cutting steps must be taken, you will be able to do so on a timely basis with the help of an annual budget and assure a profit at the end of the year.

3. **Always weigh the balance between the bottom line, service quality, and productivity.** On the one hand, you don't want the bottom line to become so overpowering that your service quality declines. Clients will notice and demand better service or go elsewhere. Ultimately you will pay a higher price by offering poor-quality service.

   On the other hand, you can easily service even a single client to the point where your entire business goes bankrupt as a result of excessive time and resources.

   You must constantly strive to strike a balance between good service and profitability. As you achieve greater productivity from more efficient business practices—and you will become more efficient through experience—you will find it easier to strike the proper balance. In addition, increased productivity will add to the cushion built in to your pricing structure because you'll be charging as much or more for work that takes less time.

4. **Keep your budgets and other financial records simple, accurate, and up to date.** As you will see in the upcoming discussions of taxes and loans, good records can be of critical importance. Also, accurate records can help you answer clients' questions about the cost of a project and remind you of how you solved a particular problem in the past.

   Once your record-keeping systems are in place, you will have financial information that can be scanned on a daily, weekly, or monthly basis. But remember, this information must correlate with short- and long-term goals to be of real value.

5. **Learn from your mistakes.** You will make mistakes—in pricing, in project cost estimating, in figuring the number of hours required to perform various tasks. You will pay the price of those mistakes. There is no way to avoid this fact of business life and every business is faced with the same predicament. The important thing is to be personally committed to learning from your mistakes and resolving not to repeat them. Study what went wrong until you can clearly identify what you would do differently to avoid the problem in the future.

   For instance, perhaps you included the cost of a freelance graphic designer's time in a Web site project, but you didn't catch the fact that the artist calculated his price on a straight hourly basis—meaning that his charges could go up if the project required additional time. Then, sure enough, the project did require additional time and you got stuck with the additional cost because you quoted your client on a fixed-project-cost basis. Make a mental note to never let this happen again with any other freelancer or outside contractor. Better yet, set up a notebook and begin collecting all your trial-and-error lessons in one permanent reference.

6. **Keep operating costs to a minimum.** Whether your company is a startup enterprise or a thriving concern, I strongly suggest that you find ways to trim unnecessary expenses. If you can pinpoint any obvious excesses, take care of those at once. But don't neglect what may seem like trivial expenses. Things like postage, office supplies, computer diskettes, and printer cartridges can mount up

and get out of control if you continue to ignore them.

As I explained earlier, cost containment is often the single most significant factor in protecting the bottom line. That's why it is essential to encourage in your employees and subcontractors an attitude of thrift while demonstrating a like approach in your own actions.

7. **Review all bills carefully.** Your suppliers and other accounts payable have as much right as you to have their bills taken care of in a timely fashion. But before you cut a check, make sure you review all invoices for mathematical errors, overcharges, or double billing.

8. **Expect the unexpected.** In business, as in any aspect of life, smooth sailing can never be guaranteed. You know the saying: "Anything that *can* happen *will* happen." I've never been much of a pessimist. Still, I've been around long enough to know that all sorts of negative events can undermine or destroy a business. Flood, fire, theft, disability—not to mention the destruction of your hard drive.

One way or another, you have to factor such negative possibilities into the mix when designing a dynamic budget. Which brings us to one of everybody's least favorite topics.

INSURANCE: TAKING CARE OF THE "WHAT-IFS"

There's a scene in the Woody Allen movie *Take the Money and Run* in which chain-gang prisoners are sent into a solitary hole with an insurance salesman as an extreme form of punishment, the obvious message being that talking about insurance is more horrendous than being thrown into solitary confinement.

Okay, so insurance isn't one of the more pleasant topics of conversation. Thinking about such unpleasantnesses as illness, disability, theft, and natural disaster is bad enough. The only thing worse is spending money to protect yourself from these remote disasters. On the other hand, if you insist on ignoring these what-ifs, you risk losing everything you worked so hard to build.

To get a basic idea of your insurance needs, I suggest you spend a few minutes thinking about the following questions:

• What areas out of your control require protective measures?

- What is your tolerance for risk versus your need for security?
- Do you know how you would handle the following unforeseen possibilities?
  - prolonged illness
  - theft, fire, or natural disaster
  - long-term disability

Weigh the peace of mind that comes from knowing you are protected from these eventualities against the expense involved. Also, consider the potential long-term consequences of not being covered. Keep in mind that insurance is not an all-or-nothing proposition. Generally speaking, the more you are willing to spend, the more coverage you can buy.

One factor to consider when insuring business property is the *deductible* you must pay before you are compensated. Some policies pay after the first $100 of loss, others after the first $250 or $500. As a rule, the higher the deductible, the less you will pay for an insurance policy.

Another question to ask when insuring property is whether the property being insured is covered at the *replacement cost* or the *estimated cash value*. If you have items of particular vintage or value, be sure that you are insured for their replacement cost.

Consider, say, the 486 computer on which you still do a great deal of work may have cost $3,500 when it was purchased seven years ago. Even though its current cash value is probably less than one tenth of that amount, it would cost you considerably more to replace that old reliable 486. Still, if that piece of hardware is not insured at its replacement value, the insurance company will compensate you on the basis of the item's original cost minus depreciation—not a very big check to take shopping for a new computer.

Four Factors to Consider When Shopping for Insurance
1. the overall cost of the policy
2. differences in deductible
3. extent of coverage
4. type of coverage

What Kind of Insurance Do You Need to Protect Your Business?

Eric Fisher was making a six-figure income as an Internet marketing consultant when an earthquake ravaged his Los Angeles home. Eric had a comprehensive homeowners' policy that covered most of the damage to his and his family's personal possessions. Unfortunately, his home-based business was not covered.

"I thought I had more than enough coverage on my homeowners' insurance to compensate me for any loss on my office and business equipment. Wrong! By the time I found out that my policy didn't cover anything connected with my business, it was too late."

In total, Eric's losses came to over $95,000, including $40,000 in equipment and supplies, $50,000 in business-interruption costs, and $5,000 in lost accounts receivable that he was unable to trace.

Six months later, Eric's business was up and running again, but the road hasn't been easy. He's still working out of an office in the basement of his new home, but this time he has all of his program and data files backed up and stored at another location. He also has made it a point to insure himself against such a financial disaster happening again—he can't do much about the earthquakes themselves!

Insurance company surveys show that the vast majority of home-business owners have no special coverage for their businesses because they mistakenly believe they are covered by their homeowners' or renters' policies. A typical homeowner policy may include some incidental business-property items, but this coverage tends to be minimal.

At the very least, entrepreneurs who work from home should add a *business endorsement rider* to their homeowners' or renters' policy. Most insurance companies now offer such plans, and the additional cost is often as little as $200–$300 a year.

In addition to a comprehensive policy that covers fire, theft, and liability, entrepreneurs should consider the following kinds of coverage:

Disability Insurance

If your business income is largely dependent on your work time, nobody is going to compensate you if you become sick or get hit by a truck. That's why many experts believe that it's a good idea to purchase as much disability insurance as you can afford.

According to a recent study, 75 percent of small-business people carry no disability insurance at all, and many more are underinsured. When I conducted my own informal survey of self-employed people, very few were able to show me how their business would survive if they were unable to work for six months.

If you decide to investigate disability policies, you will find a wide range of prices and coverage. Some policies pay your expenses plus a set amount of money for every day that you are unable to work, while others simply cover your fixed expenses. As with any kind of insurance, shop around carefully to get the most disability coverage for the least amount of money.

Business Overhead Insurance

Should you be unable to work for any length of time, a disability policy will replace only a portion of the income you would have earned. But what about the ongoing expenses of the business?

A business overhead policy does exactly what its name implies: It covers a business's fixed expenses and monthly overhead. Covered items typically include things like rent, employees' salaries, loan payments, and utilities. Such a policy, while not cheap, ensures that your business will still be intact once you recover from your disability and are able to return to work.

TAXES: LIFE'S SECOND UNAVOIDABLE TRUTH

"By means which the law permits, a taxpayer has the right to decrease the amount of what would otherwise be his taxes, or altogether to avoid them." (United States Supreme Court, *Gregory v. Helvering* (1934).

I think we can agree that the need for insurance is something many of us don't want to face, but at least we can temporarily put the potential disasters out of our minds. Taxes, however, present an altogether more concrete dilemma. Everyone has to file a tax return at least once a year, and most self-employed people have to file every three months.

There are many philosophies regarding taxes, but my advice to entrepreneurs is much like that rendered by no less an authority than former Internal Revenue Service (IRS) commissioner Russell C. Harrington: "Every taxpayer has a right to adjust his affairs so that he minimizes his tax liability…Tax evasion is illegal. Tax avoidance isn't."

In general, *tax avoidance* involves the employment of legal mechanisms to lower one's tax liability. *Tax evasion,* on the other hand, refers to the use of a wide range of illegal techniques to shield money from the IRS. On the more benign side are people who earn money by legal means and simply do not declare those earnings—like the owner of a cash business who doesn't declare a certain percentage of his income. At the other extreme are organized crime figures who deal in drugs and other contraband.

Taking a Stand Without Breaking the Law

That old saw about the inevitability of death and taxes should not be interpreted to mean that you have no control whatsoever.

There are any number of business-related tax deductions the IRS allows self-employed persons to deduct. Here is a partial list:

1. fees paid to outside contractors and freelancers
2. rent for your place of business
3. phone and utilities
4. business equipment and repairs
5. office supplies
6. travel expenses
7. postage, overnight delivery, and messenger services
8. legal, accounting, and financial services
9. dues for professional organizations
10. advertising and public relations expenses
11. moving costs
12. tuition fees for courses that relate to your work
13. computer software
14. trade publications and reference books
15. IRA, Keogh, or SEP contributions
16. printing and photocopying expenses
17. answering service
18. automobile for business purposes
19. business cards and stationery
20. a percentage of business-related meals, entertainment costs, and gifts to clients

Your accountant will advise you on exactly which deductions apply to your business. Bear in mind that you are responsible for proving all expenses, and that means keeping records. The IRS tends to be wary when it comes to the self-employed because it can't monitor their income as closely as that of employees who have taxes withheld. Should you be called in for an audit, you may be required to produce records that show where your hours are spent, what your hours have produced, and what your hours have cost.

The best way to document these things is by notations in a diary or datebook. If, for example, you took a client to dinner, proper documentation of that expense would entail writing down who you were with, where you were, and the business purpose of the occasion. The notation can be made on the back of a receipt as well as in a diary. If any one expense exceeds $25, you must have a receipt. For maximum safety, most accountants recommend both entering the expense in a diary and keeping the receipt.

There will be times when you are uncertain whether or not a particular expense is deductible. To be on the safe side, save all receipts that might be relevant to your work. When tax time arrives, your accountant will let you know if the IRS will allow that particular deduction.

Keeping records of each and every expense is not the most wonderful way to spend your time. But if you neglect to do so, you might wind up paying more taxes than necessary or leaving yourself open for trouble in the event of an audit.

Three Useful Record-Keeping Shortcuts

The good news is that there are several ways to get at least some of your record-keeping work done for you. Here are some tips for accomplishing that neat little trick:

1. Set up accounts with regular suppliers, pay them by credit card or check, and retain the monthly bills.
2. Keep a separate checking account for all business-related expenditures.
3. Use one credit card only for business—preferably one that yields a quarterly or annual statement of itemized expenses. Such statements are acceptable as documentation.

Two Crucial Issues

There are many nuances to dealing with taxes that are best left to your accountant. But, ultimately, taxes are your responsibility. In addition to record keeping, there are two crucial issues to keep in mind:

Plan ahead for your tax expense. Because consultants and other independent contractors don't have taxes with-held, it's important to remember that taxes are still due on the money that comes in. Unless you have some idea of what your tax bite will be and put an appropriate amount of money aside, you risk coming up short at tax time.

When money is tight, it's easy to forget that a nice chunk of everything you earn has to be paid to the government. Please don't fall into that trap. Sit down with your accountant and come up with an estimate of how much your taxes are likely to be in a given year or quarter. If you are going to have to pay, say, 30 percent to the government, I suggest taking that money off the top of every check you receive and putting it in a high-interest liquid account. But make no mis-take: That money is not part of your savings. It is your antici-pated tax expense. Of course this is not a complete guide to taxes, but it might be worth noting that quarterly tax *pay-ments* (estimated taxes) may be required.

Assume you will be audited. Don't get me wrong. I don't necessarily think you are in danger of being audited. Still, the whole rationale for keeping good records for tax purposes is in service of a potential audit.

On some level, the IRS trusts you. It does not require you to prove many of the assertions on your tax return. But once you are called in for an audit, the game changes. If that happens, you will be required to document everything in the area being questioned.

Remember, no matter how conservative you've been in claiming your deductions, there is still a chance that you will be audited. If you have been honest and your records are in order, there's probably nothing to worry about. Even if a deduction is disallowed, you'll only be required to pay taxes on that amount plus interest in most cases.

YOU KNOW YOU'RE A GEEK WHEN...

You dream in C++

CHAPTER
THIRTEEN

Growing the Business

Good financial record keeping is a key to maximizing your tax situation and avoiding problems with the IRS. But taxes are just one important reason why every business person needs to maintain accurate record-keeping systems. No matter how you feel about record keeping, there is no reason not to take advantage of the useful information even simple records reveal about your business.

Three Questions Your Financial Records can Answer
1. Which work is most profitable?
2. Which projects require more time than they are worth?
3. Where do the best opportunities for business growth lie?

Your answer to question 3 will depend on several factors including your business objectives and a variety of market conditions. But whatever the answer, growing your business is likely to eventually require an influx of new capital. Which brings us to yet another very good reason for keeping good records.

TRYING TO LOCK UP A LOAN

Growing a business is one of those areas where an Internet professional's resources are likely not to match his vision. Take the case of Fred Daniels.

Fred's two-year-old Internet marketing consulting business was going better than he ever expected. He showed a small profit in year one. Then, in year two, his profits increased by a factor of four.

Now, as his business enters its third year, Fred sees the possibility for significant growth. He would like to move out of the executive suite in which he has been operating to his own offices. He would also like to hire additional staff and invest in list technology instead.

Fred already has some of the capital he needs for the expansion, but he estimates that he will need an additional $25,000 to reach his objective. Where should he go to obtain those much-needed dollars? Here are five possibilities.

Borrowing from Family and Friends

As conventional wisdom has it, your loved ones are the last people you should ask for a loan. But, quite often, this appears to be most available alternative for the small entrepreneur. Like many people in his position, Fred Daniels received a cool reception at the three banks he approached. His parents, on the other hand, were excited about the prospects for his burgeoning enterprise. Fred never even asked for a loan. He simply mentioned that he was trying to raise money to expand his company.

"No problem," said Fred's father. "The twenty-five thousand is yours. Would you like me to write the check today?"

"Wow!" Fred thought to himself. "That was easy. Maybe a little too easy."

Fred's father, a successful physician, certainly had the money. Still, that wasn't the only issue. What if the expansion didn't work out as planned? Fred might not be able to repay his dad, and that might cause problems within the family.

The next day, Fred consulted his accountant, who said, "I'm not going to tell you to take your father up on his offer or to reject it. That is strictly your decision. However, if you decide to accept that money, there are a few important things to keep in mind."

Here is a summary of the well-considered advice offered by Fred's accountant—advice applicable to anyone thinking about asking family members or friends for a loan.

- To avoid personal conflicts and unfavorable tax consequences, treat a friend's or relative's loan much as you would a business transaction with anyone else.
- Should you decide to accept the loan, have your attorney draw up a loan agreement specifying the exact terms, including:

- the amount of the loan
- a complete repayment schedule
- the date the loan will be repaid in full
- the interest rate
- Insist that your family member or friend charge a fair-market-value interest rate. If the loan is being made by your parents, ask them to consult an accountant about potential gift- and estate-tax consequences.
- Ask yourself and the person you are borrowing from all the tough questions before accepting the money:
    - Are you confident you can repay the loan as expected?
    - What if repayment becomes a problem?
    - Is the lender willing to forgive the loan if you can't repay in full?
    - If not, will he take legal action to retrieve what you owe?
    - If so, can you live with your own conscience if you aren't able to repay in full?
- Keep family members apprised of how your business is progressing. Ideally, both sides should feel comfortable about the financial arrangement at all stages. Both you and the lender may start out with the best intentions. But, if you're not careful, that once-close personal relationship can be irreparably damaged.

Borrowing from Yourself

It often happens that business owners are their own best and cheapest source of credit. When you borrow against your own resources, things tend to go smoothly. And, because there is essentially no risk to the lender with these alternatives, the interest rate can often be a real bargain. Here are three self-borrowing options:

1. *Borrow against the equity in your home.* If you own a home or other real estate, you may be able to borrow against your equity. Banks generally charge interest at just above the prime rate for such loans. Better yet, the interest expense is tax-deductible—which means that Uncle Sam will be footing a healthy portion of the carrying charge.

   Of course, there is a potential downside to raising growth capital with a home equity loan. Should you run into financial problems down the road, the last thing you want to place at risk is the family abode. Nevertheless, this is an alternative worth considering.

2. *Borrow against the cash value in your life insurance.* If you have a whole-life insurance policy and need a low-interest loan on unusually favorable terms, consider borrowing against the accumulated cash value in that policy. You won't have to go through a credit check. Instead, you simply call the insurance company, tell them how much you want to borrow, and they will send you a check. Not only that, you are not even obliged to repay the loan. And, if you do decide to pay back the loan, you set the terms. Check with your insurance agent about the loan provisions in your policy, including the exact rate of interest on the loan.

    A couple of caveats: Should you die with the loan outstanding, the policy's death benefit will be reduced by what you owe. And, even though you can typically borrow up to 95 percent of a policy's cash value, you can't owe more than that amount. Should the loan balance plus unpaid interest add up to more than the policy's cash value, the policy can lapse. That's why it's always a good idea to repay at least the interest on any loan against your life insurance.

3. *Borrow against your savings.* Another way to borrow from yourself is to use a personal savings account or CD (certificate of deposit) as collateral for a loan. The interest rate is typically one or two percent more than your savings are earning, which is a bargain.

    How is this any different from simply withdrawing money from your savings account? In one sense it's not. But, by guaranteeing a loan with your own money, then paying it back on or before its due date, you establish yourself as a good credit risk with the bank. In fact, some experts recommend taking this tack before you actually need a loan.

    Say you have $10,000 in a passbook savings account and take a loan for $5,000. You will get the best rate of interest because your loan is secured by the money in the account. And, by repaying the loan early, you may be looked upon more favorably by the bank should you come looking for growth capital.

Smart Borrowing with Credit Cards

Here we come to a potentially treacherous kind of borrowing. Credit cards have become a pervasive disease in our consumer culture. Too many people get in trouble using those little pieces of plastic to buy things they can't afford—and the banks issuing credit cards take full advantage of this very human weakness.

When the average guy is deciding whether to shell out a thousand bucks in cash for, say, an expensive suit, he tends to respect the money going out of his pocket. But if all he has to do to pay for that suit is plunk down a little plastic card, it somehow doesn't feel like spending real money. At the end of the month he may owe thousands of dollars, but the bank is only asking for something like fifty bucks. Meanwhile, the unpaid balance is growing daily at high interest.

Reaping the benefits of credit card borrowing without running into trouble is a skill worth mastering. It's fine to use credit cards if you think of the money you're spending as cash and only if you trust yourself to pay all charges before interest accrues. If you are smart about using credit cards, they can be especially helpful.

Three Good Uses for Credit Cards

1. *A source of interest-free money.* If you make purchases on the day after the billing date (which appears on the top of your monthly statement), you will have between thirty and fifty-five days to pay for them without interest.

    At one time, you could also obtain cash advances on credit cards under these same favorable circumstances. In recent years, however, most banks have been charging interest from the day you obtain the cash. Still, the ability to buy products and services interest free on your credit card can be as good as actually having the cash in hand. But remember, the only way to stay on top of the credit-card game is to pay those monthly bills in full.

2. *A self-maintaining record-keeping system.* By using one card strictly for business, you get an automatic form of record-keeping that can save you time when you do your taxes. Each time you use the card you get a receipt; the same purchase information appears on your monthly itemized bill. Either of these will be accepted as valid documentation by the IRS.

3. *An essential source of identification.* There are situations where a credit card can be the only piece of valid ID that will be accepted. For example, it's almost impossible to rent a car without a major credit card.

Borrowing from Banks

With banks, the view is never rosy. These institutions tend to be extremely careful when evaluating an entrepreneur's credit worthiness. And, unlike relatives, they don't have to be reminded to take a worst-case-scenario approach.

There is a truism that goes: "Banks want to lend money only to those who can prove they don't actually need it." Not only that, banks tend to be particularly skeptical when it comes to making loans to startup businesses—or even small, successful ventures. But that doesn't necessarily mean you should rule them out as a source for growth capital. Try, rather, to look at yourself as a loan officer might—with an objective, even jaded, eye.

- Bankers want to be assured that they will be repaid if your business falters. You will be required to provide such assurance in the form of collateral. For Internet professionals this includes accounts receivable, personal assets, or business assets such as equipment.
- Generally speaking, a bank will expect you to have raised a significant portion of the money you need from private investors or personal savings prior to their getting involved.
- You may be able to prove that you are great at what you do but still be turned down for a loan. Banks often refuse loan requests to business owners who can't prove they have the necessary managerial and financial experience to run a successful business. If you anticipate being perceived in this light, one strategy is to bring someone on board who possesses the expertise you lack and make sure that person is present at all meetings with the loan officer.
- A strong business plan is a must when seeking a bank loan. This document needs to give potential lenders a clear understanding of your business, its track record, and projected plans for growth. The plan must also specify

the amount of the loan you are requesting, how you plan to use the money, and how you plan to repay it.

Any bank or prudent investor will expect to see a detailed description of your market, projected sales to potential customers, and how you intend to reach those customers. Be sure your business plan also includes financial and other data needed to support any assumptions you are presenting. (See Chapter 3 and the appendix for a full discussion of business plans.)

Raising Venture Capital

Banks are only one of several outside sources where entrepreneurs can look for financing to grow their businesses. The other possibilities are *venture capital firms* and *private investors*. As banks can be stodgy in their perception of what constitutes an acceptable risk, entrepreneurs should consider these two alternatives.

Thousands of venture capital firms have helped small businesses. Unfortunately, many of the companies owned by Internet professionals, Web developers, programmers, and new media people are simply too small to be considered. Typically, a venture capital firm's minimum investment is in the area of a half million dollars— far more than many entrepreneurs require to grow their businesses. Also, many venture capital companies have tough investment criteria and impose strict profit deadlines on the businesses in which they invest.

Private investors often turn out to be an easier way for entrepreneurs to obtain growth capital. These are private individuals or groups of individuals with money to invest in promising companies. Private investors tend to be more flexible than venture capitalists—both in their demand for timely repayment and in their expectations for increased profitability.

Unlike banks and venture capital companies, private investors can be difficult to locate. These are generally very successful men and women who prefer keeping a low profile. They realize that once word gets out that they have money to invest they will be swamped with all sorts of bizarre proposals. Most private investors would rather approach you. The problem is to make them aware of what you have to offer.

Probably the most effective way to track down these potential sources of growth capital is by effectively using the kinds of contact networks that were explored in chapter 7.

Entrepreneurs who are fortunate enough to find a private investor can often get a lot more out of the relationship than just financing. Many private investors have great expertise in various aspects of running and growing a successful business and may want to assume an active role in your enterprise. This can work out well if you and the investor have complementary talents and goals—or it can be a disaster.

So, before you agree to a relationship with any outside investor, it is essential to define the role that investor or investment group intends to take in the active running of your business. If it looks like the chemistry won't be right, it may be better to look elsewhere for growth capital.

SHOW ME THE FINANCIAL DOCUMENTS!

As you evaluate money-raising possibilities, keep in mind that any private business investor, bank, or venture capital company will ask you to prove your business is creditworthy. In addition to a sound business plan, you will be called on to present two vital pieces of financial documentation that make it possible for you and others to evaluate the present performance and future potential of your business:

1. a balance sheet
2. a profit and loss (p&l) or income statement

While you will need to consult with an accountant before presenting these documents to a potential lender, it is important to understand something about the basic accounting principles that make them relevant to your own business decisions as well as those of potential lenders.

The Balance Sheet

The balance sheet is a financial statement that shows the condition of the business as of a fixed date. Accountants often compare a balance sheet to a photograph because it presents a picture of a business's financial strength at a given point in time.

All balance sheets contain three categories: *assets, liabilities,* and *net worth*. The three are related in the following way: At any given time, a business's assets equal the total contributions by its creditors and owners minus any outstanding amount still owed. This is illustrated in the following formula:

ASSETS   −   **LIABILITIES**   =   **NET WORTH**

(anything a business owns that has cash value)   *(debts owed by the business)*   *(an amount equal to the owner's equity)*

If a business possesses more assets than debts it owes to creditors, it will have a positive net worth. If, on the other hand, the business owes more than it owns in assets, it will have a negative net worth.

The categories and subcategories on a balance sheet include:

- *Assets:* Everything owned by or owed to the business that has cash value.
  A. *Current assets:* Property that can be converted into cash within one year of the date on the balance sheet.
    - Cash: Money your business currently has on hand, including monies not yet deposited.
    - Petty cash: Monies deposited to a petty cash fund but not yet spent.
    - Accounts receivable: Monies owed to the business for goods and/or services rendered.
    - Inventory: Raw materials, work in progress, goods manufactured or purchased for resale.
    - Short-term investments: Those that are expected to be converted to cash within one year.
    - Prepaid expenses: Goods/services purchased or rented prior to use.
  B. *Long-term investments:* Stocks, bonds, and special savings accounts to be kept for one year or more.
  C. *Fixed assets:* The resources a business owns and does not intend to resell.
    - Land: Should be listed at original purchase price.
    - Buildings: Should be listed at original cost less depreciation.
    - Equipment, furniture, automobiles and other vehicles: Should be listed at original cost less depreciation.
  D. *Other assets:* Any assets not listed above. These should be listed separately and valued at their current worth.

- *Liabilities:* What your business owes; claims by creditors on your assets.
  A. *Current liabilities:* Obligations due within one operating cycle.
     - Accounts payable: Amounts owed by your business for goods purchased or services received.
     - Notes payable: Unpaid balance owed on loans.
     - Interest payable: Interest accrued on loans and credit.
     - Taxes payable: Amounts estimated to have been incurred during the applicable accounting period.
     - Payroll accrual: Current salaries, fees, and wages owed.
  B. *Long-term liabilities:* For example, a mortgage on business property.
- *Net worth (or equity):* The claims of the owner or owners on the assets of a business.

Balance Sheet
ASSETS

Current Assets

Cash	$10,000
Petty Cash	$100.
Accounts Receivable	$25,000
Inventory	0
Short-Term Investments	0
Prepaid Expenses	0
Long-Term Investments	0

Fixed Assets

Land	0
Buildings	0
Improvements	0
Equipment	$13,500
Furniture	$3,000
Autos/Vehicles	0

Other Assets

Rent and Utility Deposits	$1,500
TOTAL ASSETS	**$53,100**

LIABILITIES

Current Liabilities

Accounts Payable	$8,500
Notes Payable	0
Interest Payable	0
Taxes Payable	
Federal Income Tax	$2,000
State Income Tax	0
Self-Employment Tax	0
Sales Tax (SBE)	0
Property Tax	0
Payroll Accrual	0

Long-Term Liabilities

Notes Payable	0
TOTAL LIABILITIES	**$10,500**
NET WORTH: (TOTAL NET WORTH = Assets − Liabilities)	**$42,600**

The Profit and Loss Statement

From both your point of view and that of a potential lender, the primary purpose of a profit and loss statement is to answer one question: *Is the company profitable?*

If the answer is *no,* the statement can show you where improvement is possible. If, on the other hand, the answer is *yes,* the information can help you effectively plan for future growth.

The profit and loss statement is sometimes called an income statement or statement of operations. Its purpose is to demonstrate the financial results of operating the business for a specified period of time. The example statement shows the first three months of 1997 for a Web development firm. It contains the following components (see statement for corresponding line numbers).

The income section shows sources of income broken down by major categories appropriate for this firm which sells Web site development and promotion services as well as reselling Web hosting services. Interest earned on the firm's business savings account is also shown in the income section.

Expenses are broken down into two major subcategories: direct and indirect. Direct expenses are those expenses which can be directly related to specific projects handled by the firm. For instance, line 3 lists the revenue the firm received from the sale of banner advertising to its clients. In January the firm received $10,500. This represents amounts the firm billed for its services in creating and planning the banner ads as well as the cost of banner ad space on various Web pages. Note the corresponding expenses that can be directly related to this income amount. This expense— $7,500—is shown on line 7, Banner Advertising. Thus, the real income the firm derived from promotional fees during January was $10,500 minus its direct cost of $7,500, or $3,000.

This means that the firm only has $3,000 to work with out of the $10,500 amount—the rest was already committed to be paid to others. If the direct expenses were not separately accounted for on the income statement, it would give the impression that the firm had control over the entire $10,500 amount, which it does not. The same relationship exists with the firm's income from programming and Web hosting fees. In addition, subcontracts for programming and photography also fall into the category of direct expenses because they are incurred by the firm only on a project-by-project basis. If there were no projects the firm would not have the expenses. Direct expenses should match the amounts you negotiate with project subcontractors and advertising media prior to providing the client with a cost estimate or proposal.

By subtracting direct expenses from total income, we arrive at gross income—this is the amount the firm has available to pay the costs of its own operations. Gross income is the true income available to run the firm.

Indirect expenses (also known as overhead) are those expenses the firm would have whether it sold any projects or not. These include rent, salaries, telephone, utilities, legal and accounting fees, insurance, and so on. These costs must be paid every month just to keep the doors open and do not vary directly based on how many projects are under development. The indirect expenses are the most important area as far as cost control is concerned. If you can save money in indirect categories of expense, the savings will go straight to the bottom line—net profit before taxes. If these expenses grow uncontrolled—as they easily can—the increased costs will also show up in the bottom line—as decreased profit!

Profit and Loss Statement

Line No.		1997		
		Jan	Feb	Mar
	INCOME			
1	Web Development Fees	$15,000.00	$10,000.00	$18,000.00
2	Programming Fees	$5,000.00	$4,000.00	$6,000.00
3	Promotion Fees	$10,500.00	$22,000.00	$35,000.00
4	Hosting Fees	$1,800.00	$2,200.00	$3,000.00
5	Interest Income	$1,000.00	$500.00	$900.00
6	**TOTAL INCOME**	**$33,000.00**	**$38,700.00**	**$62,900.00**
	DIRECT EXPENSE			
7	Banner Advertising	$7,500.00	$15,000.00	$25,000.00
8	Web Hosting	$350.00	$450.00	$600.00
9	Photography	$1,500.00	$1,200.00	$500.00
10	Subcontracts	$4,500.00	$6,000.00	$4,500.00
11	**TOTAL DIRECT**	**$13,850.00**	**$22,650.00**	**$30,600.00**
12	**GROSS INCOME**	**$19,450.00**	**$16,050.00**	**$32,300.00**

	INDIRECT EXPENSE	**Jan**	**Feb**	**Mar**
13	Advertising	$300.00	$1,500.00	$1,000.00
14	Interest Expense	$0.00	$50.00	$0.00
15	Auto Expense	$300.00	$200.00	$275.00
16	Salaries, Officers	$8,500.00	$8,500.00	$8,500.00
17	Salaries, Other	$4,000.00	$4,000.00	$4,000.00
18	Contributions	$0.00	$50.00	$100.00
19	Leased Equip/Deprec	$600.00	$650.00	$650.00
20	Dues & Subs	$125.00	$25.00	$85.00
21	Insurance	$1,400.00	$1,450.00	$1,400.00
22	Legal & Accounting	$100.00	$350.00	$100.00
23	Licenses	$0.00	$0.00	$75.00

24 Misc. Exp.	$99.00	$0.00	$120.00
25 Office Expense	$300.00	$200.00	$325.00
26 Online Services/Dialup	$60.00	$85.00	$95.00
27 Rent	$1,100.00	$1,100.00	$1,100.00
28 Postage	$57.00	$65.00	$125.00
29 Taxes-Payroll	$1,800.00	$1,800.00	$1,800.00
30 Telephone	$300.00	$278.00	$350.00
31 Travel	$0.00	$28.00	$369.00
32 Entertainment	$98.00	$156.00	$177.00
33 Repairs & Maint.	$0.00	$20.00	$293.00
34 Utilities	$88.00	$65.00	$75.00
35 Shipping/Delivery	$56.00	$85.00	$110.00
36 **TOTAL INDIRECT**	**$19,283.00**	**$20,657.00**	**$21,124.00**
37 **NET PROFIT BEFORE TAXES**	**$167.00**	**($4,607.00)**	**$11,176.00**

Further Reflections on Profit and Loss

Internet professionals, Web developers, programmers, and new media people tend to be project-oriented. In turn, the project budget essentially becomes a mini–profit and loss statement. To improve profitability on each and every project, always take the following steps:

- Watch outside expenses like a hawk and keep overhead expenses to a minimum.

- Draw the line between charges that are your responsibility and charges the client should pay for, and vigorously enforce those policies.

- Learn from your pricing mistakes and resolve to estimate more accurately next time.

- Maintain tight control over the way you and everyone else in your company manages time.

DEVELOPING A PRACTICAL PLAN FOR CONTINUOUS GROWTH

There is an oft-repeated ad agency truism:"If every month is a winning month, it's hard to have a losing year." Which means if you make a profit every month, you can't lose money.

In chapters 7 and 9, I talked about the dangers of allowing your business to fall into a feast- or-famine sales cycle. Your annual profit and loss statements will reveal just when those peaks and valleys occur. What to do about such cyclical shifts is another matter.

In order to raise the valleys and achieve a more uniform level of profitability throughout the year, I suggest developing an ongoing marketing approach to smooth out those ups and downs while propelling your company to greater heights.

The Seven Commandments of Continuous Business Growth

1. Pursue some new business every day, every week, and every month.
2. Invest time and effort in making strategic partnerships work.
3. Build on cold-call selling efforts by actively seeking referrals from current and past clients.
4. Continue to expand your contact networks.
5. Choose places to hang out online where new customers can be located.
6. Continue to publicize and promote your business, even when you are not looking for additional work.
7. Advertise wisely, as your budget allows.

In addition to negotiating cyclical problems, any number of complications can pose an immediate or long-term threat to your company's health. Here are five suggestions to help you steer clear of trouble as your business continues to grow.

Maintain Your Drive/Increase Your Expertise

The same hunger that enables an entrepreneur to get a business off the ground must be sustained, no matter how much a business grows. Inevitably, there will be changes as you expand and become more profitable. But it's important never to lose the drive and motivation that made it possible for you to gain a foothold in the first place.

Many entrepreneurs are able to hit the ground running by combining talent and energy with the ability to generate a couple of successful major projects early on. In the long run, however, it usually takes a lot more than talent and good timing to perpetuate a successful business. In addition to the particular talents that make you good at what you do, it's essential to work on other entrepreneurial skills that are vital to the growth any business.

Should you find that you don't have the time or inclination to increase your expertise in one or more of the following skill groups, make sure there are people on your team whose job it is to shore up the areas where you need help. Here is a checklist to help you reflect on your level of expertise in four critical areas.

Skills You Need to Grow Your Business

- **marketing skills**
    - recognizing industry trends
    - identifying and cultivating target markets
    - researching the competition
    - retaining present customers
    - developing and updating an ongoing marketing plan
    - defining and refining your areas of expertise
    - pricing and billing
    - promoting your business
- **sales skills**
    - prospecting and networking
    - presenting in-person and written sales presentations
    - procuring new customers
    - handling objections
    - closing the sale
- **people skills**
    - recruiting and retaining good employees and freelancers
    - forming and maintaining strategic alliances
    - generating motivation and loyalty from colleagues and staff
    - maintaining customer satisfaction
- **financial management skills**
    - preparing and interpreting financial statements
    - managing cash flow
    - containing costs

- projecting profit
- creating and revising a business plan

Manage Your Money

In more than a few cases a profitable, fast-growing business has been forced into bankruptcy because of poor money management. Some companies run out of cash because they can't collect receivables; others fold because of a failure to manage credit.

The way to avoid such problems is by closely tracking all monies coming in and going out of the business. If you have to borrow in order to meet day-to-day bills, you can bet that trouble is on the horizon. Another sign that your company is at risk is decreasing sales accompanied by mounting expenses.

Many Internet professionals go into business without realizing how much money they need. Some fail to implement a no-receivables billing policy yet expect immediate payment from their customers. Entrepreneurs who make this mistake soon discover that they often have to wait 60 days or more for that money to come in. Meanwhile they are forced to meet their own financial obligations.

One way to avoid this kind of cash crunch is to establish a revolving line of credit as soon as possible. But remember, the best time to get money from a bank is *before* you need it—not after you're desperate.

Manage Your Time

Effective time management is critical to the success of any enterprise. Despite the many books and seminars on this topic, this process is based on common-sense principles that I have boiled down to a short list of general guidelines.

Do's and Don'ts for Effective Time Management

1. Aim to make 80 percent of your time billable. You won't always be able to achieve this, but it should be your goal nevertheless.
2. Plan your time and establish priorities on a daily to-do list. The key to prioritizing is simply doing what is most important first.
3. Pinpoint your prime time for various tasks and arrange them accordingly. If, for example, you do your best cre-

ative work in the late afternoon, schedule your sales calls and other meetings in the morning.

4. Avoid interruptions. If you don't have a secretary to screen your calls, press the appropriate button on your answering machine when you need to be left alone. Make family, friends, and colleagues aware that you will only accept emergency calls during these times.

5. Eliminate time-wasters. Everyone has at least a few major time-wasters that can be done away with. These include: procrastination, poor scheduling, too much paperwork, problems dealing with multiple projects, and the misguided notion that you have to do everything yourself.

6. Delegate whenever possible. Time management experts recommend placing a dollar value on your time and delegating all tasks that can be billed at a lesser amount. If, for example, a Web site designer charges $100 per hour for her time, she has no business spending the better part of a morning going to the bank or running off Xerox copies.

7. Schedule your time. Even if you often don't stick to a schedule, writing things down gives you a greater measure of control over those irretrievable hours. Keep a monthly calendar that includes your long-term goals and a daily calendar to remind you of appointments and other tasks.

8. Time must be budgeted just like money. Every project will have a certain number of hours and any more will mean a loss. Knowing how much time it will take to do any given task is something that only comes from experience. There are two sides to the time issue.

> The most difficult thing for the artist to know is when to stop painting.

The key to time management in the creative department: if you have two hours budgeted, do it in two hours. If you have twenty hours budgeted, do it in twenty. This may sound simpleminded and unrealistic, but the fact is, accepting and coming to terms with the discipline of time can make all the difference in being able to earn a high hourly rate. The bottom line: when time is up, stop working. Make the ruthless decisions that are necessary to make it work in the available time.

Another key: being able to do the same quality of work at ten different speeds. This is one of the most difficult concepts to learn. Some never do. If you can master this, you will have complete control over your time, your budget, and your profitability. The trick lies in being able to look at a problem and simultaneously see a range of possible solutions, some simple to implement, some complex. If you're pressed for time with an impossible deadline, pick the simplest possible solution. If you have plenty of time to undertake a more complex solution, consider it.

9. Don't spend too much time and effort managing your time. Find a simple system that works for you and stick with it.

10. For the most part, all of your activities should relate to your long-term business or personal goals. Take a minute to stand back and ask yourself: Is what I'm doing furthering these goals? Or would my time be better spent doing something else?

11. Don't burn yourself out. Schedule in times for creative rest. This can include some form of physical exercise or short naps to recharge the battery. Remember, you are your business's most important asset. Learn to balance your professional and personal life—and don't compromise your health.

Pace Your Company's Growth

Alison and Neal Johnson, a husband-and-wife team who started their own Internet service provider (ISP) business, decided to expand their market after two profitable years in business. The results were disastrous.

Six months after investing heavily in additional high-tech communications equipment and doubling their staff, the Johnsons discovered that their enterprise was losing money. Instead of steering a ship that was moving ahead at a nice, steady pace, they suddenly found themselves about to capsize in turbulent waters.

All business owners want to grow their companies as quickly as possible. Still, it's easy to mistake a few profitable periods as a sign that it's time to expand your market.

Pacing the growth of your business is an art—one that many

entrepreneurs have not mastered. Things are even less predictable on the Internet than in many other business environments and therefore require an even more careful decision-making process. Before deciding to undertake any sort of expansion, study your financial records and consult with your accountant. Should you decide to proceed, do so with confidence—tempered by a measure of objectivity and caution.

Stay Focused

A friend whose Web site design business has been thriving recently told me that she was thinking about launching her own Internet service provider company. My advice to her was to hold off. In the first place, there was already a glut of ISPs in her area. Even if that were not the case, she did not have the necessary capital or expertise such a move requires.

If your company has been growing at a good pace, chances are that success is due to your ability to provide one or two services better than your competitors. Should you lose that edge, it can be extremely difficult to get it back.

Naturally, there are times when it is a good idea to add new services and products. But remember, it's always risky to undertake any enterprise that draws resources and customers from your core business.

YOU KNOW YOU'RE A GEEK WHEN...

You get a tatoo that reads, "This body best viewed with Netscape Navigator 3.0 or higher."

Sample Business Plan

What follows is a sample business plan for National WebSite, a fictitious Internet consulting, Web page development, and hosting business. The sample plan shown here was developed with the assistance of Business Plan Pro by Palo Alto Software `http://palo-alto.com`.

　　While every effort has been made to provide a complete business plan, the example presented here is by no means exhaustive. It presents a clear picture of a typical firm engaged in offering a combination of Internet consulting, Web development, and hosting services. It is intended to be illustrative only and does not represent the plan of an actual business.

National WebSite

P.O. Box 9999
Orlando FL 32899

Business plan

Prepared August 1997

PRIVATE AND CONFIDENTIAL

NATIONAL WEBSITE

1.0 Executive Summary

National WebSite is a World Wide Web site development agency to be established as a Florida corporation in January 1998 and will serve local and national companies. It will have main offices in the Orlando, Florida area. Services will be sold directly by the company's principals and additional sales personnel.

1.1 Goal of the Plan

The Company is seeking a working capital equity investment in the amount of $104,000 for purposes of startup operations and to cover estimated operating costs for a six-month period. Proceeds of the investment will be treated as a loan and will be repaid over three years at 10 percent annual interest. Ten percent of the Company's stock is offered in exchange for the working capital investment. The Company shall retain an option to buy back its stock at an amount which will yield an annual rate of return on investment equal to 20 percent (in addition to loan interest). The Company may exercise its buyback option anytime after the loan has been repaid in full.

1.2 Market Potential

In spite of the phenomenal growth of the Internet since 1993 and the fact that tens of thousands of businesses have established a presence on the Internet, the vast majority of businesses do not yet have a site on the Internet's World Wide Web. Our research indicates that as many as 80 percent of companies with revenues of $3 million or more do not yet have a Web site. Of those, 20 percent indicate they are ready to move forward with a Web site within the next six months. Only 5 percent indicate they have no plans or interest in developing a Web site at anytime in the foreseeable future. National Website will concentrate its sales efforts on those companies with revenues of $3 million or more who are ready to move forward with an Internet project—a market segment numbering more than 7,500 firms in the Orlando area alone, more than 30,000 throughout Florida.

In addition, the Company will market its services nationally to mail order catalog companies who desire to establish a Web site. The Company's research indicates there are more than 2,500 catalog companies with revenues of $10 million or more. These companies are being hurt by rising costs of paper, printing, and postage and are prime prospects for doing business via a Web site. Web site catalog projects are a lucrative source of business for the Company.

1.3 Strategic Advantages

National WebSite principals have extensive experience selling, developing, and promoting Web sites and have worked together in the development of more than 45 Web sites since 1995, and have developed effective procedures for streamlining the process of creating and implementing Web site projects on a fast-track basis, allowing the Company to achieve economies of scale superior to competing firms.

In addition, one of the Company's principals has more than 10 years of experience in advertising and corporate communications, including 5 years of experience selling to business owners and CEOs. This alone distinguishes the experience and capabilities of the firm from competitors.

1.4 Objectives

- Establish a high profile in the marketplace through public relations, advertising, and community involvement.
- To establish market dominance in Orlando and the state of Florida as the foremost Web development agency.
- To increase sales to reach $77,000 per month by June 1998 and $657,000 for the year ending December, 1998.
- To grow sales during the second year to reach $1.1 million by year end.

1.5 Keys to Success

The keys to success in this business are:

- Aggressive selling posture
- High creative standards exemplified by the ad agency philosophy, "it's not creative unless it sells"

- Fully functioning Web sites that serve a valid marketing purpose for our clients' businesses
- Outstanding customer service
- Prompt collection of all moneys owed

1.6 Financial Summary

In 1998 the Company intends to sell approximately 90 Web site projects generating sales exceeding $650,000 with first year cash flows exceeding $580,000 and netting more than $200,000 before depreciation, taxes, and repayment of investment. In addition, first year sales will produce a residual income stream of $69,000 in Year Two. The Company will reach its break-even point in the fourth month of operations and will earn net revenues equal to the amount of working capital in the eighth month of the first year.

In the second year, the Company plans to sell approximately 135 Web site packages generating sales exceeding $1.1 million and annual cash flow of $1 million with a net profit of $301,000 and third year residual income of $129,000. Cumulative net by the end of the second year is projected to exceed $429,000 (before depreciation, taxes and repayment of investment).

	1998	1999
Projects Sold	90	135
Cash Receipts	$587,650	$1,088,300
Net Income Before Taxes	$200,255	$301,278
Net Profit Margin	34.08%	27.68%

2.0 Company Summary

National WebSite will sell Internet Web site development services to the business community. The company is being founded on the idea that every business, regardless of size, can benefit from a properly conceived and developed Web site.

The core sales offering comprises two pre-established service packages consisting of 10 or 15 Web pages, bundled with a number of related Internet e-mail and promotional services. Any number of additional pages may be added to any of the packages.

Package prices range from $3,000 to $5,000 for Web development. Accompanying Web hosting services will also be offered and will range from $100 to $150 per month (equal to $1,200 to $1,800 per project per year), depending on the size of the project.

A wide array of custom marketing, creative, and programming services will also be offered to meet the needs of any company desiring to maximize the marketing and communications potential of the Internet.

2.1 Company Ownership

National WebSite will be a privately held Florida "C" corporation based in Orlando, Florida, owned by its managing employees and investors.

2.2 Startup Summary

Our startup costs total an initial outlay of $59,000 which covers the costs of opening a modest office and hiring initial staff. Additional startup capital of $45,000 will be required to fully fund operations until break-even sales levels are achieved in the fourth month of operations (April 1998). These costs are to be financed by capital investment.

Startup Expenses	Jan-98
Working Capital	$30,000
Office Equipment	
4 Fax Machines	$ 2,400
Computers	
5 Desktop PCs & Monitors	10,000
1 Laser Printer	850
4 Color Inkjet Printers	2,000
2 Laptop Computers	8,000
Misc. Memory Upgrades, Cables, Modems, etc.	1,500
21" Monitor	950
Software	3,000
Total Startup	**$ 28,700**

Startup Funding Plan

Investment	$104,000
Total investment	**$104,000**
Short-term borrowing	
Unpaid expenses	0
Short-term loans	0
Interest-free short-term loans	0
Subtotal Short-term borrowing	0
Long-term borrowing	0
Total borrowing	0
Loss at startup	**(33,600)**
Total equity	**70,400**
Total debt and equity	**70,400**

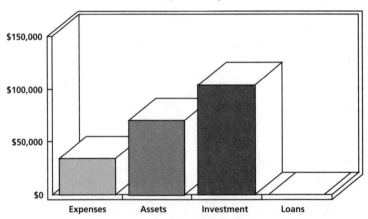

Startup Financing

2.3 Company Locations and Facilities

During the initial year of operation, to keep costs to a minimum, the Company will function essentially as a "virtual corporation" — a modest office will be rented in an executive suite facility, but all employees will work from home. The office will be used to receive phone calls and mail and for occasional conferences with clients.

In the second year of operations, Company headquarters will be located in professional office space of approximately 2,000 square feet within the Orlando area.

3.0 Services

National WebSite will sell Web site development services and Web site hosting, including all creative and technical services such as copywriting, creative direction, graphic design, illustration, HTML coding, CGI and JavaScript programming, and Web site administration. We will expand our services to include Intranet development services.

We will provide customers with a total solution turn-key service to ensure the success of their Internet presence and Internet marketing efforts. We will also offer advanced services such as shopping cart technology and database-driven Web sites. We will expand our services to include intranet development services.

National WebSite will offer its customers a strategic creative communications resource that effectively assists them in integrating Internet marketing into their existing marketing strategies, whether to generate additional revenue, enhance customer service and technical support, or as an enhancement to public relations such as for media relations or investor relations.

3.1 Service Description

Local Sales

Our services to local companies in the Orlando area consist primarily of two bundled packages of services as follows:

10-Page Package	Home Page Plus 9 Additional Pages
Project fee	$3,000
Maintenance/hosting fee $100 per mo	$1,200
Hosting setup fee	$ 50
Annual Total	**$4,250**

Services included in above fees:

- Layout/design of Web pages
- HTML coding
- Copy editing
- 3–5 Color Scans/logo conversions per page
- 1 image map
- 1 response form
- E-mail capabilities
- One-time registration of site with top 6 search engines
- All necessary project coordination and customer service

15-Page Package	Home Page Plus 14 Pages
Project fee	$5,000
Maintenance/hosting fee $150 per mo	$1,800
Hosting setup fee	$ 50
Annual Total	**$6,850**

Includes all 10 Page Package Services above

National Sales

For sales to companies located across the nation, we will target catalog companies with sales of $10 million or more. Projects for these clients will typically consist of shopping cart sites designed to enable consumers to conveniently browse and purchase products directly via the Internet.

Typical catalog shopping cart project annual fees will range from $10,000 to $30,000

In addition, we will offer a wide range of additional creative and promotional services to address the needs of any company's Internet marketing strategy. Our expertise in this area, our understanding of the need for these services, and ability to implement them successfully is a major reason we will stand above our competitors.

Additional Services

Copywriting

Design and coding of additional pages

Additional scans/graphics and logo conversions

Additional image maps

Additional forms

Local Internet access dialup accounts

Autoresponder e-mail accounts

Shopping cart site design

Animated graphics

Photography

Intranet development

Database development

Coordinated Web/print packages

Internet public relations services

Internet advertising campaign creative and media buying services

Virtual server hosting

Domain name registration

Basic search engine registration

Advanced search engine registration

Newsgroup/online forum announcements

Newsgroup/online forum representation

Personal Internet training for executives and other staff

3.2 Competitive Comparison

National WebSite services are designed to deliver high perceived value to the customer while remaining affordable to all but the very smallest business enterprise. A full year of hosting plus initial Web development can be purchased for as little as $4,300, less than the cost of a single placement of a small ad in a newspaper and less than a typical three-day flight of radio advertising.

Our Web sites will utilize the latest state-of-the-art design and technology and will feature fast-loading graphics for easy use by any Internet browser software.

We include basic search engine registration services to register each site with the six major Internet search engines for easy location by Internet users.

We will also offer an exclusive proprietary advanced search engine registration service (at an additional fee) that is designed to put a customer's site at the top of the search engine listings, a key factor in achieving a high number of site visitors, and especially important to companies desiring to use the Web as a direct selling channel. No other Web site development firm has access to the proprietary system we have developed.

We will have outstanding customer service unparalleled in the industry. Rather than interfacing with technical personnel not attuned to the needs of the customer, we will provide experienced customer personnel dedicated to customer satisfaction and backed by a management commitment to the same. This is a strategic asset which will free up sales staff to acquire additional sales.

We will offer clients Internet marketing expertise backed by more than 10 years of professional marketing, advertising, and public relations experience. In the Orlando area, no other Web development firm or advertising agency can match the combined expertise we offer in these areas. Competitors will, at best, excel in only one of these areas. Only National WebSite has complete mastery over all forms of traditional advertising and promotion as well as Internet marketing.

Although the Internet is obviously the hottest new marketing medium to come along in decades, and despite the clear advantages both in terms of market expansion and cost savings that the Internet makes possible for practically any company, our research shows that 80 percent of companies with revenues of $3 million or more do not have a Web site. To counter this we will focus only on the 20 percent who indicate they are ready to move forward now. We believe ultimately every company will have a Web site and we plan to follow the wave as it moves forward to touch all companies over the next 5 to 7 years.

The competition will come in several forms:

1. Internet service providers (ISPs)—dial-up access for e-mail and Web browsing. Although these providers do not typically offer Web development, those that do are not competitive on price or quality; nevertheless, when most businesspeople think "Internet" they think of local dialup providers. ISPs are actually good potential strategic partners for National WebSite, but will be perceived by customers as competitors.

2. Other Web developers. As one skeptic put it, "everyone with a computer and an AOL account is a Web designer." This category includes everything from high school students to accomplished graphic designers as well as full-time, professional Web consulting firms. We estimate there are approximately 50 competitors in this category of which 10 represent significant competition in terms of technical and design capabilities. However, none of the other firms can match our experience and understanding of business owners' wants and desires with respect to any type of marketing expenditure and our marketing communications capabilities and experience far exceed that of any other firm in the market, enabling us to overcome objections and negotiate win-win agreements. Having a strong partner with credentials in traditional marketing who can be relied on for professional Internet marketing advice has already proven to be a determining factor for many companies in choosing a Web development firm. We are uniquely qualified to be that firm.

3. Ad agencies. Nationally and locally, agencies have been slow to add Internet marketing to their mix of services. Few national agencies, and no local Orlando agencies, have achieved professional capabilities in Internet services. However, our combined experience in traditional advertising as well as our extensive Internet experience will enable us to compete favorably with most agencies.

4. Other miscellaneous categories, largely representing future competitors, such as the local daily newspaper.

3.3 Advertising and Public Relations

We will launch an aggressive advertising campaign designed to position the company as the dominant leader in Web site development, increase awareness, stimulate demand, and generate qualified leads for sales force follow-up. The campaign will begin in March 1998, and continue through October 1998, with expenditures of approximately $5,000 per month. Primary emphasis will be placed on the local Orlando market with ads in the business press accompanied by direct mail to the top 1,000 companies. A smaller campaign in selected national publications will also be conducted.

An aggressive public relations campaign will be carried out beginning with an announcement of the formation of the company and personnel appointments and culminating with local and national feature stories. In addition, a release will be prepared on a monthly basis announcing all Web sites recently completed. As a courtesy to out-of-town clients, we will prepare a standard release suitable for client distribution to local and trade publications.

We will seek opportunities to gain media recognition as knowledgeable experts on Internet marketing issues. This will further extend our reach and influence on prospects to assure they are already familiar with the company as a market leader when our staff calls to make the sale.

3.4 Resources

National WebSite will be virtually self-sufficient in terms of resources required to deliver services to clients, with two exceptions.

1. Outside freelance graphic design assistance and outside programming assistance will likely be required. We believe it is prudent to postpone any additional personnel expense until the business is established and profitable.

    In addition, we anticipate the opportunity to sell additional graphics and programming services to clients that are not included in the scope of our established Web site packages. We have already identified a number of qualified professionals available to work under our direction. Typical markups of outside services will range between 75% and 100%. Note that no sales of these additional services has been assumed in the Sales Forecast.

2. Web hosting services will initially be purchased from outside sources. Typical markup of Web hosting services purchased from outside sources will be 300%. While theoretically the markup would be higher and control greater if handled on an in-house basis, the costs of equipment, software, bandwidth connectivity, and qualified personnel add up to a fixed cost of at least $10,000 per month. We do not anticipate that level of expenditure for outside Web hosting services until the third year of operations. In addition, while the costs of equipment is coming down, the cost of software and bandwidth over the long term

are unknown. Break-even and "make vs. buy" analysis will be performed periodically to identify the point at which it will make sense to bring these services in-house.

3.5 Technology Considerations

National WebSite is in the business of providing creative marketing solutions and does not rely on process technology or patentable inventions. Our business will depend on providing custom solutions to client needs. As Internet technology continues to change, we will strive to keep up. Because the pace of change in this area continues to be rapid, we are determined not to get locked into obsolete technology or be wedded to any particular proprietary platform.

3.6 Future Services

1999–2000	Intranet Development
2001 and beyond	Pursuit of related business opportunities such as acquisition of Internet Access Providers, Sponsored Internet-Media Content Creation

Full and complete business plans will be developed prior to pursuing these additional businesses.

4.0 Market Analysis Summary

Companies throughout the United States will continue to build Web sites. According to our estimates, market potential exceeds $100 million per year through 2005.

In addition, the market for intranets is growing at tremendous rates as companies are turning to Internet technology for internal employee communications and productivity. We estimate the intranet market to be equal in size to, if not larger than, the market for Web sites due to the larger scope and higher average sale.

A third category, that of extranets, is also growing rapidly and is a market we plan to enter during 2000–2001.

4.1 Market Segmentation

The Web site development market has been largely undifferentiated. However, we see the following segments:

Local

Businesses of all types, with revenues of $3 million and up. The affordable nature of our packages puts a high performance Web site within reach of all but the smallest local businesses. With two sales reps, and average per-site sales of $4,250, we expect first year sales in this area to exceed 60 sites and $255,000 in revenue.

National

Catalog companies with revenues of $10 million and up, largely targeted towards those with sales up to $50 million since those companies are feeling the greatest squeeze on margins from continual increases in printing, paper, and postage costs. First year sales are projected at more than 20 projects and more than $300,000 in revenue at an average price of $15,050 per project.

4.2 Sales Methods

Consistent with appropriate and effective sales techniques for professional consulting, local sales will be conducted through a combination of sales by telephone and fax, and personal sales calls. We will seek to keep in-person sales calls to a minimum, however, we are determined to do whatever it takes to bring in the sale and will act accordingly.

National sales will be almost entirely conducted via phone and fax. In most cases, we will encourage out-of-town clients to visit our offices. However, the size of some projects may justify out-of-town travel on the part of our national sales rep, and possibly additional agency staff, to close the sale. Such travel has been estimated and included in the expense projections.

4.3 Competition

A survey of local Web developers and advertising agencies—the two categories of nominal competition—shows that Web developers lack marketing savvy and the professional training needed to counsel clients on the most beneficial application of the Internet, and ad agencies lack the familiarity and understanding of the Internet and Web development creative and production procedures.

In addition, in neither category of competitors is there a single instance of any company pursuing the market with the aggressive sales posture National WebSite will be implementing. Thus, while there is significant nominal competition, the lack of sophistication, lack of management capability, and lack of organized sales efforts on the part of the competition mean that National WebSite will easily dominate the market over these two categories.

The daily newspaper is developing an online subsidiary. This subsidiary will be a Web-based publishing business that combines newspaper editorial, local online "communities," and sponsorship by local companies. It is not clear at this time whether the newspaper will also be in the Web site development business. While this is a possibility, it must be recognized that any efforts on the newspaper's part to promote the Internet represents a direct threat to its print publishing business. Thus, it is likely that the newspaper will price Web services well above our package prices giving us plenty of margin to compete favorably on price alone. And the newspaper will find it difficult to respond to the daily changing environment of the Internet, whereas our smaller size and superior knowledge of Internet technology will give us complete flexibility to change and adapt to changing market conditions and technology. Nevertheless, this is a competitor which must be recognized.

However, we can see in the newspaper's publishing and direct mail businesses that its prices are high and value is achieved only at advertiser expenditures exceeding $100,000 per year. Many local businesses resent the paper's monopoly and perceived high cost of advertising. We will be prepared to fully position ourselves against the paper as a cost-effective and results-oriented alternative, just as local radio stations, television, direct mail, and other print publications already successfully do.

There are fewer than 100 national firms that combine the requisite creative and Internet marketing capabilities to rival our effort. The number of prospects far outweighs such firms. The market is wide open and ripe for exploitation. Whereas we may not be able to dominate the national market, neither will any other firm.

5.0 Marketing Strategy

Overall marketing strategy consists of

- Emphasizing total-solution Internet marketing services
- Aggressive sales push
- Focus on targeted local and national markets

Marketing Programs

We will utilize a combination of direct mail, newspaper/business journal advertising, and radio to reach our local target market.

We will utilize a combination of direct mail and business publication advertising to reach our national and vertical markets.

5.2 Sales Strategy

Within the context of professional consulting firms, our sales strategy is an aggressive one. John Doe, managing partner of the firm, will be primarily responsible for all sales. He will personally handle all local sales of the firm's services. In addition, a national sales representative will be hired and trained to sell Web development services. A national rep will be sought who has direct experience in selling advertising agency services or national advertising media such as radio, television, newspaper, or magazines. This type of background will provide the best preparation for the additional training that will be necessary in order to sell the firm's services and achieve desired sales goals.

John Doe will supervise the national sales rep in establishing effective sales techniques, overcoming objections, and closing sales.

Sales Forecast

The following chart shows the breakdown of first year sales by segment.

Local Sales (Avg. $4,250 per Sale)	**$284,750**
National Sales (Avg. $15,050 per Sale)	**$346,150**
Promotion, Sell-ups & Misc. (Avg. $300 per site)	**$26,400**
Total Sales	**$657,300**

Total Receipts by Month in Year 1

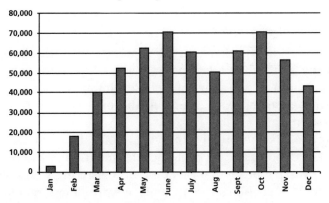

Business Plan Milestones

Milestone	Date
Initial Staff	1-1-98
Office Setup	1-1-98
National Sales Rep Hired	1-1-98
Local Sales Literature Complete	1-15-98
Local Sales Begin	1-15-98
National Sales Literature Complete	1-20-98
National Sales Begin	1-20-98
Ad Campaign Launch	3-1-98
Sales > $50,000/mo.	3-31-98
Phase II Staff Hired	4-1-98
Cash Rcpt. > $50,000/mo.	4-30-98

6.0 Organizational Structure

National WebSite is organized into four main functional areas: Sales and Marketing, Creative, Customer Service, and Finance and Administration. Actual production falls under the Creative area. Customer contact falls under the Sales and Customer Service areas.

6.1 Management Team

John Doe (Managing Partner)

With 10 years of experience in the ownership and management of advertising and public relations agencies, six years of experience selling online, and two years of Web development experience, Mr. Doe brings a strong background in the management of creative organizations.

Mr. Doe is thoroughly knowledgeable about all aspects of Internet marketing and Web site development. He was one of the first to develop a proprietary method of registering Web sites with search engines enabling sites to achieve a prominent ranking at or near the top of search engine query results. He has developed effective Internet public relations strategies to achieve a high awareness of Web sites among Internet users.

Mr. Doe is an award winning advertising copywriter and an accomplished public relations professional and public relations writer. He has provided the creative direction and copywriting for more than 30 Web sites.

Jane Smith (Customer Service Manager)

With experience and background in customer service, Ms. Smith is ideally qualified to head up National WebSite's customer service department. Ms. Smith was previously in charge of the customer service department for a large professional photo lab in and served as Production Coordinator for a start-up Internet advertising agency. She is thoroughly versed in all aspects of the Web site development process and, under John Doe's direction, developed a streamlined Web site development production procedure.

Joe Johnson (Web Designer)

Mr. Johnson has extensive experience in print production and graphics. He began working on Internet Web sites in 1995 and has achieved an advanced level of skills in the preparation of graphics and coding of Web pages. He has personally developed more than 30 Web sites during the past two years.

6.3 Personnel Plan

Personnel will be added in two phases during the first year: Start-up and Phase II.

Startup personnel will consist of:

Manager

National Sales Rep

Customer Service Manager

Web Designer

Bookkeeper

Phase II personnel will consist of:

Assistant HTML Coder

Graphic Designer

Additional personnel will be hired in the second year:

Startup Personnel	1998	1999
Managing Partner	50,000	75,000
Customer Service Mgr	35,000	50,000
Web Designer	35,000	50,000
National Account Rep	45,961	79,180
Bookkeeper	22,000	22,000
Payroll - Phase II		
Asst. HTML Coder	18,750	35,000
Graphic Designer	18,747	35,000
Year 2 Staff Additions		
Executive Secretary		29,000
Receptionist		15,000
Asst. HTML Coder		22,500
Asst. Customer Service Mgr		30,000
Total	206,711	311,180

7. 0 Financial Plan

Enclosed are National WebSite's financial plans for Years 1 and 2 and a pro-forma balance sheet.

Web Site Projects Sold Per Month

	Year 1													
	Jan-98	Feb-98	Mar-98	Apr-98	May-98	Jun-98	Jul-98	Aug-98	Sep-98	Oct-98	Nov-98	Dec-98	Total	A/R
Local Sales	2	4	6	7	7	7	5	5	6	6	6	6	67	
National	0	1	2	2	3	3	2	2	3	3	1	1	23	
Month Total	2	5	8	9	10	10	7	7	9	9	7	7	90	
Y-T-D Total	2	7	15	24	34	44	51	58	67	76	83	90		
Sales From Projects														
Local Sales (Avg. $4250 per Sale)	8,500	17,000	25,500	29,750	29,750	29,750	21,250	21,250	25,500	25,500	25,500	25,500	284,750	
National Sales (Avg. $15050 per Sale)	0	15,050	30,100	30,100	45,150	45,150	30,100	30,100	45,150	45,150	15,050	15,050	346,150	
Promotion, Sell-ups & Misc. Avg. $300 per site		1,500	2,400	2,700	3,000	3,000	2,100	2,100	2,700	2,700	2,100	2,100	26,400	
Total Sales	8,500	33,550	58,000	62,550	77,900	77,900	53,450	53,450	73,350	73,350	42,650	42,650	657,300	
Cash Receipts														
Web Projects - Billed 50% Adv./50% Final														
50% Deposit	3,000	12,900	22,800	24,300	31,200	31,200	21,300	21,300	29,700	29,700	15,900	15,900	259,200	
Remaining 50%		3,000	12,900	22,800	24,300	31,200	31,200	21,300	21,300	29,700	29,700	15,900	243,300	
Web Hosting - Billed Quarterly in Advance														
Setup Fees - $50 per site		100	250	400	450	500	500	350	350	450	450	350	4,150	
First Q Hosting		600	1,500	2,400	2,700	3,000	3,000	2,100	2,100	2,700	2,700	2,100	24,900	
Second Q Hosting					600	1,500	2,400	2,700	3,000	3,000	2,100	2,100	17,400	
Third Q Hosting								600	1,500	2,400	2,700	3,000	10,200	
Fourth Q Hosting											600	1,500	2,100	A/R
Promotions, Sell-ups & Misc.	0	1,500	2,400	2,700	3,000	3,000	2,100	2,100	2,700	2,700	2,100	2,100	26,400	
Total Receipts	3,000	18,100	39,850	52,600	62,250	70,400	60,500	50,450	60,650	70,650	56,250	42,950	587,650	69,650
Expenses:														
Direct Costs														
Web Hosting	100	310	610	900	1,220	1,520	1,670	1,880	2,190	2,460	2,630	2,840	18,330	
Freelance Graphic Design	200	200	200	300	300								1,200	

													Total
Programming	200	500	500	1,000	1,000	1,500	1,500	1,500	1,500	1,500	1,500	1,500	13,700
Total Direct Costs	500	1,010	1,310	2,200	2,520	3,020	3,170	3,380	3,690	3,960	4,130	4,340	33,230
Indirect Costs													
Payroll - Phase I													
Managing Partner 50M	4,167	4,167	4,167	4,167	4,167	4,167	4,167	4,167	4,167	4,167	4,167	4,167	50,000
Customer Service Mgr 35M	2,917	2,917	2,917	2,917	2,917	2,917	2,917	2,917	2,917	2,917	2,917	2,917	35,000
Web Designer 35M	2,917	2,917	2,917	2,917	2,917	2,917	2,917	2,917	2,917	2,917	2,917	2,917	35,000
National Account Rep 20M+7.5%	1,667	2,795	3,924	3,924	5,053	5,053	3,924	3,924	5,053	5,053	2,795	2,795	45,961
Bookkeeper 22M	1,833	1,833	1,833	1,833	1,833	1,833	1,833	1,834	1,834	1,834	1,834	1,834	22,000
Payroll - Phase II													
Asst. HTML Coder 25M				2,083	2,083	2,083	2,083	2,083	2,083	2,083	2,083	2,083	18,750
Graphic Designer 25M				2,083	2,083	2,083	2,083	2,083	2,083	2,083	2,083	2,083	18,747
Total Payroll	13,500	14,628	15,757	19,923	21,052	21,052	19,924	19,924	21,053	21,053	18,796	18,796	225,458
Payroll Taxes & Fringe @18%	2,430	2,633	2,836	3,586	3,789	3,789	3,586	3,586	3,790	3,790	3,383	3,383	40,582
Rent Executive Suite	500	500	500	500	500	500	500	500	500	500	500	500	6,000
Telephone	200	300	300	300	400	400	400	400	400	400	400	400	4,300
Office Supplies	300	200	200	200	300	200	200	200	200	200	200	200	2,600
Postage	75	100	100	100	100	100	100	100	100	100	100	100	1,175
Advertising/Prospect Lists	0	1,000	5,000	5,000	5,000	5,000	2,500	2,500	5,000	5,000	0	0	36,000
Accounting/Legal	100	100	200	200	200	200	200	200	200	200	200	200	2,200
Business Insurance	200	200	200	200	200	200	200	200	200	200	200	200	2,400
Entertainment	0	200	200	200	200	200	200	200	200	200	200	200	2,200
Mileage	100	200	300	350	350	350	350	350	350	350	350	350	3,750
Out of Town Travel	0	0	0	1,500	1,500	0	0	0	1,500	1,500	0	0	6,000
Miscellaneous	1,000	1,000	1,500	2,000	2,000	2,000	2,000	2,000	2,000	2,000	2,000	2,000	21,500
Total Expenses	18,905	22,072	28,403	36,259	38,112	37,012	33,330	33,540	39,183	39,453	30,459	30,669	387,395
Net Cash Flow from Operations (before taxes)	(15,905)	(3,972)	11,447	16,341	24,138	33,388	27,170	16,910	21,467	31,197	25,791	12,281	200,255
Cumulative Net from Operations (before taxes)	(15,905)	(19,876)	(8,430)	7,911	32,049	65,438	92,608	109,518	130,985	162,183	187,974	200,255	

	Jan-98												
Start Up:													
Working Capital	30,000												
Office Equipment													
4 Fax Machines	2,400												
Computers													
5 Desktop PCs & Monitors	10,000												
1 Laser Printer	850												
4 Color Inkjet Printers	2,000												
2 Laptop Computer	8,000												
Misc. Memory Upgrades, Cables, Modems, etc.	1,500												
21" Monitor	950												
Software	3,000												
Total Start Up	(58,700)												
Phase II Staff Addition													
Computers													
2 Desktop PCs					4,000								
2 Color Inkjet Printers					800								
2 21" Monitors					1,800								
Software					2,000								
Total Phase II Equipment					(8,600)								
Total Cumulative Net (before taxes)	(58,700)	(74,605)	(94,481)	(102,910)	(103,599)	(71,550)	(6,112)	21,058	37,968	59,436	90,633	116,424	128,705

Web Site Projects Sold Per Month	Year 2													
	Jan-99	Feb-99	Mar-99	Apr-99	May-99	Jun-99	Jul-99	Aug-99	Sep-99	Oct-99	Nov-99	Dec-99	Total	
Local Sales	4	6	10	12	12	10	5	4	4	8	4	4	87	0
National Sales	3	3	5	6	6	6	3	2	4	5	3	2	48	
Month Total	7	9	15	18	18	16	8	6	10	13	9	6	135	
Y-T-D Total	7	16	31	49	67	83	91	97	107	120	129	135		
Sales From Projects														
Local Sales (Avg. $4250 per Sale)	17,000	25,500	42,500	51,000	51,000	42,500	21,250	17,000	25,500	34,000	25,500	17,000	369,750	
National Sales (Avg. $15050 per Sale)	45,150	45,150	75,250	90,300	90,300	90,300	45,150	30,100	60,200	75,250	45,150	30,100	722,400	
Promotion, Sell-ups & Misc. Avg. $300 per site	2,100	2,700	4,500	5,400	5,400	4,800	2,400	1,800	3,000	3,900	2,700	1,800	40,500	
Total Sales	64,250	73,350	122,250	146,700	146,700	137,600	68,800	48,900	88,700	113,150	73,350	48,900	1,132,650	
Cash Receipts														
Residual Income From Previous Year														
Project Fees (Dec. 98 Sales)	15,900	15,900												
Web Hosting Fees														
Setup Fees (Dec. 98 Sales)	350												350	
Fourth Q	2,400	2,700	2,100	2,100	2,100	2,100	2,700						16,200	
Third Q	3,000				2,700	2,100	2,100						9,900	
Second Q	2,700	2,700	3,000	3,000				2,700	2,100	2,100			18,300	
First Q	2,100	2,100	2,100	2,700									9,000	
Total Residual	26,450	23,400	7,200	7,800	4,800	4,200	4,800	2,700	2,100	2,100	0	0	85,550	
Web Projects - Billed 50% Adv./50% Final														
50% Deposit	26,700	29,700	49,500	59,400	59,400	56,400	28,200	19,800	36,600	46,500	29,700	19,800	461,700	
Remaining 50%		26,700	29,700	49,500	59,400	59,400	56,400	28,200	19,800	36,600	46,500	29,700	441,900	
Web Hosting - Billed Quarterly in Advance													0	
Setup Fees - $50 per site		350	450	750	900	900	800	400	300	500	650	450	6,450	
First Q Hosting		2,100	2,700	4,500	5,400	5,400	4,800	2,400	1,800	3,000	3,900	2,700	38,700	
Second Q Hosting					2,100	2,700	4,500	5,400	5,400	4,800	2,400	1,800	29,100	
Third Q Hosting								2,100	2,700	4,500	5,400	5,400	20,100 A/R	
Fourth Q Hosting											2,100	2,700	4,800	
Total Current Year Receipts	26,700	58,850	82,350	114,150	127,200	124,800	94,700	58,300	66,600	95,900	90,650	62,550	1,002,750	
Total Current & Residual	53,150	82,250	89,550	121,950	132,000	129,000	99,500	61,000	68,700	98,000	90,650	62,550	1,088,300	129,900

Expenses	1	2	3	4	5	6	7	8	9	10	11	12	Total
Direct Costs													
Web Hosting for last year's sales of 90 sites	2,700	2,700	2,700	2,700	2,700	2,700	2,700	2,700	2,700	2,700	2,700	2,700	32,400
Web Hosting	350	660	1,230	1,830	2,370	2,810	2,890	3,030	3,410	3,860	4,050	4,170	30,660
Freelance Graphic Design	200	200	200	300	300	500	500	500	500	500	500	500	4,700
Programming	2,000	2,000	2,000	2,000	2,000	2,000	2,000	2,000	2,000	2,000	2,000	2,000	24,000
Total Direct Costs	5,250	5,560	6,130	6,830	7,370	8,010	8,090	8,230	8,610	9,060	9,250	9,370	91,760
Indirect Costs													
Payroll - Phase I													
Managing Partner 75M	6,250	6,250	6,250	6,250	6,250	6,250	6,250	6,250	6,250	6,250	6,250	6,250	75,000
Customer Service Mgr 50M	4,167	4,167	4,167	4,167	4,167	4,167	4,167	4,167	4,167	4,167	4,167	4,167	50,000
Web Designer 50M	4,167	4,167	4,167	4,167	4,167	4,167	4,167	4,167	4,167	4,167	4,167	4,167	50,000
National Account Rep 30M+7.5%	5,470	5,470	7,727	8,856	8,856	8,856	5,470	4,341	6,598	7,727	5,470	4,341	79,180
Bookkeeper 25M	1,833	1,833	1,833	1,833	1,833	1,833	1,833	1,833	1,834	1,834	1,834	1,834	22,000
Executive Secretary 29M	2,417	2,417	2,417	2,417	2,417	2,417	2,417	2,417	2,417	2,417	2,417	2,417	29,000
Receptionist				1,667	1,667	1,667	1,667	1,667	1,667	1,667	1,667	1,667	15,000
Asst. HTML Coder 35M	2,917	2,917	2,917	2,917	2,917	2,917	2,917	2,917	2,917	2,917	2,917	2,917	35,000
Asst. HTML Coder 30M				2,500	2,500	2,500	2,500	2,500	2,500	2,500	2,500	2,500	22,500
Graphic Designer 35M	2,917	2,917	2,917	2,917	2,917	2,917	2,917	2,917	2,917	2,917	2,917	2,917	35,000
Asst. Customer Service Mgr 30M	2,500	2,500	2,500	2,500	2,500	2,500	2,500	2,500	2,500	2,500	2,500	2,500	30,000
	32,636	32,636	34,893	40,189	40,189	40,189	36,803	35,674	37,932	39,061	36,804	35,675	442,680
Payroll Taxes & Fringe @18%	5,874	5,874	6,281	7,234	7,234	7,234	6,624	6,421	6,828	7,031	6,625	6,421	79,682
Rent - 2000 Sq. Ft. @$14/ft.	2,333	2,333	2,333	2,333	2,333	2,333	2,333	2,333	2,333	2,333	2,333	2,333	28,000
Telephone	1,400	400	400	400	400	400	400	400	400	400	400	400	5,800
Office Supplies	600	600	600	300	300	300	300	300	300	300	300	300	4,500
Postage	200	200	200	200	200	200	200	200	200	200	200	200	2,400
Advertising	1,000	10,000	10,000	10,000	10,000	5,000	5,000	1,000	5,000	5,000	0	0	62,000
Accounting/Legal	200	300	300	300	300	300	300	300	300	300	300	300	3,500
Business Insurance	400	400	400	400	400	400	400	400	400	400	400	400	4,800
Entertainment	200	500	500	500	500	500	500	500	500	500	500	500	5,700
Mileage	300	400	500	500	500	500	500	500	500	500	500	500	5,700
Out of Town Travel	0	2,500	2,500	2,500	2,500	2,500	2,500	2,500	2,500	2,500	2,500	2,500	27,500
Miscellaneous	1,000	2,000	2,000	2,000	2,000	2,000	2,000	2,000	2,000	2,000	2,000	2,000	23,000
Total Expenses	51,394	63,704	67,038	73,686	74,226	69,866	65,950	60,758	67,803	69,585	62,112	60,900	787,022
Net Cash Flow from Operations (before taxes)	1,756	18,546	22,512	48,264	57,774	59,134	33,550	242	897	28,415	28,538	1,650	301,278
Cumulative Net from Operations (before taxes)	1,756	20,303	42,815	91,079	148,853	207,987	241,536	241,778	242,674	271,089	299,627	301,278	301,278

Additional Capital Expense

Office Equipment	
11 Desks & Chairs	6,600
4 Filing Cabinets	1,600
Conference Room Table & Chairs	2,500
Misc. Office Furniture	5,000
Computers	
7 Desktop PC's & Monitors	14,000
1 Laser Printer	850
4 Color Inkjet Printers	2,000
Misc. Memory Upgrades, Cables, Modems, etc.	5,000
2- 21" Monitors	2,000
Software - New & Upgrades	5,000
Telephone Equipment & Installation	3000
Rent Deposit	3,000
Telephone Deposit	1000
Leasehold Improvements	3000
Total Additional Capital Exp.	**(54,550)**

Prev. Yr. Cumulative Balance Fwd.	128,705											
Total Cumulative Net (before taxes)	74,155	75,911	94,457	116,970	165,234	223,007	282,141	315,691	315,932	316,829	345,244	373,782	375,432

CASH FLOW VARIABLES

Beg Cash	20000
Mark Up1	1
Mark Up2	1
Mark Up3	1
Mark Up4	1
Frt Pct1	1
Frt Pct2	1
Frt Pct3	1
Frt Pct4	1
CommRt	1
Withhold_Rate	0.2
Cash Reserve	20,000

Pro-forma Balance Sheet

	Starting Balances	Jan-98	Feb-98	Mar-98	Apr-98	May-98	Jun-98	Jul-98	Aug-98	Sep-98	Oct-98	Nov-98	Dec-98	Dec-98	Dec-98
Short-term Assets															
Cash	70,400	59,922	57,341	69,249	82,923	100,208	122,932	139,837	151,413	170,199	192,547	204,737	212,841	212,841	432,470
Accounts receivable	0	0	0	0	0	0	0	0	0	0	0	0	0	0	0
Inventory	0	0	0	0	0	0	0	0	0	0	0	0	0	0	0
Other Short-term Assets	0	0	0	0	0	0	0	0	0	0	0	0	0	0	0
Total Short-term Assets	70,400	59,922	57,341	69,249	82,923	100,208	122,932	139,837	151,413	170,199	192,547	204,737	212,841	212,841	432,470
Long-term Assets															
Capital Assets	0	0	0	0	0	0	0	0	0	0	0	0	0	0	0
Accumulated Depreciation	0	0	0	0	0	0	0	0	0	0	0	0	0	0	0
Total Long-term Assets	0	0	0	0	0	0	0	0	0	0	0	0	0	0	0
Total Assets	70,400	59,922	57,341	69,249	82,923	100,208	122,932	139,837	151,413	170,199	192,547	204,737	212,841	212,841	432,470
	Starting Balances	Jan-98	Feb-98	Mar-98	Apr-98	May-98	Jun-98	Jul-98	Aug-98	Sep-98	Oct-98	Nov-98	Dec-98	Dec-98	Dec-98
Debt and Equity															
Accounts Payable	0	2,751	4,448	9,071	11,789	12,270	11,253	9,080	9,274	13,260	13,509	7,656	7,850	1,998	1,999
Short-term Notes	0	0	0	0	0	0	0	0	0	0	0	0	0	5,852	15,122
Other ST Liabilities	0	0	0	0	0	0	0	0	0	0	0	0	0	0	0
Subtotal Short-term Liabilities	0	2,751	4,448	9,071	11,789	12,270	11,253	9,080	9,274	13,260	13,509	7,656	7,850	7,850	17,121
Long-term Liabilities	104,000	104,000	104,000	104,000	104,000	104,000	104,000	104,000	104,000	104,000	104,000	104,000	104,000	104,000	104,000
Total Liabilities	104,000	106,751	108,448	113,071	115,789	116,270	115,253	113,080	113,274	117,260	117,509	111,656	111,850	111,850	121,121
Paid in Capital	104,000	104,000	104,000	104,000	104,000	104,000	104,000	104,000	104,000	104,000	104,000	104,000	104,000	104,000	104,000
Retained Earnings	-137,600	-137,600	-137,600	-137,600	-137,600	-137,600	-137,600	-137,600	-137,600	-137,600	-137,600	-137,600	-137,600	-137,600	-3,009
Earnings	0	-13,229	-17,507	-10,222	734	17,538	41,279	60,356	71,739	86,539	108,637	126,680	134,591	134,591	210,358
Total Equity	-33,600	-46,829	-51,107	-43,822	-32,866	-16,062	7,679	26,756	38,139	52,939	75,037	93,080	100,991	100,991	311,349
Total Debt and Equity	70,400	59,922	57,341	69,249	82,923	100,208	122,932	139,837	151,413	170,199	192,547	204,737	212,841	212,841	432,470
Net Worth	-33,600	-46,829	-51,107	-43,822	-32,866	-16,062	7,679	26,756	38,139	52,939	75,037	93,080	100,991	100,991	311,349

Index